The Anthem Companion to David Ricardo

Anthem Companions to Sociology

The Sociology programme takes a fresh and challenging sociological look at the interactions between politics, society, history and culture. Titles transcend traditional disciplinary boundaries. This programme includes a variety of book series.

Anthem Companions to Sociology offer authoritative and comprehensive assessments of major figures in the development of sociology from the last two centuries. Covering the major advancements in sociological thought, these companions offer critical evaluations of key figures in the American and European sociological tradition, and will provide students and scholars with an in-depth assessment of the makers of sociology and chart their relevance to modern society.

Series Editor

Bryan S. Turner – City University of New York, USA / Australian Catholic University, Australia / University of Potsdam, Germany

Titles in the Series

The Anthem Companion to Alexis de Tocqueville
The Anthem Companion to Auguste Comte
The Anthem Companion to C. Wright Mills
The Anthem Companion to Ernst Troeltsch
The Anthem Companion to Everett Hughes
The Anthem Companion to Ferdinand Tönnies
The Anthem Companion to Gabriel Tarde
The Anthem Companion to Georg Simmel
The Anthem Companion to Hannah Arendt
The Anthem Companion to Karl Mannheim
The Anthem Companion to Karl Marx
The Anthem Companion to Maurice Halbwachs
The Anthem Companion to Max Weber
The Anthem Companion to Philip Selznick
The Anthem Companion to Philip Rieff
The Anthem Companion to Pierre Bourdieu
The Anthem Companion to Raymond Aron
The Anthem Companion to Robert N. Bellah
The Anthem Companion to Robert K. Merton
The Anthem Companion to Robert Park
The Anthem Companion to Talcott Parsons
The Anthem Companion to Thorstein Veblen

The Anthem Companion to David Ricardo

Edited by John E. King
Emeritus Professor, La Trobe University,
Melbourne, Australia

ANTHEM PRESS

Anthem Press
An imprint of Wimbledon Publishing Company
www.anthempress.com

This edition first published in UK and USA 2023
by ANTHEM PRESS
75–76 Blackfriars Road, London SE1 8HA, UK
or PO Box 9779, London SW19 7ZG, UK
and
244 Madison Ave #116, New York, NY 10016, USA

British Library Cataloguing-in-Publication Data
A catalogue record for this book is available from the British Library.

Library of Congress Cataloging-in-Publication Data
A catalog record for this book has been requested.

ISBN-13: 978-1-83998-291-0 (Hbk)
ISBN-10: 1-83998-291-8 (Hbk)

Cover Credit: Portrait of David Ricardo by Thomas Phillips

This title is also available as an e-book.

CONTENTS

Notes on Contributors vii

Chapter 1. Introduction 1
John E. King

Chapter 2. On Some Myths about Ricardo's Theory of Money 9
Ghislain Deleplace

Chapter 3. Ricardo on Foreign Trade 29
Gilbert Faccarello

Chapter 4. 'A Tolerably Correct Law Respecting Proportions': Ricardo on Income Distribution 51
Christian Gehrke

Chapter 5. Ricardo on Economic Policy 73
John E. King

Chapter 6. (Mis)Interpreting Ricardo 91
Heinz D. Kurz

Chapter 7. Ricardo's Business Activities 125
Wilfried Parys

Chapter 8. Political Economy 'Through a Glass Hive'? The Encounter of Ricardian Ideas with Nineteenth-Century Australia 143
William Coleman

Chapter 9. Ricardo and Classical Political Economy 163
Alex M. Thomas

Chapter 10. Ricardo and Marx 181
Michael C. Howard

Chapter 11. Malthus and Ricardo on the Dismal Science 195
Bryan S. Turner

Further Reading 209

Index 213

NOTES ON CONTRIBUTORS

William Coleman is Reader at the Research School of Economics of the Australian National University. He is the author, or co-author, of eight books; and his scholarly output spans biography, oral history, economic history, political economy, political theory, demography, evolution, the history of ideas, the history of medicine, religious prejudice, technological change and protectionism. He was the 1996 winner of the (U.S.) History of Economics Society Award for the Best Article on the History of Economics. In 2016, he edited *Only in Australia: The History, Politics and Economics of Australian Exceptionalism* (Oxford University Press).

Ghislain Deleplace is Emeritus Professor of Economics at the University Paris 8. He has worked on the history of monetary theory, with special emphasis on Ricardo, Sraffa, Keynes and Steuart, and on the history of international bimetallism. His books include *Private Money and Public Currencies: The 16th Century Challenge* (with M. T. Boyer-Xambeu and L. Gillard, 1994); *Money in Motion: The Post Keynesian and Circulation Approaches* (co-edited with E. J. Nell, 1996); *Ricardo on Money: A Reappraisal* (2017); *Histoire de la pensée économique* (3rd edition, 2018); and *New Perspectives on Political Economy and Its History* (co-edited with M. C. Marcuzzo and P. Paesani, 2020).

Gilbert Faccarello is Emeritus Professor at Panthéon-Assas University, Paris. His publications (https://gilfac.eu) include articles and books in the history of economic thought. Recently, he edited *Handbook on the History of Economic Analysis* (with H. D. Kurz, 3 volumes, Edward Elgar, 2016) and *Malthus Across Nations: The Reception of Thomas Robert Malthus in Europe, America and Japan* (with M. Izumo and H. Morishita, Edward Elgar, 2020). He is a co-founder of *The European Journal of the History of Economic Thought* and acted as a chairman of the Council of the European Society for the History of Economic Thought.

Christian Gehrke is Associate Professor at the Department of Economics of the University of Graz, Austria, and Co-Director of the Graz Schumpeter Centre. He has published several papers in the major history of economic thought journals, mostly on classical economics, and edited a number of books, including *Sraffa and Modern Economics* (2 volumes, Routledge, 2011). Currently he also serves on the editorial boards of *Metroeconomica*, *Oeconomia*, *The European Journal of the History of Economic Thought*, and *Bulletin of Political Economy*, and as member of the executive committee and vice-president of the *European Society for the History of Economic Thought*.

Michael C. Howard is Distinguished Professor Emeritus at the University of Waterloo and Fellow at the Balsillie School of International Affairs, both of which are located in Waterloo, Ontario, Canada. He has also held academic positions at the Universities of Lancaster and Leicester in the UK, the University of California, Riverside in the USA, the University of British Columbia in Vancouver, Canada, and the Netherlands Institute for Advanced Study in Holland. His research has been concentrated in the areas of economic theory and political theory, as well as the intellectual history of both subjects. He has published extensively, including with his co-author of many years, John King of La Trobe University in Victoria, Australia.

John E. King is Emeritus Professor at La Trobe University. His principal research interests are in the history of heterodox economic thought, especially Marxian political economy and Post Keynesian economics. Recent publications include *The Distribution of Wealth* (2016; with Michael Schneider and Mike Pottenger), *A History of American Economic Thought* (2018; with Samuel Barbour and James Cicarelli) and *The Alternative Austrian Economics* (2019), dealing with socialist economic thought in Austria between 1900 and the present day.

Heinz D. Kurz is Professor Emeritus of Economics at the University of Graz and founder of the Graz Schumpeter Centre. He studied Economics and Political Science in Munich, wrote his PhD thesis in Kiel, Germany, and was a visiting fellow of Wolfson College, Cambridge. In 1979, he was appointed to a chair in economics at the University of Bremen. In 1988, he joined the University of Graz. In 1990–1991, he served as Theodor Heuss Professor in the Graduate Faculty, New School for Social Research, New York. He held numerous visiting professorships in many universities around the world. He is a managing editor of *Metroeconomica* and was a founding member and former managing editor of *The European Journal of the History of Economic Thought*. Together with Neri Salvadori, he wrote *Theory of Production* (Cambridge University Press, 1995).

Wilfried Parys spent his whole career at the University of Antwerp (Belgium), where he is now Professor Emeritus. His research concentrated on the history of economic thought, especially on the theories of value of Ricardo and Marx, the linear systems of Leontief and Sraffa and their precursors (Potron, Charasoff, Remak and Hawkins). In recent years, he also did detailed research on Ricardo's financial activities. His publications include papers in the *Quarterly Journal of Economics*, *American Economic Review*, *European Journal of the History of Economic Thought*, *Economic Systems Research*, *Cambridge Journal of Economics* and various other scholarly journals.

Alex M. Thomas teaches economics at Azim Premji University, Bengaluru, India. He studied economics at the Universities of Madras, Hyderabad and Sydney. He has published his research in several journals, including the *European Journal of the History of Economic Thought*, *History of Economic Ideas*, *History of Economics Review* and *Journal of Interdisciplinary Economics*. His co-edited book with Ajit Sinha *Pluralistic Economics and Its History* was published by Routledge in 2019. In 2021, Cambridge University Press published his textbook *Macroeconomics: An Introduction*.

Bryan S. Turner is Professor of Sociology at the Australian Catholic University, Professor Emeritus at the Graduate Center CUNY and Honorary Professor at Potsdam University. He won the Max Planck award in 2015 and directs the Centre for Social Citizenship at Potsdam. He is the founding editor of two journals – *Citizenship Studies* and *Journal of Classical Sociology*. He was awarded a Doctor of Letters from the University of Cambridge in 2009. His recent publications include Jürgen Mackert, Bryan S. Turner and Hannah Wolf, eds., *The Condition of Democracy* (2021), and Rob Stones and Bryan S. Turner, 'Successful Societies: Decision-making and the Quality of Attentiveness', *British Journal of Sociology* (2020).

Chapter 1

INTRODUCTION

John E. King

David Ricardo was born in London on 18 April 1772 into a prosperous family of Sephardic Jews. He died on 11 September 1823 from an ear infection. His father, Abraham Israel Ricardo (1733–1812) worked as a broker in the City of London and left a fortune of about £45,000. Some years ago, I made a back-of-the-envelope estimate that this would amount to approximately £23 million today (King 2013: 3). Abraham and his wife Abigail had at least seventeen children, of whom all but three were still alive when David died. Two of his younger brothers lived to the ripe old age of 89: Raphael or Ralph (1785–1875) and Moses (1776–1886), who wrote a celebrated 'Memoir' of his famous elder brother (X: 3–15). The reference is to volume X of the eleven-volume *Works and Correspondence of David Ricardo*, and this format will be used in all references to the *Works* throughout this book.

Surprisingly little is known about David Ricardo's youth. He did not have a particularly good education. As his brother Moses recalled, their father

> [...] was a man of good intellect but uncultivated. His prejudices were exceedingly strong; and they induced him to take the opinions of his forefathers in points of religion, politics, education, &c, upon faith, and without investigation. Not only did he adopt this rule for himself, but he insisted on its being followed by his children. (X: 5)

The young David, on the other hand

> [...] never yielded his assent on any important subject, until after he had thoroughly investigated it. It was perhaps in opposing these strong prejudices, that he was first led to that freedom and independence of thought for which he was so remarkable, and which indeed extended itself to the other branches of the family. (X: 5)

In December 1791, he married Priscilla Ann Wilkinson, a Quaker, which caused considerable tension with his devoutly Jewish parents. By this time, he was a convinced liberal who had no remaining commitment to Judaism.

Even more than his father, David Ricardo was highly successful in his business activities. 'Ricardo, at the time of his marriage, was a poor man', Max Hartwell wrote. However,

> [...] at the time of his death, thirty years later, his total estate was worth between £675,000 and £775,000. How did he make such a large fortune? In three ways: as a Stock Exchange jobber, as a loan contractor, as an investor in land and French bonds. (Hartwell 1971: 40)

In 1815, he added significantly to his already large fortune by betting successfully on an English victory over the French at the Battle of Waterloo, and then retired from business to live at Gatcombe Park, a country mansion set in 5,000 acres of Gloucestershire countryside that he had purchased in the previous year. Ricardo was now an extremely wealthy country squire. In the last four years of his life, he enjoyed an annual income of £28,000 (Hartwell 1971: 42). Using the same rule of thumb as I applied to his father, I estimated David Ricardo's income in twenty-first century terms as approximately £15 million per year, and the value of his estate on his death in 1823 as £350–400 million (King 2013: 7).

As Hartwell notes

> The picture that has come down to us of the rural Ricardo, with his family and friends, is a charming one; that of a gracious and kindly father and neighbour, living well, entertaining with pleasure, and devoting his spare time to the reading and writing of political economy. (Hartwell 1971: 38)

He was elected High Sheriff of Gloucestershire in 1818, and in the following year he entered Parliament when he bought the Irish seat of Portarlington, a 'rotten borough' that was sold to him by its *de facto* owner, Lord Portarlington. Ricardo was a conscientious MP and used the forum that was provided by the House of Commons to propagate his views on social and economic policy. Two of his sons, Osman (1795–1881) and David Jr. (1803–64), followed their father into Parliament.

By his mid-twenties, Moses recalled, David Ricardo was devoting a great deal of time and energy to 'mathematics, chemistry, geology, and mineralogy. He fitted up a laboratory, formed a collection of minerals, and was one of the original members of the Geological Society' (X: 6). He soon moved into economics, his interest being 'first awakened by his taking up a copy of the *Wealth of Nations* by chance while on a visit to Bath in 1799' (X: 35). His first publications in political economy came in 1809, when he wrote a series of articles on monetary issues for the *Morning Chronicle*, which soon appeared as a pamphlet on *The High Price of Bullion*. He now began to correspond with leading economists like Robert Malthus and James Mill, publishing three more pamphlets, one of which was the very important *Essay on the Influence of a Low Price of Corn on the Profits of Stock* in 1815. A good account of all of Ricardo's pamphlets is provided by Max Hartwell (1971: 22–28).

James Mill now encouraged him to write a full-length book. 'In the late summer of 1815, Mill began to press for a treatise [...] The letters now unfold the picture of a strict but kindly master dealing with a brilliant but unconfident and procrastinating pupil' (Stigler 1953: 589). Ricardo was, however, well aware of his disagreements with both Smith and Malthus on the questions of rent, profits and wages, and he soon began work on the *Principles*. The book was published on 19 April 1817, one day after the author's forty-fifth birthday; a second edition appeared in February 1819 and a significantly revised third edition in March 1821. The third edition contained thirty-two chapters and amounted (in the canonical Sraffa edition, in which it was volume I of the *Works and Correspondence*) to 429 pages. It 'falls into roughly equal parts on theory, taxation, and the errors of other writers' (Aldrich 2004: 384). The first seven chapters deal with theoretical issues (value, rent, wages and foreign trade), while the next eleven are devoted to taxation and the final fourteen chapters are diverse and rather poorly planned.

Ricardo was not a literary stylist. As one early critic complained, the book is

> [...] disfigured by blemishes and defects of very many kinds. Not only is it remarkable for infelicity of language, with all its fatal consequences of exaggeration and obscurity, but the grammar itself is halting and the accuracy often apparent, fallaciously apparent, rather than real. (Gonner 1923: xxiv)

His formal models are presented without any algebra or diagrams, but with no less than thirty-eight numerical examples, which are not always clearly explained. The book is certainly not an easy read.

It was not quite his final publication. In 1816, he had written another pamphlet, *Proposals for an Economical and Secure Currency*, and four years later he produced an entry on fiscal policy for the *Encyclopaedia Britannica*. A pamphlet *On Protection of Agriculture* was published in 1822, and his *Plan for the Establishment of a National Bank* appeared posthumously in 1824. Almost everything that Ricardo had written was eventually published between 1951 and 1955 in the first ten of the eleven volumes of his *Works and Correspondence* (as explained in 'Further Reading', pp. 209).

The ten principal chapters of this book deal in various ways with all the major themes to which Ricardo had devoted himself. In Chapter 2, Ghislain Deleplace argues that it was only after 1815 that Ricardo developed a mature theory of money, criticising many earlier writers for focusing instead on the (rather immature) ideas set out in the 1809 'Bullion Essays'. Deleplace maintains instead that the failure to take account of the entirety of Ricardo's writings on money, which continued to appear right down to his death in 1823, has nurtured some myths related to his thinking on monetary questions. These include the argument that Ricardo was principally concerned with a non-monetary (barter) economy and that his acceptance of Say's law required that he adhere to a strict version of the quantity theory of money in which the general price level varies directly, and exclusively, with changes in the quantity of money. Instead, Deleplace suggests, Ricardo's theory of money was both specific (being neither a commodity- nor a quantity-theory) and coherent, in the important sense that it was consistent with his theory of value and distribution.

A rather similar approach is taken by Gilbert Faccarello in Chapter 3 to the huge literature on Ricardo's theory of international trade, which was both more complex and more satisfactory than the 'principle of comparative advantage' to which it has too often been reduced. Faccarello deals at some length with Ricardo's celebrated numerical example of the gains from trade that arise when Portugal specialises in the production of wine and England in the production of cloth. He points to the existence of two competing interpretations of the four 'magic numbers' set out in the *Principles*, one originating with James Mill and John Stuart Mill and the other with Piero Sraffa. Faccarello is critical of both interpretations, which fail adequately to explain the microeconomics of trade, neglect the monetary aspects of international exchange and fail to explain how the relative prices of wine and cloth are determined. He sets out Ricardo's treatment of destabilising shocks, both temporary and permanent, which raises the fascinating possibility that England might specialise in wine production and Portugal in the clothing industry. Faccarello concludes that Ricardo's writings on trade constitute an elaborate jigsaw puzzle, which cannot be reduced to the simple principle of comparative advantage.

Christian Gehrke maintains in Chapter 4 that Ricardo's thinking on the distribution of income, while it was full of theoretical insights and represented a major theoretical achievement, also contained significant weaknesses. In fact Ricardo changed his analysis quite significantly between the 1815 *Essay on Profits* and the *Principles*, giving up the simplifying device of a 'corn model' and instead invoking the labour theory of value. In the process, he developed a novel 'share concept' of wages, which needs to be carefully distinguished from the more conventional notions of 'money wages' and 'real wages'. Gehrke demonstrates that Ricardo's treatment of the inverse wage–profit relationship was erroneous, before turning to his admission that in his model the share of rent was indeterminate. He concludes by discussing the textual changes that Ricardo made to the third edition of the *Principles* under the influence of Malthus and the critical secondary literature on these issues that has since emerged.

My own discussion on Ricardo and economic policy issues in Chapter 5 begins with a brief outline of English society at the end of the eighteenth century, which provided the political, social and economic context in which Ricardo thought and wrote on these questions. I deal in turn with his views on monetary policy, fiscal policy, social policy and international trade. Unlike Deleplace, I regard Ricardo as an 'extreme Bullionist', who saw the over-issue of paper currency as the cause (and the only cause) of inflation and a falling exchange rate. On fiscal policy, too he revealed himself to be a 'small government, low tax' advocate, and this spilled over into his thinking on social policy, where he opposed both government interference in the operation of the labour market and the use of 'poor relief' to provide a minimal level of social security. He did, of course, argue for free international trade, though with some temporary continuing support for English farmers. I conclude by turning to the work of the so-called Ricardian Socialists (John Francis Bray, John Gray, Thomas Hodgskin, William Thompson and others), who drew very different, very much more egalitarian policy conclusions from Ricardo's theory of value and distribution, which they shared with him.

In Chapter 6, Heinz Kurz criticises a number of common misunderstandings of Ricardo. (This is the only chapter that has been previously published, having appeared in the *European Journal of the History of Economic Thought* in 2015). He begins by critically examining the proposition that Ricardo was a purely abstract theorist, with his head in the clouds. After summarising his method of analysis and his use of numerical examples, Kurz assesses Ricardo's theory of value and distribution, which paved the way for Piero Sraffa's later and analytically more satisfactory work on the 'Standard commodity' and the 'Standard system'. Kurz considers and rebuts the contention that Ricardo's treatment of the different forms of technical progress is hopelessly muddled. This is followed by a critical appraisal of Ricardo's theory of differential rent, a discussion of some of the misunderstandings in the literature on his analysis of machinery, and a thoughtful account of the theory of comparative cost in international trade. Kurz concludes that the case of David Ricardo demonstrates very clearly that the market for economic ideas is by no means a perfect selection mechanism.

In Chapter 7, Wilfried Parys makes extensive use of several archives in London and Cambridge to explore Ricardo's business activities. He begins by outlining Ricardo's work as a jobber on the Stock Exchange, in which his unusual combination of integrity and financial talent proved extremely successful. Parys continues by describing the first loan contract that Ricardo raised for the British government in 1807 and discussing the work of his consortium and its mysterious fourth member. He explores the influence and prestige that Ricardo enjoyed on the Stock Exchange and critically assesses Norman Silberston's notorious and completely unfounded attack on his business ethics. After a discussion of Ricardo's seven British loan contracts, Parys continues by outlining the extent of his sales and purchases as recorded in the archives of the Bank of England and by setting out the investment strategies that he used. The chapter ends with some remarks on the contrasting characters of David Ricardo and Nathan Mayer Rothschild. Unlike the latter, Ricardo treated his business activities less as an end in themselves than as a means of obtaining a better quality of life as a country gentleman and a political economist.

In Chapter 8, William Coleman surveys the efforts made by nineteenth-century economists to make sense of Ricardo's theoretical and policy work in a colonial context. The *Principles* appeared in the same year that the colony's name was changed from New Holland to Australia and its first bank was established. Coleman notes that Ricardo's work offered food for thought to both the Colonial Office and the colonists, the former having a strong interest in the possibility of taxing land to meet the costs of administering the settlement. An early, highly critical attempt to apply Ricardian thinking to Australia came from Edward Gibbon Wakefield, who was soon followed by Robert Torrens and by Gladstone's later Chancellor, Robert Lowe, who spent most of the 1840s in Sydney. John Stuart Mill touched on some of the issues that they raised in his *Principles*, while Henry George wrote at length about Australia, which he toured in 1890 and where he enjoyed some influence over taxation policy in New South Wales. On the whole, however, Coleman concludes the response of the economists to nineteenth-century Australia was analytically very weak.

Ricardo's relationship with classical political economy is the theme of Alex Thomas's Chapter 9. Thomas focuses on Ricardo's explanation of relative prices and the distribution of income, set in the context of his theory of economic growth and with particular reference to the work of Smith, Sismondi and Malthus. He begins by highlighting the role that value theory plays both in Ricardo's political economy and for economics more generally. After providing a substantial overview of Ricardo's analytical method, emphasising the vital importance of the concept of social surplus in every aspect of his economics, Thomas explains his critical engagement with the concepts of use value and exchange value. Following a detailed discussion of Ricardo's theory of value and distribution, which again draws heavily on the notion of the surplus product and its distribution among the social classes, Thomas turns to growth theory, and in particular to the role that demand plays in it. He concludes by noting the stark contrast between Ricardo's objective approach to value, distribution and growth and the subjective theory later developed by marginalist economics, which gave his own political economy a firm sociological foundation that has not always been fully appreciated in the literature.

In Chapter 10, Michael Howard assesses the intellectual relationship between Ricardo and Karl Marx. Although Marx had great respect for Ricardo, and was more deeply influenced by him than by any other economist, he was also severely critical of Ricardo's analysis of value, distribution, cyclical instability and long-run economic development. Howard documents these criticisms at some length, noting also that the most impressive aspects of Marx's own political economy lay in areas untouched by Ricardo. He also maintains that Marx interpreted Ricardo's thinking within his own, broadly Hegelian, conceptual framework, which was of course very different from Ricardo's version of classical liberalism. Howard further criticises the twentieth-century claim that it was possible to resurrect a 'Classical-Marxian' approach to economic theory based on the work of Piero Sraffa, arguing instead that Sraffa's work was purely critical in nature and could not be used as the foundation for an alternative theoretical system that synthesised Ricardo and Marx. He concludes that Marx's theoretical achievements were largely independent of his reading of Ricardo, whose influence on Marx was either non-existent or very limited indeed.

In Chapter 11, 'Malthus and Ricardo on the dismal science', Bryan Turner argues that these two great intellectuals were not just political economists but also founders of sociology. Ricardo's treatment of the class conflict between capitalist and workers that resulted from the replacement of human labour by machines provided the foundations for Marx's class analysis, and was later taken up by Max Weber and other German sociologists of his generation. Turner's account of the role of Malthus draws heavily on recent historical research, which has led to a re-evaluation of both his importance and his relevance to the sociology and political theory of his day, not least with respect to the significance of demography in the history of modern societies. Turner also maintains that the distinction that is often drawn between economics and sociology is artificial, as clearly demonstrated by the history of the theory of money. He criticises Joseph Schumpeter for denying that Malthus had any sociological appreciation of the role played by institutions in the regulation of population growth. Turner concludes that Malthus and Ricardo had in fact developed an economic sociology of unintended consequences, which in Ricardo's case hinged on his theory of the falling rate of profit, so that economics was indeed regarded as a *dismal* science.

References

Aldrich, J. 2004. 'The Discovery of Comparative Advantage'. *Journal of the History of Economic Thought* 26, no. 3, September: 379–99.

Gonner, E. C. K. 1923. 'Introduction'. In *Economic Essays by David Ricardo*, i–xxx. London: Frank Cass, 1966.

Hartwell, R. M. 1971. Introduction to D. Ricardo. *On the Principles of Political Economy and Taxation*, 7–43. Harmondsworth: Penguin.

King, J. E. 2013. *David Ricardo*. Basingstoke: Palgrave Macmillan.

Ricardo, D. 1951–1973. *The Works and Correspondence of David Ricardo*, eleven volumes. Cambridge: Cambridge University Press.

Stigler, G. J. 1953. 'Sraffa's Ricardo'. *American Economic Review* 43, no. 4, 1 September: 586–99.

Chapter 2

ON SOME MYTHS ABOUT RICARDO'S THEORY OF MONEY

Ghislain Deleplace

1. Introduction

Judging by the Sraffa edition of his *Works and Correspondence* (Ricardo 1951–73), more than one half of Ricardo's writings was devoted to money. However, many commentators in this domain only consider his early publications, what Sraffa called his 'Bullion Essays' of 1809–11. It is as if Ricardo's turn to the study of value and distribution from 1815 onwards changed nothing in his monetary views or at worst made them more confused. Such an attitude obviously downplays his *Proposals for an Economical and Secure Currency* (Ricardo 1816) and the monetary aspects of *On the Principles of Political Economy, and Taxation*, which cannot be reduced to the sole Chapter XXVII 'On Currency and Banks'.[1] It also neglects many interventions by Ricardo from 1819 until his death in 1823, whether in print, speeches or correspondence.[2] This is not only to be regretted because the 'Bullion Essays' were written in the exceptional circumstances of the suspension of convertibility while the later contributions were concerned with the conditions and effects of the return to a normal system of convertible notes. Focusing on the 'Bullion Essays' also postulates that Ricardo's theory of money was disconnected from his theory of value and distribution. On the contrary, when in 1815 he shifted from monetary issues to political economy at large, Ricardo was conscious that the understanding of commodity price required coordinating these two theories.[3] To know whether he succeeded in doing so one must assess the logical consistency between them. I will contend that only after 1815 did Ricardo develop a mature theory of money, both specific and coherent.

Failing to take account of the whole of Ricardo's writings on money has nourished some myths about his monetary theory. Indeed, myths have been common for long in the literature on his other theories, but nowhere are they more frequent than on money. Just to mention a few: most of Ricardo's economics is concerned with a non-monetary economy (barter); Ricardo held a commodity-theory of money (money is gold); he also held a strict quantity theory of money (in which the general level of prices varies proportionally with the quantity of money); according to him paper money (banknotes) behaves like metallic money, with its quantity adjusting automatically thanks to convertibility and international gold flows; his precept for the issuing bank was to maintain a 100 per cent proportionality between issues and metallic reserves.

Some of these statements obviously contradict Ricardo's explicit and repeated contentions, for example about the desirability of paper money rather than a metallic one and the relevance of a note-issuing rule that made international gold flows and proportionality between note issues and reserves unnecessary. Others contradict one another, such as the alleged commodity-theory of money (in which the value of gold-money determines its quantity in circulation) and the quantity theory of money (in which the causality goes the other way round), or the alleged automaticity of monetary adjustment contradicted by the 100 per cent reserve requirement. Since to be effective, myths require an appearance of consistency, a reading key is usually resorted to: the distinction between short run and long run. In the short run (the time of practice and observation), any increase in the quantity of bank issues above the equilibrium level may stimulate output and employment but also leads to a rise in the price level which triggers correcting effects – the export of gold and the corresponding shrinkage of bank reserve forcing a contraction of the note issue – and brings back the economy to the equilibrium output, employment and price level. In the long run (the time of economic laws and abstract theory), paper money only represents gold, the quantity of which is distributed among nations according to their needs. The value of money only varies with the relative price of gold (determined by its conditions of production), without any effect on output and employment. Money neutrality strictly rules and the economy behaves as if commodities exchanged against one another through the medium of one of them (gold). According to whether one is inclined to praise or to criticise Ricardo, this short run/long run reading key strengthens his importance in the history of monetary thought or is another proof of the 'Ricardian vice' blamed by Schumpeter (1954: 472–73).

The purpose of this chapter is to challenge these myths and to suggest another view in which the relationship between the value and the quantity of money owes nothing to a commodity-theory of money (Section 2) or to the Quantity Theory of Money (Section 3) but puts the market price of the standard of money centre-stage (Section 4). Ricardo's applied pronouncements on money then appear as direct consequences of this theory (Section 5).

2. Ricardo's Monetary Theory Is *Not* a Commodity-Theory of Money

2.1. A search for consistency

The question of the consistency between the theory of value and the theory of money has not been much discussed in the literature on Ricardo (nor on other Classical authors), something that contrasts with its importance in the literature on modern general equilibrium theory, where the so-called problem of integration of money in the theory of value has been explored in depth. In fact, this problem is not raised in the same way in the two frameworks. In modern general equilibrium theory, relative prices are supposed to be determined for a non-monetary economy and money is 'integrated' at a later logical step, under the constraint that this integration should both be consistent with the general law of supply and demand *and* leave relative prices unaltered (neutrality). This method of reasoning was not Ricardo's.[4] When he exposed his theory of value and distribution, he did not refer to an economy where money was supposed to be *absent* but to one where its value was supposed to be *constant*.[5] The proper object of the theory of money was then to inquire into the conditions under which this assumption could be considered as valid, so that money was 'perfect'. Although in a different perspective from the modern general-equilibrium one, this also raises the question of the consistency in Ricardo between the theory of value and the theory of money.

However, the most common attitude is to evaluate this question in the following way: the theory of value is concerned with the determination of natural prices and applies in the long run, where money is simply confused with a particular commodity (gold), while the theory of money is concerned with the regulation of its quantity and applies to the short run, where this quantity affects the general price level but is disconnected from the variations in individual market prices (the so-called gravitation). This sharp distinction reinforces the belief that Ricardo's understanding of money is actually split in two theories inconsistent with each other, one for the long run (a commodity-theory of money) and the other for the short run (the quantity theory of money).

As far as I know, the first attempts at considering the consistency between Ricardo's theory of natural prices and his theory of money may be found in two texts that are not available in the English language: Cartelier (1987) and Benetti (1990). They both concluded that this consistency was out of reach in Ricardo. To inquire into the presence of a commodity-theory of money in Ricardo implies asking this question again.

Two main issues must be discussed: that of the conditions of production of the commodity chosen arbitrarily as money and that of the variation in its quantity to meet the requirements of the circulation of all other commodities. In the line of the introduction to his edition of Ricardo's *Works and Correspondence*, Sraffa has proposed a reconstruction of Ricardo's theory of natural prices in which the quantities of the commodities used in their production are substituted for the labour values (Sraffa 1960). Since it is a well-known feature of Ricardo's approach to money that a change in its quantity is supposed *not* to affect natural prices and distribution, a commodity-money may only be consistent with such a reconstruction if a change in its quantity does *not* affect the price system and distribution.

Let us consider an economy producing n basic commodities – that is, entering directly or indirectly into the production of all commodities – called $1, \ldots, i, \ldots, n$. In the natural state they are produced in quantities $q_1, \ldots, q_i, \ldots, q_n$ with $a_{ji}\, q_i$ the quantity of commodity j and l_i the quantity of direct labour required to produce q_i of commodity i. Prices $p_1, \ldots, p_i, \ldots, p_n$ and the wage rate w are measured in the nth commodity (e.g. gold), the price of which is thus fixed equal to 1. With r the uniform rate of profit, the system of natural prices is composed of n independent equations having the general form:

$$q_i p_i = (1+r)\sum_{j=1}^{n} a_{ji} q_i p_j + l_i w \tag{1}$$

If, as in Sraffa (1960), the rate of profit r is given exogenously, the system of n equations determines the $n - 1$ real prices and the wage rate w, all in terms of gold. By contrast, if, as in Ricardo's *Principles*, the quantities of goods in which the wage rate is spent in the natural state are given exogenously, one must add a corresponding independent equation and the system now determines both distribution variables w and r. Since the requirements to apply the price system to a monetary economy are the same, the simplicity of exposition calls here for the adoption of Sraffa's assumption.[6]

If this economy is a monetary one and gold is supposed to be the money-commodity all prices are now money prices. An equation must be added, which accounts for the circulation of all quantities of commodities at their natural money prices (including the quantity of gold not used as money) by means of the quantity q_n^M of gold-money, for a given velocity of circulation V:

$$q_n^M = \frac{1}{V}\frac{1}{p_n}\left[\sum_{i=1}^{n-1} q_i p_i + \left(q_n - q_n^M\right) p_n\right] \tag{2}$$

The question now is whether the system described by the n equations of type (1) and Equation (2) accepts a solution.

2.2. Gold-money and the surplus product

In a Sraffa system any change in the quantity of a basic commodity used in the production of another one affects the whole system of prices and the level of the endogenously-determined distribution variable. Hence, the condition of consistency we are looking for cannot be found in a situation where the change in the quantity of the commodity-money would alter the quantities of this commodity that are used in the production of the basic commodities. Since it is a characteristic property of a Sraffa system that the utilisation of the surplus – composed of the quantities of the basic commodities above what is strictly required by the self-replacement of their quantities consumed productively – does *not* affect the price system and distribution, one concludes that the necessary and sufficient condition for a change in the quantity of the commodity-money *not* to alter the price system and distribution is that this quantity should be taken from the surplus.

Two alternative assumptions may satisfy this condition: either gold is a basic product the quantity of which used as money belongs to the surplus in gold produced, or gold is a non-basic product. The first alternative implies that some sort of mechanism exists which separates the quantity of gold-money from the quantity of gold-metal entering in the production of the basic commodities. Nothing in Equation (1) or (2) hints at such a mechanism: it might be said that coining gold into specie allows distinguishing between gold-money and gold-metal but this calls for the introduction of the legal price of gold when it is coined, something that modifies completely the formalisation of circulation (see Section 4). The reasonable candidate is thus the second alternative of gold as a non-basic product – something in accordance with its usual description as a luxury good in the classical meaning of the word.

The system of n equations of type (1) is now replaced by $n-1$ equations of type (1a) and Equation (1b) of the natural price of gold (which does not affect the equations of type (1a)):

$$q_i p_i = (1+r)\sum_{j=1}^{n-1} a_{ji} q_i p_j + l_i w \tag{1a}$$

$$q_n p_n = (1+r)\sum_{j=1}^{n-1} a_{jn} q_n p_j + l_n w \tag{1b}$$

Equation (2) is left unchanged but one should notice that the quantity $q_n - q_n^M$ of gold not used as money is now exclusively used as final good or as means of production of non-basic commodities. Supposing that the system formed by the equations of type (1a) admits a (real) solution, a monetary solution exists for a given quantity q_n of gold produced at a price p_n determined by (1b) if and only if:

$$q_n^M \leq q_n \tag{3}$$

It can immediately be seen that there is no reason why this condition should be fulfilled in the generality of cases, that is, for any given quantity q_n of gold produced. For example, given the same quantities produced of all commodities, there may exist a monetary solution for a certain level of the exogenous distribution variable and not for another, because the price system and hence q_n^M will be different.

If the quantity of gold produced is not enough to answer the requirements of its use as money, can it increase until it does? In other words, can the quantity of money increase without affecting the price system and distribution? Since gold is a non-basic commodity, its quantity is produced by the use of the surplus quantities of the basic commodities. An increase in the quantity of money requires more of these surplus quantities to be diverted from the production of the quantities of the other commodities belonging to the surplus (whether basic or non-basic). The limit to an increase in the quantity of money is reached when all surplus quantities of the basic commodities are used to produce gold-money, that is, when the surplus of the economy is entirely composed of gold, which is exclusively used as money. The monetary equation (Equation (2)) then simplifies to:

$$q_n^M = \frac{1}{V}\frac{1}{p_n}\sum_{i=1}^{n-1} q_i\, p_i \tag{2a}$$

Beyond the point described by (2a), for which $q_n^M = q_n$, no increase in the quantity of gold-money is possible without jeopardizing the self-replacement of the production system. The solution to the real system of production is no longer consistent with the requirements of circulation: there is no monetary solution to the system of natural prices.

One might think of three ways to overcome this limit. The first is to take into account the physical durability of gold and to rely on its existing stock, not only on its newly-produced flow.[7] Equation (2a) may be reformulated on this basis, but, even if the constraint is displaced, the condition of compatibility between the system of production and the requirements of circulation ceases to be satisfied when the whole stock of gold is used as money. The second way is a reduction in the production levels of the basic commodities, so as to free some quantities of them to increase the production of gold. To such a reallocation it may be objected that this non-neutrality of money in respect to economic activity only leaves the price system and distribution unaltered under the assumption of constant returns, something at odds with Sraffa's emphatic denial of such assumption (Sraffa 1960: vi). The third way to loosen the constraint imposed by the availability of gold is to complement the commodity-money with paper money; after all, this device is often presented in the history of money as a way to economize on gold-money by increasing its velocity of circulation. However, if the paper is issued with a 100 per cent backing in gold – so that it is only a gold certificate – the limit is not displaced. And if the issue is not 100 per cent backed by gold, one needs an issuing principle guaranteeing that the paper adequately 'represents' gold. Obviously, this direction leads beyond the domain of a commodity-theory of money.

One may conclude that the quantity produced of the commodity-money cannot be made consistent with the requirements of its circulation.[8] Formally, even if the conditions of the existence of a real solution to the system built by the $n - 1$ equations of type (1a) and equation (1b) are fulfilled, they do not guarantee the existence of a monetary solution compatible with (2). This negative result, however, should not be interpreted as a critique of Ricardo's theory of money but as an indication that Ricardo did *not* have a commodity-theory of money. Notwithstanding the importance of the issuing principle of paper money in Ricardo's monetary writings (see Section 5), a proof of this absence may be given *a contrario*. If the above system had an adequate monetary solution, one should apply to gold the adjustment mechanism described by Ricardo for *any* commodity produced in competitive conditions: the regulation of its market price by its natural price. This would contradict a central idea in Ricardo's theory of money, namely that the market price of gold as commodity is regulated, not by its (variable) natural price but by its (constant) legal price as money. This was why, as he proclaimed in evidence before the Commons' Committee on Resumption of Cash Payments on 4 March 1819, 'In a sound state of the currency the value of gold may change, but its price cannot' (V: 392). As already noted, the above system leaves no room for the legal price of gold as money and this testifies to the fact that Ricardo's monetary theory was not a commodity-theory of money.

However, this negative conclusion does not rule out *any* causal relationship between the value of gold and the value of money. Rejecting a commodity-theory of money means denying that gold might be *money*. However, another role should be considered for gold: that of *standard of money*. The relationship between money and its standard implies that in Ricardo the value of money is not *exclusively* determined by the value of gold but is *in some way* dependent on it. And to understand this dependency, we will have to analyse the specific regulation of the market price of gold as commodity by the legal price of gold when coined into money (see Section 4).

3. Ricardo's Monetary Theory Is *Not* a Quantity Theory of Money

3.1. A dead end for monetary theory: Say's Law

It is often postulated in the literature that Ricardo's adherence to Say's law and to the quantity theory of money is one and the same thing.[9] Strictly speaking, Say's law denies that the level of aggregate output might be lowered because of a deficient aggregate demand. Since in modern times the rejection of Say's law has been associated with a Keynesian point of view, in which money usually plays an important role in the deficiency of aggregate demand, one has become accustomed to equating the adherence to Say's law with the neutrality of money in respect to the level of aggregate output. Ricardo has been a victim of such association, all the more so since the crude quantity theory of money often attributed to him – with which the level of aggregate output is supposed to be given whatever the quantity of money – provides an illustration of both Say's law and neutrality. It will here be contended that relying on Say's law – an already intricate issue in Ricardo[10] – is of no help to prove the attribution to him of the quantity theory of money.

In order to clarify this issue, one needs to disentangle the possible effects attributed to a change in the quantity of money on aggregate output in two opposite situations: when a sudden shortage of money triggers a depression and when a monetary expansion fuels inflation.[11] It is striking that the commentators who focus on the latter situation usually concentrate on the 'Bullion Essays' and disregard the monetary chapters of *Principles*,[12] which by contrast are privileged by those who focus on the former one.[13] This is not only a matter of historical gap, Ricardo being in 1809–11 more concerned with inflation and in 1819–23 with deflation. Theory is involved.

Those who focus on inflation wish to show that the causal relationship between an increase in the quantity of money and the general rise in prices is not 'mechanical' (as they say) but obtained through an increase in the demand for commodities allowed by the availability of more money but constrained by their given supply. The purpose is to endow Ricardo's alleged quantity theory of money with more flexibility (see below) and to relax Say's law by introducing a cause of change in aggregate demand independent of production – so as to substitute 'Say's Equality' for 'Say's Identity'. However, these two amendments have nothing to do with each other: the assumed effect of a change in the quantity of money on aggregate demand is to *increase* it while Say's law is concerned with its *deficiency*.

Those who focus on depression should admit that for Ricardo a money shortage triggers a depression because of the effects on production, *not* on demand. To introduce an effect of money on aggregate demand that could be responsible for a depression, one would have to consider a store-of-value function of money which is at odds with the only two roles of money in Ricardo as unit of account and circulating medium. So doing, the depression would be caused by something happening on the side of the demand for money (as in the Keynesian liquidity-preference theory), *not* on the side of the money supply. This is going far away from Ricardo, where a function of demand for money based on the store-of-value behaviour of its users is clearly absent.

To sum up, whatever the chosen interpretation of Say's law in Ricardo's economics, it can in no way sustain the attribution to him of the quantity theory of money. Besides, there are other more positive reasons to deny such an attribution.

3.2. The direct or indirect link between the quantity of money and commodity prices

The attribution of the quantity theory of money to Ricardo takes two forms in the literature. One is to blame a 'rigid' (Schumpeter 1954, 724) or 'hard-line' (Blaug 1995, 31) version of it, in which all nominal prices vary with the quantity of money in the same direction and proportion as a logical consequence of the combined assumptions of neutrality, constancy of the velocity of circulation, and exogeneity of the supply of money. The second form credits Ricardo with an adjustment process in which an increase in the quantity of money raises the demand for consumption goods thanks to a primitive real-balance effect[14] and the demand for investment goods through a decline in the rate of interest charged by banks,[15] so that a temporary effect on output may occur, although the economy will eventually return to the initial real situation at a higher level of nominal prices. In both cases, the assumption is that a change in the quantity of money directly affects all prices. Since money may purchase any commodity, all commodities play the same role as far as the relationship between the quantity of money and prices is concerned.

However, it is well known that Ricardo repeatedly insisted on the fact that an excess quantity of money was reflected in the rise of a *specific* price, namely the market price of bullion. This was already illustrated by the title of his first published pamphlet: *The High Price of Bullion, A Proof of the Depreciation of Bank Notes* (Ricardo 1810–11). Later, in his *Proposals for an Economical and Secure Currency*, he introduced a distinction between a situation in which the value of the currency 'conforms' to the value of the standard and a situation in which it does not; in the latter money was either 'depreciated' or 'appreciated'. The market price of bullion provided a test of the ruling situation:

> While these metals [gold and silver] are the standard, the currency should conform in value to them, and, whenever it does not, and the market price of bullion is above the mint price, the currency is depreciated. This proposition is unanswered, and is unanswerable. (IV: 62–63)[16]

One could be tempted to recognise here a distinction between equilibrium and disequilibrium. But in the quantity theory of money, the causality goes from the quantity of money to its value in both cases. There is nothing of the kind in Ricardo: in the (so to speak) conformable situation, the value of money is determined by the value of the standard and the quantity of money adjusts accordingly: the causality between the value and the quantity of money is the reverse of what, according to the quantity theory of money, it is in equilibrium. Only out of this conformable situation does an increase in the quantity of money cause a fall in its value, reflected in a market price of bullion higher than the legal mint price, what Ricardo called a depreciation of the currency.

It is common in the literature to assert that the market price of gold was only in Ricardo a proxy of the general price index, at a time when the measure and even the notion of the latter were lacking (see, e.g., Hollander 1979: 416; Laidler 1987: 291). As will be shown in Section 4, it may be more interesting to take the relationship between the quantity of money and the market price of gold seriously and to give it a central role in the commodity-price changes that have a monetary origin.

This is not a mere amendment to Ricardo's alleged quantity theory of money, which would substitute another link between the quantity of money and nominal prices for the usual one. Focusing on the market price of gold paves the way to a completely different theory of money as can be inferred from the reversal of the relationship between the value of money and nominal prices. In the adjustment process mentioned above an increase in the quantity of money raises the nominal price of a commodity because it raises its demand; here money plays its role as medium of exchange and the adjustment directly concerns every commodity it may purchase. The fall in the value of money is thus only a consequence of the rise in the nominal prices of all commodities, under the heroic assumption that this rise is equiproportional (to comply with neutrality as regards relative prices).[17] By contrast, when the price of gold is put centre-stage, an increase in the quantity of money first raises the market price of bullion and then indirectly the nominal prices of all other commodities, whose rise is a consequence of the fall in the value of money, not the other way round. Money is here considered in its unit-of-account function, and this explains why all prices rise at the same rate as the price of gold, because the value of money has fallen in terms of its standard. The market price of gold bullion being quoted twice a week in London and published in John Castaing's *The Course of the Exchange*, all sellers of commodities could know exactly how much it changed when it did and pass this change on to their money prices in the same proportion, leaving relative prices unaltered.[18] This bullion-price channel of transmission of a monetary shock to the value of money and hence to commodity prices not only contrasts with other transmission channels sometimes credited to Ricardo in modern literature (based on the real-balance effect or the rate of interest); it is thus also at odds with the attribution to Ricardo of the quantity theory of money.

We saw in Section 2 that rejecting the attribution to Ricardo of a commodity-theory of money did not rule out *any* causal relationship between the value of gold and the value of money. Similarly, rejecting the attribution to Ricardo of the quantity theory of money does not rule out *any* causal relationship between the quantity of money and its value. And here also the central notion to be considered is the market price of gold bullion. It is now time to weave these two threads into an explicit relationship between money and the standard of money (gold), so as to account for Ricardo's statement: 'The only use of a standard is to regulate the quantity, and by the quantity the value of a currency'. (IV: 59)

4. The Relationship between Money and Its Standard

The first to have drawn attention to the market for gold as standard of money in Ricardo are Maria Cristina Marcuzzo and Annalisa Rosselli in their 1991 pioneering book *Ricardo and the Gold Standard*. Other scholars have since contributed to a reappraisal of Ricardo's theory of money along this line, so that, even if they still are a minority, one may speak of an 'unorthodox view' on this theory (see Deleplace 2020). According to this view, Ricardo's central proposition is that, in a monetary system where the currency is convertible both ways into the (gold) standard, the market price of gold bullion is stabilised thanks to an appropriate regulation of the quantity of money. This stability brings the monetary system as close as possible to perfection, even if it does not guarantee the constancy of the value of money, which may still vary with the conditions of production of the standard. The golden rule of the issuing of money was thus for Ricardo to ensure that the market price of the standard was brought in line with its legal price, so that the value of money was always kept equal to the value of the standard. In Deleplace (2017) I have attempted to bring together Ricardo's many statements on money so as to provide a firm theoretical basis to that central proposition.

In *Proposals for an Economical and Secure Currency* Ricardo stated the three conditions of a perfect currency: 'A currency may be considered as perfect, of which the standard is invariable, which always conforms to that standard, and in the use of which the utmost economy is practised' (Ricardo 1816, 55). The proper object of monetary theory was to determine under which conditions the second requisite may be fulfilled, that is, the currency 'conforms' to its standard. Such conformity is characterised by three equivalent equalities between: a) the value of money and the value of the commodity selected as standard;

b) the market price of this commodity and its legal price; and c) the actual quantity of money and the quantity required by 'the wants of commerce'.[19] To know whether money did conform to the standard, it was thus unnecessary to calculate their respective values (with the index-problems generated by such calculation) or the actual and required quantities of money (with the difficulties generated by their definition and observation). It was enough to compare the market price and the legal price of gold – two observable magnitudes – and to vary the note issue according to the sign of the difference, if any (see Section 5).

The core model of Ricardo's theory of money, that is, the relationship between the quantity of money and its value may be summarised as follows.[20] Let me consider a situation at time 0 in which the currency conforms to the standard, so that the value of money $V_{M(0)}$ is equal to the value of gold $V_{G(0)}$, the market price of gold $P_{G(0)}$ is equal to its legal (mint) price $\overline{P_{GC}}$, and the actual quantity of money $M_{(0)}$ is equal to the quantity $M_{(0)}^*$ required by 'the wants of commerce'. If in time t a quantity of money $M_{(t)}$ is circulating, the market price of gold and the value of money change according to the following equations:

$$\frac{P_{G(t)} - P_{G(0)}}{P_{G(0)}} = \frac{M_{(t)} - M_{(0)}}{M_{(0)}} - \frac{M_{(t)}^* - M_{(0)}^*}{M_{(0)}^*} \tag{4}$$

$$\frac{V_{M(t)} - V_{M(0)}}{V_{M(0)}} = \frac{V_{G(t)} - V_{G(0)}}{V_{G(0)}} - \frac{P_{G(t)} - P_{G(0)}}{P_{G(0)}} \tag{5}$$

Equation (4) expresses that, if the rate of change in the actual quantity of money between 0 and t deviates from the rate of change required in t by the wants of commerce, the market price of gold bullion rises or falls in accordance with the sign and the amount of this deviation. As a consequence, the value of money changes by a rate that reflects positively the change in the value of gold (if any) and negatively the change in its market price (Equation (5)).

After a lag of duration n, the actual quantity of money adjusts inversely with the sign of the spread between the market price of gold in time t and its legal price:

$$\frac{M_{(t+n)} - M_{(t)}}{M_{(t)}} = f^{-1}\left(\frac{P_{G(t)} - \overline{P_{GC}}}{\overline{P_{GC}}}\right) \tag{6}$$

The process goes on until the conformable situation is restored, meaning that the actual quantity of money is again equal to the level required by the wants of commerce (whether it had changed or not between 0 and t) and the market price of gold is again equal to the mint price.

One should observe that the theory of money in Ricardo is concerned with the determination of the value of money V_M, its actual quantity M, and the market price of the standard P_G. In this theory, the value of the standard V_G, the quantity of money M^* required by the wants of commerce, and the legal price of the standard $\overline{P_{GC}}$ are independent variables, which call for a separate analysis implying to take into account various technical and institutional factors (including the state of credit). However, these aspects are outside Ricardo's theory of money, for which they should be considered as given.

Equation (5) embodies Ricardo's theory of the value of a standard-based currency. This money-standard equation, as I call it (MSE in short),[21] derives from Ricardo's crucial distinction between 'a fall in the value of money' and 'a depreciation of money':

> 'The term "depreciation", I conceive, does not mean a mere diminution in value, but it means a diminished relative value, on a comparison with something which is a standard; and therefore I think it quite possible that a bank note may be depreciated, although it should rise in value, if it did not rise in value in a degree equal to the standard, by which only its depreciation is measured. [...] A currency might be depreciated, without falling in value; it might fall in value, without being depreciated, because depreciation is estimated only by reference to a standard'. (Evidence of 4 March 1819, in Ricardo 1951–73, V: 393–94; speech of 11 June 1823, ibid., 311)

The MSE illustrates this distinction: it means that the value of money varies positively with the value of the standard and negatively with its market price, which the legal price of the standard being fixed, indicates by how much money depreciates or appreciates, that is, varies in value less or more (respectively) than the standard. The two causes of change in the value of money can thus be clearly distinguished. The real cause – a change in the difficulty of production of the standard – manifests itself in the first element of the right-hand side of the MSE (a change in the value of the standard). The monetary cause – a quantity of money departing from its conformable level, as illustrated by Equation (4) – manifests itself in the second element. In accordance with what Ricardo said, money might 'rise in value' (the left-hand side of Equation (5) is positive) although it 'might be depreciated' (the second element of the right-hand side is positive), whenever 'it did not rise in value in a degree equal to the standard' (the first element of the right-hand side is greater than the second). The MSE is the key to the consistency between Ricardo's theory of money and his theory of value and distribution.

5. Some Applied Consequences of the Theory

Three of them may be quickly described (for more details, see Deleplace 2017, 2020): the exteriority of the standard of money, the small importance of international bullion flows, and the rule of monetary policy.

As seen in Section 2, money in Ricardo is *not* a commodity. However, the standard of money (gold) *is* a commodity in Ricardo's sense, that is, it has both a natural price and a market price. Here, one is confronted with a riddle. Since gold is a competitively-produced commodity, Equation (1) above applies to its natural price, which regulates its market price. Since gold is the standard of money, it has a legal price $\overline{P_{GC}}$ which regulates its market price P_G according to Equations (4) and (6). How can the same market price P_G of gold bullion be regulated both by a natural price that varies with changes in the difficulty of production and the rate of profit *and* by a legal price that is required to be constant? There is only one way to solve this riddle, by assuming that gold used as standard of money in a given economy (e.g. England) is produced in another economy where it is *not* the standard of money (e.g. Spanish America on a silver standard).[22] The peculiarity of the standard of money is that, although it is produced as a commodity, it is exterior to the system of production of the economy that uses it as standard of money.

It is usually believed that monetary stability is ensured in Ricardo by international bullion flows, according to the price-specie flow mechanism. This is true under inconvertibility – the type of regime mostly considered in the 'Bullion Essays' of 1809–11 – but no longer in Ricardo's mature theory of money after 1815, which applies to a standard-based monetary system. The reason is that, when the Bank of England note was convertible into the standard, its depreciation did in the first place trigger an export of gold obtained at the legal price against notes at the Bank, but only so long as the Bank was not forced to purchase it in the market to replenish its reserves. Then it became more profitable for the bullion traders to sell gold to the Bank rather than to export it, because this saved the cost of transporting it to a foreign market: 'Guineas would still be demanded [from the Bank], but instead of being exported would be melted and sold to the Bank at an advanced price'. (Ricardo 1810–11, 58) The consequence was what I called a 'Penelope effect' after the image borrowed by Ricardo from Adam Smith.[23] The Bank was trapped in a loss-making activity, since it purchased bullion in the market above the price at which it was legally compelled to give coins against its notes. The only way to get out of this trap was for the Bank to reduce its issues at the discount window, so that fewer notes were returned to be converted into coin: 'The Bank would be obliged ultimately to adopt the only remedy in their power to put a stop to the demand for guineas. They would withdraw part of their notes from circulation'. (ibid., 59) The exportation of bullion, which under inconvertibility was the driving force of the adjustment process, only played a role at the beginning of it under convertibility where sooner or later a domestic adjustment did the job: the contraction of the Bank issue under the pressure of the Penelope effect, until the market price of bullion fell to the mint price of coined gold.

This effect of a change in the note issue on the adjustment process was already described by Ricardo in one of the few passages of the 'Bullion Essays' devoted to convertibility. However, it only got a rational foundation in the *Proposals* of 1816, with the dynamic system formed by Equations (4) and (6). And there was more: the adjustment generated by the Penelope effect did operate albeit inefficiently, since, not being automatic but based on the behaviour of the Bank of England, it might take quite a long time, depending on the lag with which the Bank first purchased bullion to replenish its reserve, and second contracted the issue after having experienced losses. A better system could be implemented thanks to a change in the convertibility principle combined with a rule of monetary policy: this was the Ingot Plan. Firstly this plan substituted a circulation exclusively composed of notes convertible into gold bullion – that is, the non-circulating standard – for a mixed system of coins and notes convertible into coins: 'A currency is in its most perfect state when it consists wholly of paper money, but of paper money of an equal value with the gold which it professes to represent' (Ricardo 1821, 361). The currency became not only 'economical' but also 'secure' (the two adjectives in the title of *Proposals*) because domestic circulation (of notes) was now separated from foreign payments (in bullion) – an advantage that would be credited to Ricardo many decades later during the debate on the Indian gold-exchange standard (see Deleplace 2023). Secondly, the centralised control over the issuing of notes allowed implementing a rule of monetary policy, especially if the issuing bank was public, as argued in the posthumously-published *Plan for the Establishment of a National Bank* (Ricardo 1824). This rule – varying the note issue inversely with the difference between the market price and the legal price of gold, so as to give Equation (6) a normative meaning – triggered an adjustment in the quantity of money without having to rely on international bullion flows:

> The most perfect liberty should be given, at the same time, to export or import every description of bullion. These transactions in bullion would be very few in number, if the Bank regulated their loans and issues of paper by the criterion which I have so often mentioned, namely, the price of standard bullion, without attending to the absolute quantity of paper in circulation. (Ricardo 1816, 67; reproduced in Ricardo 1821, 357–58)

As shown by the end of the quotation, this rule also dispensed with any requirement about the size of the quantity of money – hence the size of metallic reserves. Contrary to what is too often found in the literature, there is no continuity between Ricardo's plans and the currency principle embodied in the 1844 Bank Charter Act, which imposed on the Bank of England a rule that specified the aggregate quantity of notes it could issue and provided the foundation of monetary orthodoxy.

To sum up, the fecundity of Ricardo's monetary views for the day-to-day working of an economy was made possible because, contrary to long-lasting myths, his theory of money was both specific – it was neither a commodity- nor a quantity-theory of money – and coherent – it was consistent with Ricardo's theory of value and distribution.

Notes

1 In what follows I will refer to the third edition of *Principles* (Ricardo 1821).

2 For an exhaustive list of Ricardo's contributions on money from 1809 to 1823, see Deleplace (2017: 75–80).

3 'It appears to me that there are two causes which may cause a rise of prices, – one the depreciation of money, the other the difficulty of producing.' (letter to Malthus of 27 June 1815, in VI: 233) 'Before my readers can understand the proof I mean to offer, they must understand the theory of currency and of price. They must know that the prices of commodities are affected two ways one by the alteration in the relative value of money, which affects all commodities nearly at the same time, – the other by an alteration in the value of the particular commodity, and which affects the value of no other thing, excepting it enter into its composition'. (letter to James Mill of 30 December 1815, ibid., 348).

4 In a manuscript written in 1932, Piero Sraffa suggested that no economist used such a method until Hayek published *Prices and Production* in 1931; see *Sraffa Papers* D3/9/181.

5 See, for example: 'The reader is desired to bear in mind, that for the purpose of making the subject more clear, I consider money to be invariable in value, and therefore every variation of price to be referable to an alteration in the value of the commodity'. (Ricardo 1821: 110; see also ibid., 46–47, 87).

6 As is well known, Sraffa's argument for adopting this assumption is that the wage is not only 'consisting of the necessary subsistence of the workers' but also 'may include a share of the surplus product' (Sraffa 1960: 9) so that, contrary to the rate of profit which is a ratio, it 'does not acquire a definite meaning until the prices of commodities are determined' (ibid., 33). Sraffa also suggests – without developing this point – that the rate of profit may be determined 'in particular by the level of the money rates of interest' (ibid.), a suggestion which has been taken up by some of his followers as a way to link a price system *à la* Sraffa and money. Since such a view is at odds with Ricardo's contention that in the natural state the rate of interest depends on the rate of profit and not the other way round, it will not be considered here.

7 On the basis of indications given by Ricardo himself in *Principles*, some commentators give a central role to this aspect; see for example in the recent literature Takenaga (2013).

8 This conclusion was already present in Cartelier (1987) and Benetti (1990). In a recent joint paper, these authors (Benetti and Cartelier 2020), take up again the problem of the integration of a classical theory of money in a Sraffa theory of prices. This time they introduce the legal price of the monetary standard (gold) and reach the same conclusion of inconsistency. However, their formalisation assumes that the market price of gold is *always* equal to the legal price, something which they acknowledge as being unfaithful to Ricardo. We will see below that the possible divergence between these two prices of gold is indeed central to Ricardo's theory of money. For a discussion of this point, see Deleplace (2021) followed by their reply and my rejoinder.

9 See for example King (2013: 120): 'There is a very clear link between Ricardo's position on Say's Law and his approach to monetary theory, and here again there is strong support for the conventional interpretation', which King summarises as follows: '[Say's Law] induced Ricardo to deny the existence of "general gluts," and with them any possibility that output might be constrained by deficient effective demand. This also led Ricardo to endorse a strict version of the Quantity Theory of Money and thereby also to accept the neutrality of money' (ibid., 112–13). Speaking of the 'group [of Bullionists] led by Ricardo', Green (199: 137) observes that it 'maintained that exogenous changes in the money supply would be reflected in corresponding variations in the price level, which followed from their assumption of a fixed level of output and monetary velocity. In other words, their short-run quantity "theory" of money was no theory at all but simply a logical outcome of assuming Say's Law'.

10 On these intricacies see King (2013), Meacci (2015).

11 See Samuel Hollander's conclusion to the chapter of his book *The Economics of David Ricardo* entitled 'The quantity theory and the law of markets': 'My analysis of the quantity theory earlier in this chapter has demonstrated a conscious allowance on Ricardo's part for depressions generated by sudden contraction of the money supply, and a conscious treatment of the effects on prices generated by money supply increases in terms of an initial pressure on commodity demand in commodity markets' (Hollander 1979: 512).

12 See, for example Patinkin (1956: 376): 'As against the purely mechanical exposition of the quantity theory in his *Principles*, we have the other passages already cited [from the "Bullion Essays"] that show that he fully understood the effect of an increase in the quantity of money in increasing demand'. Gootzeit (1975: 9) stresses that in *Principles* Ricardo 'did not think it necessary to include a carefully coordinated analysis of his monetary system, which was more descriptive than theoretical'. However, 'Ricardo's monetary writings [the "Bullion Essays"] exhibited a "sophisticated" version of Say's Law because his analysis of the market clearing relationship in a growing inflationary economy concentrated on short run maladjustments generated from the money to the output market' (ibid., 19).

13 Although he maintains that on monetary matters Ricardo was only 'an empirical economist', Davis (2005, 185) refers to his positions during the resumption debate of 1819–21 to show that 'Ricardo's preference for stable prices above all other monetary objectives does not imply that he was blind to the effects of money on output and employment. His ingot plan, his allowance for devaluation if the currency was highly depreciated, and his criticism of the Bank's return to gold all demonstrate that he recognised the nonneutrality of money'.

14 Patinkin was the first to ascribe such effect to 'the classical quantity-theory tradition of Cantillon, Thornton, Ricardo, and [John Stuart] Mill', although it was not 'in the fullest sense of the term' (Patinkin 1956: 98).

15 See for example Hollander (1979: 479–83); Panico (1988: 17); Davis (2005: 9).

16 When this pamphlet was written, there were still legally two standards of money in England, gold and silver. Gold was made the sole legal standard by the Proclamations of February 1817.

17 In the Classical tradition since Adam Smith, the market price of a commodity is determined by dividing the 'effectual demand' of this commodity – the purchasing power in money addressed to the market of the commodity at its natural price – by the quantity of it brought to market. An increase in the quantity of money raises the demand for the commodity above its initial level while its available quantity does not change, so that the market price rises. However, this rise may only maintain *relative* prices constant (neutrality) if the demand increases at the same rate for all commodities, that is, if the supplement of purchasing power in money is allocated to all markets in the initial proportions. This would be a heroic assumption.

18 The competition of capitals – the driving force behind the uniformity of the rate of profit – forced them to do so, whether the market price of gold bullion rose above or fell below the mint price. Ricardo maintained that the lag between a change in the market price of gold bullion and the same change in the money prices of all other commodities was not great, whether upwards or downwards. Being examined by the House of Lords Committee on Resumption on 26 March 1819, he replied to a question on the 'length of time [after which] the prices of commodities conform to the fluctuations in the market price of gold': 'They do not immediately conform, but I do not think it very long before they do' and 'I think the prices of commodities fall from a reduction of the paper circulation quite as soon as gold falls' (V: 452). This channel of transmission between the market price of the standard and all commodity prices operated even when the standard had ceased to regulate the quantity of money (that is, when the convertibility of the Bank of England note had been suspended) because the pound in notes was now depreciated in comparison with the pound in coin. When in 1811 the market price of an ounce of gold bullion paid in notes was quoted £4.12s., as compared with the mint price of gold in coin of £3.17s.10½d., Ricardo wrote: 'Now, as 4*l.*12*s.* of paper currency is of no more value than an ounce of gold bullion, prices are actually raised to the purchaser 18 per cent., in consequence of his purchase being made with paper instead of coin of its bullion value. Eighteen per cent is, therefore, equal to the rise in the price of commodities, occasioned by the depreciation of paper' (Ricardo 181: 239).

19 For a demonstration that a) implies, b) see Deleplace (2017: 94–97) and that a) and b) imply c), see ibid., 245–47.

20 This summing-up is taken from Deleplace (2020); for demonstrations see Deleplace (2017).

21 This equation appears for the first time in Deleplace (2008: 26). An equation linking the purchasing power of money over commodities, its purchasing power over gold, and the relative price of gold in terms of commodities, may be found in Marcuzzo and Rosselli (1994: 1254) and Sato (2013: 56). However, their interpretation of this equation is different from that of the money-standard equation (see Deleplace 2017: 126 n 5).

22 In Chapter XIII 'Taxes on Gold' of *Principles* Ricardo considers the case of the King of Spain who 'were to lay a considerable tax on gold [and] would very much raise its natural value', and he details the consequences 'as its market value in Europe is ultimately regulated by its natural value in Spanish America' (Ricardo 1821: 195).

23 '"The operations of the bank", observed Dr. Smith, alluding to an analogous case, "were upon this account somewhat like the web of Penelope, the work that was done in the day was undone in the night"' (Ricardo 1810–11: 58). In this passage Ricardo also credited Thornton for the same idea.

References

Benetti, Carlo. 1990. *Moneda y Teoria del Valor (Money and the Theory of Value)*. Mexico: Universidad Autonoma Metropolitana / Fondo de Cultura Economica.

Benetti, Carlo. Cartelier, Jean. 2020. 'From Ricardo to Sraffa: Gold as Monetary Standard in a Classical Theory of Money'. In *New Perspectives on Political Economy and Its History*, edited by Maria Cristina Marcuzzo et al., 241–60. Cham: Palgrave Macmillan.

Blaug, Mark. 1995. 'Why Is the Quantity Theory of Money the Oldest Surviving Theory in Economics?' In *The Quantity Theory of Money: From Locke to Keynes and Friedman*, edited by Mark Blaug et al., 27–49. Aldershot: Edward Elgar.

Cartelier, Jean. 1987. 'Emission et valeur de la circulation chez Ricardo'. *Cahiers d'économie politique* 13: 91–104.

Davis, Timothy. 2005. *Ricardo's Macroeconomics: Money, Trade Cycles, & Growth*. Cambridge: Cambridge University Press.

Deleplace, Ghislain. 2008. 'Les deux plans monétaires de Ricardo'. *Cahiers d'économie politique* 55: 13–33.

———. 2017. *Ricardo on Money: A Reappraisal*. Abingdon: Routledge.

———. 2020. 'Orthodox *versus* Unorthodox Views on Ricardo's Theory of Money'. *The European Journal of the History of Economic Thought* 27, no. 6: 819–36.

———. 2021. 'From Ricardo to Sraffa: A Quest for a Modern Classical Standpoint on Money'. In *A Reflection on Sraffa's Revolution in Economic Theory*, edited by Ajit Sinha, 499–514. Cham: Palgrave Macmillan.

———. 2023. 'Power Relations and Monetary Ideas: The Case of the Gold-Exchange Standard in India'. *Review of Political Economy*: forthcoming.

Green, Roy. 1998. 'Money and banking'. In *The Elgar Companion to Classical Economics*, edited by Heinz D. Kurz and Neri Salvadori, vol. 2: 136–41. Cheltenham: Edward Elgar.

Hollander, Samuel. 1979. *The Economics of David Ricardo*. London: Heinemann.

King, John E. 2013. *David Ricardo*. Basingstoke: Palgrave Macmillan.

Laidler, David. 1987. 'Bullionist Controversy'. In *The New Palgrave. A Dictionary of Economics*, edited by John Eatwell et al., vol. I: 289–94. London: Macmillan.

Marcuzzo, Maria Cristina. Rosselli, Annalisa. 1991. *Ricardo and the Gold Standard: The Foundations of the International Monetary Order*. London: Macmillan.

———. 1994. 'Ricardo's Theory of Money Matters. *Revue économique* 45, no. 5: 1251–67.

———. 2015. 'Natural quantity of money'. In *The Elgar Companion to David Ricardo*, edited by Heinz D. Kurz and Neri Salvadori: 370–75. Cheltenham: Edward Elgar.

Meacci, Ferdinando. 2015. 'Say's Law'. In *The Elgar Companion to David Ricardo*, edited by Heinz D. Kurz and Neri Salvadori: 508–15. Cheltenham: Edward Elgar.

Panico, Carlo. 1988. *Interest and Profit in the Theories of Value and Distribution*. New York: St. Martin's Press.

Patinkin, Don. 1956. *Money, Interest, and Prices: An Integration of Monetary and Value Theory*. Evanston: Row, Peterson and Company.

Ricardo, David. 1810–11. *The High Price of Bullion: A Proof of the Depreciation of Bank Notes*. In Ricardo (1951–73), vol. III, 1951.

———. 1811. *Reply to Mr. Bosanquet's 'Practical Observations on the Report of the Bullion Committee'*. In Ricardo (1951–73), vol. III, 1951.

———. 1816. *Proposals for an Economical and Secure Currency*. In Ricardo (1951–73), vol. IV, 1951.

———. 1821. *On the Principles of Political Economy, and Taxation*, 3rd ed. In Ricardo (1951–73), vol. I, 1951.

———. 1824. *Plan for the Establishment of a National Bank.* In Ricardo (1951–73), vol. IV, 1951.
———. 1951–73. *The Works and Correspondence of David Ricardo,* edited by Piero Sraffa with the collaboration of Maurice H. Dobb. Cambridge: Cambridge University Press, 11 vols.
Sato, Yuji. 2013. 'Old and New Interpretations of Classical Monetary Theory'. In *Ricardo on Money and Finance: A Bicentenary Reappraisal*, edited by Yuji Sato and Susumu Takenaga: 53–74. Abingdon: Routledge.
Schumpeter, Joseph A. 1954. *History of Economic Analysis*. New York: Oxford University Press.
Sraffa, Piero. 1960. *Production of Commodities by Means of Commodities: Prelude to a Critique of Economic Theory*. Cambridge: Cambridge University Press.
——— *Sraffa Papers*. Cambridge: Trinity College, Wren Library.
Takenaga, Susumu. 2013. 'Labour Theory of Value and Quantity Theory in Ricardo's Economic Theory'. In *Ricardo on Money and Finance: A Bicentenary Reappraisal*, edited by Yuji Sato and Susumu Takenaga: 77–114. Abingdon: Routledge.

Chapter 3

RICARDO ON FOREIGN TRADE

Gilbert Faccarello

Among David Ricardo's theoretical developments, one is still accepted today, while also the subject of recurring discussions: his views on international trade. These views, however, are most of the time not reported in their complexity but reduced to what was called later the 'principle of comparative advantage', allegedly stated in a few paragraphs of the chapter 'On foreign trade' of his *Principles of Political Economy and Taxation*.[1] Taken out of the context of this chapter and of his other writings as well – and seemingly playing no role in the rest of the book – this 'principle' became the basis of international trade theories.

As will be seen, however, the so-called 'principle of comparative advantage' is a questionable interpretation of Ricardo's text. Ricardo's writings, admittedly, are sometimes ambiguous and he himself recognised this: 'My speaking is like my writing too much compressed', he wrote to Malthus (VI: 335). 'I am too apt to crowd a great deal of difficult matter into so short a space as to be incomprehensible to the generality of readers'. Over the last few decades, however, his works have been the subject of more accurate readings, which show both that the traditional interpretation of this 'principle' is flawed and that a more faithful interpretation is possible. This chapter analyses the basic features of both interpretations, their main points of disagreement and their logical consequences. It will be seen that the alleged 'principle' is no principle at all: it cannot form the basis of any specific economic policy trying to influence the direction of trade, and the benefits a country receives from its participation in international exchanges are just the unintended consequences of the decisions of the many individuals who, in markets, only act for their own benefit.[2]

1. Prelude. Ricardo's Text

In his chapter on foreign trade, Ricardo introduces an exchange between two countries, England and Portugal, each being able to produce two commodities: cloth and wine.[3] The costs of production of these commodities are given in each country: Portugal requires 80 and 90 units of labour per year, respectively, to produce wine and cloth, while England requires 120 and 100 units of labour per year respectively. As Ricardo writes:

> England may be so circumstanced, that to produce the cloth may require the labour of 100 men for one year; and if she attempted to make the wine, it might require the labour of 120 men for the same time. England would therefore find it her interest to import wine, and to purchase it by the exportation of cloth.
>
> To produce the wine in Portugal, might require only the labour of 80 men for one year, and to produce the cloth in the same country, might require the labour of 90 men for the same time. It would therefore be advantageous for her to export wine in exchange for cloth.

With this decisive statement:

> This exchange might even take place, notwithstanding that the commodity imported by Portugal could be produced there with less labour than in England. Though she could make the cloth with the labour of 90 men, she would import it from a country where it required the labour of 100 men to produce it, because it would be advantageous to her rather to employ her capital in the production of wine, for which she would obtain more cloth from England, than she could produce by diverting a portion of her capital from the cultivation of vines to the manufacture of cloth. (I: 135)

Ricardo's view is thus in line with what was called 'the eighteenth-century rule'[4] (Viner 1937: 440) for international trade. In international exchanges, according to this rule, what should be compared are not the real costs of production of a given commodity at home and abroad (as in the absolute advantage approach) but the domestic real costs of the imported and exported commodities. It is thus advantageous to import a quantity of a foreign commodity in exchange for a quantity of a good produced domestically, if the latter is produced at a lower real cost than the domestic production of the imported commodity would entail. Ricardo, however, adds an important statement: this trade is beneficial to the country even if the imported commodity could have been produced at home at a lower cost than that required to produce it abroad.

The advantage that each country gets from free foreign trade is better allocation and accumulation of capital (I: 132–33) and an increase in the quantities and varieties of use values at its disposal (III: 331–32). International trade, however, never increases the value of the annual product of the country (I: 128, 319–20) and never directly influences the rate of profits (this being said in contradiction to Adam Smith and Thomas Robert Malthus) (I: 132). This influence, if any, can only be indirect, for example when the importation of cheap corn from abroad reduces the cultivation of land of worse quality at home, lowers the ground rent and favours profits in consequence.

> It has been my endeavour to shew [...] that the rate of profits can never be increased but by a fall in wages, and that there can be no permanent fall of wages but in consequence of a fall of the necessaries on which wages are expended. If [...] by the extension of foreign trade, or by improvements in machinery, the food and necessaries of the labourer can be brought to market at a reduced price, profits will rise [...] but if the commodities obtained at a cheaper rate [...] be exclusively [...] consumed by the rich, no alteration will take place in the rate of profits. (I: 132)

Ricardo also states that what happens in the exchange between two nations is the same as what happens between two individuals in domestic trade:[5] the benefits obtained by each country are just the result of the division of labour. Adapting an example from the *Wealth of Nations* in which Smith presents the advantages of the division of labour between a tailor and a shoemaker (1776: 456-7), he reports the case of two men making shoes and hats, one of them having greater productivity in both goods but being relatively more productive in making shoes than hats (I: 136n). In this case, he notes, it is in the interest of the first man to specialise in shoes and buy hats from the second, the reverse being advantageous to the second. In the case of countries as in the case of individuals, it is better not to attempt to produce everything at home but instead to specialise in certain productions and to exchange.

However, Ricardo stresses, while the gains from trade follow the same logic at home and between countries, there is an important difference between domestic and international exchange: as the example of the exchange between England and Portugal suggests, the relative international price is not determined by the labour theory of value – 'the quantity of wine which she [Portugal] shall give in exchange for the cloth of England, is not determined by the respective quantities of labour devoted to the production of each' (I: 134–35). Hence the general statement, discussed below: 'The same rule which regulates the relative value of commodities in one country, does not regulate the relative value of the commodities exchanged between two or more countries' (I: 133). This is due, he writes, to the relative international immobility of capital and labour caused by a 'fancied or real insecurity of capital' abroad and a 'natural disinclination which every man has to quit the country of his birth and connexions' (I: 136).

Finally, foreign exchange induces a process of specialisation in the trading nations. But how far can it go? Ricardo never went into details on this topic, but, in one of his simple two-country examples, he admits that in specific cases a country can fully specialise in one of the two goods (I: 138). However, there could logically be cases of partial specialisation, for example when one of the commodities traded is produced with increasing difficulty and also, more relevantly, in more complex and realistic situations where there are more than two goods and two countries.

2. Counterpoint. Two Conflicting Interpretations

Two alternative interpretations of Ricardo's text have been advanced, based on different understandings of the four numbers – or 'four magic numbers', as P. A. Samuelson (1969: 4) called them – which appear in Ricardo's example. The first dates from Ricardo's times, while the second is much more recent.

2.1. The traditional interpretation of Ricardo's example

What is the meaning of the four numbers? The traditional interpretation understands them as the respective autarky costs of production of a unit of each commodity. In other words, the 'magic numbers' are seen as the technical coefficients prevailing in the production processes in the two countries (Table 3.1) before they open to trade. According to the labour theory of value developed in the previous chapters of the *Principles*, they are also the respective labour values of the commodities in each country.

It seems at first sight that an exchange cannot take place between the two countries because in England the cost of production of each commodity is higher than in Portugal. Yet, when the countries open to trade, an exchange is supposed to take place. This is because trade is not based on some 'absolute advantage' a country could have in the production of a commodity but on some 'relative advantage' in its production, that is, an advantage in 'comparative costs'. In England, the pre-trade relative cost of wine in terms of cloth is 120/100, while it is lower in Portugal (80/90); and the relative cost of cloth in terms of wine is 100/120 in England while it is higher in Portugal (90/80). The ratios are different between countries – identical relative costs in both

Table 3.1 Ricardo's example according to the traditional interpretation

	One unit of wine	**One unit of cloth**
Portugal	80	90
England	120	100

nations would not allow any trade – and in the present example, England has a relative advantage in producing cloth (it produces it relatively cheaper than Portugal) and Portugal in producing wine.

The ratios determine the directions of trade: a country exports the commodity that is produced there with the lower relative cost – this is what is called its 'comparative advantage' – and imports the other one. The exchange of commodities in which each country has an absolute advantage is just a special case of this rule. In the present case, England exports cloth to – and imports wine from – Portugal, and Portugal exports wine and imports cloth. And if trade takes place, this is because each country benefits from it: (1) England because it supplies cloth, the unit cost of production of which is 100, in exchange for wine, which it can only produce with a unit cost of 120; (2) and Portugal for a similar reason: it supplies wine, the unit cost of which is 80, in return for cloth, which it can only produce at a unit cost of 90. However, this reasoning is not really conclusive, because at this stage the possible gains from trade will depend on the quantities exchanged, not yet specified. Finally, this interpretation concludes, the two countries are induced to specialise in the production of one commodity. Thus, with given productive resources, they can each enjoy a greater amount of use values.

2.2. The origins of the traditional view

This interpretation of Ricardo's text is basically due to James Mill and was stated in various ways in the three editions of his *Elements of Political Economy* (1821, 1824, 1826) (Faccarello 2022). As Ricardo was not easy to read, and as Mill was close to Ricardo and his *Elements* was supposed to be a 'School Book' explaining the main points developed in Ricardo's *Principles* – 'I have been making good progress with my School Book of Political Economy. In fact I have got over all the knotty points; and, as I think, clearly; so that any body will understand them' (Mill to Ricardo, 28 December 1820, VIII: 327) – his text was taken as the expression of Ricardo's ideas, especially on 'comparative advantage', a subject on which Mill multiplied the examples. As John Ramsey McCulloch put it, 'The study of Mr Ricardo's work […] has been much facilitated by the labours of late writers […] Mr Mill's *Elements of Political Economy* is a work of a higher order' (McCulloch 1824: 71). Four decades later, the readers of the *The New American Cyclopaedia. A Popular Dictionary of General Knowledge* could read that Mill's *Elements* 'presented the views of Ricardo in a precise and clear style' (Ripley and Dana 1861: 502).

Two additional facts are worth noting at this point. In the first place, reasoning in terms of ratios to express the comparative advantage of each country cannot formally be found in Ricardo. These ratios are advanced by James Mill (1821: 88), who also speaks of 'the purchasing power of one commodity with respect to another' in each country (1824: 118; 1826: 124).

In the second place, the phrase 'principle of comparative advantage' is also not to be found in Ricardo. The words 'comparative' or 'comparatively' are, it is true, extensively used in the *Principles* with the meaning of 'relative', for example when Ricardo refers to the 'comparative value' or 'comparative quantity' of commodities. The phrase 'comparative advantage' is however not to be found in his chapter on foreign trade but appears incidentally once in the context of an open economy (I: 172, 263). 'Comparative disadvantage' is also used once, in the context of taxation (I: 172). As regards costs in relation to international trade, the phrases 'comparative difficulty of production' and 'comparative facility [of] production' are employed (Works I: 343, 374). But the final and systematic meaning of the phrases emerged in the writings of James and John Stuart Mill and Robert Torrens. James Mill wrote of 'comparative facility' of production (J. Mill 1821: 84) and contrasted 'greater absolute' with 'greater relative, facility' of production (1821: 87). He also spoke of 'peculiar advantages' with the meaning of comparative advantage (1821: 84). For his part, in the third and fourth editions of his *Essay on the External Corn Trade* (1826, 1827), Torrens started to clearly designate the doctrine with the phrases 'comparative advantage' or 'disadvantage' (1826: vii) and 'comparative costs' (1827: 401). The young Stuart Mill also used the phrase 'comparative cost(s)' (1829–30: 233, 235–36, 254) and, to speak of comparative advantage, wrote of a commodity in which the 'advantage is least' or the 'advantage is greatest' (ibid: 233).

2.3. Some difficulties

Mill's interpretation, however, presents some difficulties that were immediately spotted by his son. The main problem was that, once the 'magic numbers' are interpreted as technical coefficients, some important questions are left unanswered. In particular, the quantities exchanged between the two countries and the price at which this exchange is made are unknown. From this point of view, Ricardo's approach is allegedly incomplete. The magnitude of the possible benefits each country obtains from foreign trade, which depends on the quantities exchanged and the international relative price, are also unknown. The young J. S. Mill tried to solve the problem by introducing the reciprocal demands of the countries into the picture. In his 1829–30 essay 'Of the laws of interchange between nations, and the distribution of the gains of commerce among the countries of the commercial world' – later published in his 1844 *Essays on Some Unsettled Questions of Political Economy* – he considered different price-elasticities of the countries' demands for imports. Each country's demand for imports, he stated, is assumed to depend on the possible barter ratios between the commodities: once the reciprocal demands are known, the international equilibrium relative price, the quantities exchanged and the benefits obtained by each nation can be determined. This relative price must lie within the interval bounded by the countries' autarky relative prices of the commodities, and the closer (further away) this rate is to a country's relative autarky price, the smaller (the greater) are this country's gains from trade – these gains being nil when the two coincide. This approach was developed afterwards by generations of economists.[6]

However, another difficulty arises that can also be found in Ricardo's texts but on which commentators remained silent. The analysis is made at the macro level, and what seem always at stake are the interests of the countries: once its comparative advantage is known, a country is assumed to act accordingly, orienting trade in consequence. 'Under a system of perfectly free commerce, each country naturally devotes its capital and labour to such employments as are most beneficial to each' (Works I: 133). Portugal and England are seemingly the protagonists in the game. 'England would […] find it her interest to import wine, and to purchase it by the exportation of cloth', and similarly 'it would […] be advantageous' to Portugal 'to export wine in exchange for cloth' (Works I: 135). But the countries are not themselves the agents of trade: they do not decide to import and export such or such commodity with a view to obtaining the benefit indicated by the 'principle'. Economies are market-based and the traders are individual agents: they act in markets according to their own private interests and only engage in international trade if it is profitable for them. In this perspective, the 'principle of comparative advantage' is of no use to them – except perhaps if we imagine traders making arbitrages in real terms on commodities (Faccarello 2015a: 760–61), but this approach turns out to be a blind alley.

Finally, it must be noted that, in the chapter on foreign trade, the most extensive developments mainly deal with money prices and gold flows between countries, but this aspect of the analysis is not taken seriously in the traditional interpretation of Ricardo's text. Although James (1821, Chapter 3, Sections XII–XV) and John Stuart Mill (1829–30: 241 et seq.) did try to deal with this question, their analyses only confirm the traditional view conducted in real terms (Faccarello 2022). Yet, are Ricardo's monetary developments purely decorative? Is it legitimate to ignore them and to isolate Ricardo's celebrated example – expressed in real terms and generally interpreted as a barter between the two countries – from the rest of the chapter?

2.4. The challenging view: Ricardo's example in a new perspective

The above presentation of Ricardo's views on foreign trade was challenged some decades ago. A new interpretation emerged, basically due to Sraffa (1930) – who however did not develop it – and Yukizawa (1974, 1978), restated by Ruffin (2002) and developed by Maneschi (2004) and Faccarello (2015a).[7]

At first sight, the differences between this analysis and the traditional one appear to be of trifling importance. It states that the 'magic numbers' cannot be interpreted as technical coefficients and that, in his example, Ricardo is not dealing with countries in situations of autarky – which would afterwards open to exchanges on the basis of their comparative advantages – but is instead directly starting with an actual exchange between England and Portugal. The quantities exchanged are known – 'the quantity of [Portuguese] wine', not specified, is exchanged against 'the cloth of England' (I: 134) – and the exchange ratio between the two countries is thus also given.

In modern terms, *a* units of Portuguese wine are exchanged for *b* units of English cloth. In this perspective, the 'four magic numbers' are the respective costs of production, actual or potential, of the quantities exchanged: if each country had to produce these same quantities of both commodities, Portugal would employ 80 and 90 units of labour respectively to produce *a* units of wine and *b* units of cloth, while England would need 120 and 100 units of labour respectively (Table 3.2). These numbers, in each country, are also the respective labour values of these quantities. As before, and for the same reasons, the fact that Portugal has lower real costs in the production of both quantities does not prevent the exchange from happening.

Now what can be said of the gains from trade? As in the traditional interpretation, the exchange between England and Portugal is not only possible but profitable to both countries – and possible because profitable. However, contrary to the traditional view, the gains from trade are immediately determined, without the need to introduce reciprocal demand schedules or any additional hypotheses. For one country, the gains consist in the difference between the cost of production – here the units of labour – the country would have spent in the home production of the quantity of foreign commodity it imports and the cost of the quantity of the home commodity it exports in exchange. Portugal's gains from trade are thus 10 units of labour – Portugal gives *a* units of wine, the product of 80 units of labour, for *b* units of cloth which would have required 90 units to produce at home. England's gains from trade are determined in a similar way: they amount to 20 units of labour. The immediate calculation of the gains from trade illustrates in a very

Table 3.2 The 'four magic numbers' in Ricardo's text

	***a* units of wine**	***b* units of cloth**
Portugal	80	90
England	120	100

clear and straightforward manner the 'eighteenth-century rule' adapted by Ricardo. While the gains from trade are not equal on both sides, both countries nevertheless benefit from trade and save resources – and this aspect is also immediately clear in the present perspective.

3. Variations. Further Questions and Developments

While more faithful to Ricardo's text, the new interpretation of his views on foreign trade tells only part of the story, sticking as it does to Ricardo's always quoted few paragraphs of the *Principles*. It leaves important problems unsolved, some of them similar to the difficulties met by the traditional view. In a nutshell: (1) the analysis is still conducted at the macro level, and does not explain why the decisions of selfish individual traders in free markets lead to this result; (2) the analysis is still made in real terms, and thus neglects the extended monetary developments of the chapter on foreign trade; (3) while the analysis now starts from an actual exchange between England and Portugal – the quantities exchanged and the international relative price thus being known – and allows an immediate calculation of the gains from trade, it is not clear how this price is determined. These difficulties, as will be seen, are interconnected: a change of perspective in the analysis actually opens the way to their solution.

3.1. A change of perspective: money and markets

The traditional view is a macroeconomic and ex-ante approach to foreign trade: the countries are first in autarky, calculate their comparative advantages and open to trade in consequence. Ricardo's approach is the reverse. It presents an ex-post situation – the exchange has already taken place – but what happens before and leads to the final result at the macro level can only be grasped at the micro level. Ricardo often insisted that economic phenomena have to be explained on the basis of the individual choices of free agents in search of profitability. 'It is self-interest which regulates all the speculations of trade', he wrote in *The High Price of Bullion* (Works III: 102). The objection that agents might not act in such a way is off the mark, he wrote to Malthus, 'because that is a question of fact not of science, and might be urged against almost every proposition in Political Economy' (VI: 64). And this is as true for foreign transactions as it is for domestic trade: whenever there is an outflow of specie, for example, 'a very little reflection will convince us that it is our choice, and not our necessity, that sends it abroad' (III: 55). The same words are used in the *Principles*: 'When merchants engage their capitals in foreign trade […] it is always from choice, and never from necessity' (I: 293). Finally, in his *Reply to*

Mr. Bosanquet's 'Practical Observations on the Report of the Bullion Committee', Ricardo warns his readers against the fallacies of aggregate analysis: the countries are not the agents of trade (III: 207–8):

> Mr. Bosanquet speaks as if the nation collectively, as one body, imported corn and exported gold […] not reflecting that the importation of corn […] is the act of individuals, and governed by the same motives as all other branches of trade. What is the degree of *compulsion* which is employed to make us receive corn from our enemy? I suppose no other than the want of that commodity which makes it an advantageous article of import; but if it be a voluntary […] and not a compulsory bargain between the two nations, I […] maintain that gold would not, even if famine raged amongst us, be given to France in exchange for corn, unless the exportation of gold was attended with advantage to the exporter.

We must thus introduce individual traders into the picture, but also money. Merchants deal with money prices, they do not barter: 'Every transaction in commerce is an independent transaction' (Works I: 138). When they buy abroad and import, they settle the transaction with a bill of exchange which they buy in a specialised market, and they receive such a bill when they export commodities. The business of a Portuguese merchant who buys cloth in England 'is simply to purchase English cloth, and to pay for it by a bill of exchange, which he purchases with Portuguese money. It is to him of no importance what becomes of this money: he has discharged his debt by the remittance of the bill' (Works I: 138). The monetary context is an ideal gold standard,[8] in which gold is freely traded domestically and abroad and banknotes are convertible into gold on demand.

Merchants engage in trade only if it is profitable for them to do so. In order to buy and sell commodities, they consider their prices and they make a transaction if they expect to sell them at a higher price than they bought them, the transportation costs being included in the computation (Works I: 138, 170). They compare gold prices of the same commodity at home and abroad and thus do not follow the logic of the macroeconomic 'eighteenth century rule': 'The motive which determines us to import a commodity, is the discovery of its relative cheapness abroad: it is the comparison of its price abroad with its price at home' (Works I: 170). To refer to Ricardo's example, English merchants import (Portuguese merchants export) wine if and only if the price of wine is higher in England than in Portugal and English merchants export (Portuguese merchants import) cloth if and only if cloth is dearer in Portugal than in England (Works I: 137). Let p_w and p_w^* be the gold prices of wine in England and in Portugal respectively, and p_c and p_c^* the respective prices of cloth in these countries. Portuguese merchants export wine or import cloth (English merchants export cloth or import wine) if $p_w^* < p_w$ and $p_c^* > p_c$, hence if:

$$\frac{p_w^*}{p_c^*} < \frac{p_w}{p_c}$$

These ratios between the prices of wine and cloth in the two countries respect the inequality, on which the traditional approach insists, between the unit cost ratios in the different countries – in each country, the ratio is even equal to the ratio of labour values because the currency is the same for both commodities. It thus seems that the 'principle of comparative advantage' is found again at the individual level. But this is an illusion. The above inequality between the ratios is just the consequence of – and an arbitrary connection between – two independent transactions, and the notion of a 'comparative advantage' as traditionally understood does not explain anything here. This is certainly the reason why Ricardo does not refer to it in the rest of the *Principles* and in his other writings – this fact was puzzling for the traditional interpretation and raised the vexed question of the authorship of the 'principle'.

In Ricardo's example, however, an important question arises because it seems that the above structure of prices supposes that each country has an absolute advantage in one commodity, which is not the case. In other words, while, owing to the respective costs of production of (*a* units of) wine in the two countries, it seems intuitively true that the price of wine will be higher in England than in Portugal, this is not the case with (*b* units of) cloth: could its price in Portugal be higher than in England, while its cost is (much) lower? Yet 'cloth cannot be imported into Portugal, unless it sell there for more gold than it cost in the country from which it was imported' (I: 137). As an example, Ricardo supposes that the price of one pipe of wine is respectively £50 in England and £45 in Portugal, and 'a certain quantity' of cloth is £45 in England and £50 in Portugal (I: 138). What could explain the comparative level of these prices, so different from that of the real costs?

The reason is, Ricardo states, that gold does not necessarily have the same relative value in different countries (I: 142–43). It is important, Ricardo insists in contradiction to Henry Thornton and James Mill, to keep in mind the distinction between the price and the (relative) value of gold. The monetary units of nations are defined by specific weights of gold, and currencies are convertible into each other at the rate given by the mint prices: as for all commodities, the price of gold is its price in terms of currency. The relative value of gold is its exchange ratio with such or such commodity: 'when we speak of the [relative] value of bullion we mean a very different thing – we mean […] to measure it by some other commodity, – corn, coffee […] or any amongst the thousands of commodities which may be exported' (to Mill, VI: 54–55).[9] In a perfect gold standard, the price of gold is uniform 'throughout the globe' thanks to the variations of the price of the bills of exchange and the foreign exchange. Contrary to its price, its relative value does not have this uniformity.

As a matter of fact, while being the standard, gold remains a commodity produced and traded like any others: 'There does not appear to me to be any substantial difference between bullion and any other commodity, as far as regards the regulation of its value, and the laws which determine its exportation or importation' (to Malthus, VI: 24). Its relative value thus depends on its natural or market value, which themselves depends on two factors (I: 143–46): (1) the distance of the country from the gold mines (I: 144) and (2) the comparative skill of the home producers vis-à-vis their foreign competitors I: 146), which determine the flows of international trade. This second reason is predominant at an advanced stage of development (I: 144). However, these two causes do not play the same role: (1) the first regulates the natural value of gold in different nations and (2) the second, through variations in the quantity of gold available in a country, determines its market value and thus the gold prices of commodities. The first is stable in the short run, while the second, depending on the flows of international trade, is constantly at work, affecting countries in different ways. These fluctuations in the market value of gold and thus in the gold prices of commodities, Ricardo writes, are the great regulator of foreign trade (I: 343).

Now, if gold does not have the same relative value everywhere, gold prices of commodities will generally be higher, all other things being equal, where this value is lower, and lower where it is higher. This means that commodities produced in exactly the same conditions in terms of labour value could well not have the same gold price. This is the reason why, in international trade, the labour theory of value does not seem to work. This does not mean that exchanges within and between countries are regulated by different principles. In both cases, they are governed by gold prices. But, within a country, the value of gold is approximately uniform – or could sometimes differ between two regions but to a much lesser extent (III: 87) – and relative prices are thus determined by labour values. This is also the reason why, when the differences between countries are great, as we can suppose they are in Ricardo's example, it could happen that a commodity (cloth) having a lower labour value can have a higher price in one country (Portugal) than the same commodity with a superior labour value in the other country (England).

3.2. International prices

The initial international exchange ratio (*a* Portuguese wine = *b* English cloth) is taken for granted in Ricardo's example. But how is it determined? In the first place, it is important to note that, asked in this traditional way, the question is inaccurate because this ratio is just the result of two independent transactions made in money terms, and not a direct exchange between the two quantities of commodities. To state how international prices of commodities are determined, we must thus revert as before to the rationale of single transactions. In the second place, we have to return to Ricardo's statement that the labour theory of value is of no use because of the relative international immobility of capital and labour.

While the explanation of a possible difference with labour values has just been given above, this second point must nevertheless be addressed because it focused the attention of commentators and, in the end, has been an obstacle to a correct solution of the problem. Ricardo's statement has been accepted as obvious. But it is not: why should the relative immobility of 'capital and population' (I: 134) imply that the theory of value is no longer valid in international exchanges? His reasoning on this point is ambiguous and prone to mislead commentators, in particular because he leaves the ground of the labour theory of value and switches to his alternative theory of natural prices based on the principle of the uniformity of the rate of profit: the so-called prices of production.[10] In this perspective, the relative immobility of capital between countries implies that the rates of profit – which tend to uniformity in a single country 'or differ only as the employment of capital may be more or less secure and agreeable' (I: 134) – cannot be equalised between nations: what happens between London and Yorkshire cannot take place between England and 'Holland, or Spain, or Russia' (I: 134). But the argument is not conclusive because, even supposing an internationally uniform rate of profit, commodities would anyway *not* have been exchanged according to their labour values – we know that, except in very special cases, the two theories of natural prices (labour value and production prices) imply different exchange ratios, even if Ricardo thought that the first was a good approximation of the second. As a consequence, the hypothesis of an international immobility of capital and labour cannot justify the invalidity of the theory of labour value in foreign trade. This hypothesis is not necessary to Ricardo's approach, nor is it respected by Ricardo himself, who, in many places, admitted this mobility as a real fact (see, e.g. VIII: 357–58).[11]

Now, as regards the establishment of international prices, a clear solution exists: it is developed in Chapters 25 ('On Colonial Trade') and

28 ('On the Comparative Value of Gold, Corn, and Labour, in Rich and in Poor Countries') of the *Principles*. There, Ricardo insists that, if we disregard the transportation costs, the price of an imported good in the home market is basically the same as in the exporting country:

> It may […] be again remarked, that […] no more will be paid for commodities by foreign purchasers than by home purchasers; the price which they will both pay will not differ greatly from their natural price in the country where they are produced. England, for example, will, under ordinary circumstances, always be able to buy French goods, at the natural price of those goods in France. (I: 340–41)

Let the price of one unit of corn be £3 in France but £6 in England because of a prohibition on the importation of corn to this country. If this prohibition were removed, importation from France would change the price of corn in England. To what extent? All other things being equal, until the English consumer pays the French price:

> If […] the prohibition of importation were removed, corn would fall in the English market, not to a price between 6*l.* and 3*l.*, but ultimately and permanently to the natural price of France, the price at which it could be furnished to the English market, and afford the usual and ordinary profits of stock in France; and it would remain at this price, whether England consumed a hundred thousand, or a million of quarters. (I: 374–75)

Of course, if the quantity imported were so great that the French producers were obliged to cultivate less fertile land in order to increase their production, the price of corn would then rise in both countries. But this does not change the principle of the determination of prices: 'it is the natural price of commodities in the exporting country, which ultimately regulates the prices at which they shall be sold, if they are not the objects of monopoly, in the importing country' (I: 375). Finally, all this logically implies that, in the end, 'exportable commodities' each have the same gold price in the different trading nations, corrected by various costs – which can be substantial, especially if duties, taxes, etc., are added – incurred by the merchants.

4. Postlude. Back to the Macro Level

The international flows of commodities, generated at the individual level, are of material importance for the country because they globally determine its state of equilibrium. Reciprocally, a global disequilibrium and the induced variations of prices are likely to change the magnitude and direction of these flows and the possible specialisation of the country. It is thus time to turn to the macroeconomic side of Ricardo's analysis, which illustrates when and why gold does not have the same market value in different countries and describes the dynamics of exchanges.

4.1. Equilibrium in trade

Ricardo calls a global state of equilibrium 'a trade of barter' (I: 137, 140, 142). The use of the word 'barter' is surprising because, for him, 'every transaction in commerce is an independent transaction'. Yet he writes of 'a trade of barter, which all commerce, both foreign and domestic, really is' (I: 220). For a country, this is in fact the case when there are no international flows of bullion, that is, when the total price of exports balances the total price of imports. 'England might possibly import more goods from, than she would export to, France', Ricardo writes, 'but she would in consequence export more to some other country, and France would import more from that country; so that the exports and imports of all countries would balance each other' (III: 53–54; see also VI: 64). There are not necessarily bilateral equilibria between them, except by chance, and the equilibrium is reached by the compensation of deficits by surpluses through the circulation of bills of exchange. A country thus acts *as if*, at the macroeconomic level, it were bartering bundles of goods with all the other countries taken as a whole. Ricardo (I: 141–42, 145) also uses the phrase 'equilibrium of money' to depict such a situation because 'the distribution of the precious metals' among nations is stable.

This state of equilibrium, however, is a fiction showing where free market forces would lead all other things being equal. However, Ricardo writes to Malthus, these other things are never equal: 'there is no degree of permanence in the proportions between the currencies and the commodities of nations, – they are subject to constant fluctuations always approaching an absolute level but never really finding it' (VI: 39–40). Destabilising shocks constantly occur, which change the distribution of gold among nations and impact foreign trade. The logic at work is always the same: a destabilising shock suddenly changes the relative amount of circulating medium in the country, which, all other things being equal, becomes either 'redundant' or scarce. This 'superabundance' or scarcity generates price movements which in turn provoke changes in the flows of trade.

A destabilising shock can be monetary if it results from an excessive or over-restrictive emission of notes, or real if it is caused, for example, by a bad harvest or by a change in the technology of the economy. Bad harvests or technical progress, just like an over-issue of notes, also provoke an excess of circulating medium, either because fewer commodities are circulated during the period (bad harvest) or because of the fall in certain prices (technical progress). The disruptions they provoke can be temporary (bad harvest, monetary shock) or persist in the longer term (technical progress) and lead to a new equilibrium in trade. Taxes, tariffs, subsidies, bounties or treatises of commerce also induce disruptive effects on trade: they are analysed along the same lines (I: 141–42, 343) and can be either temporary or long-lasting, depending on the persistence of the policy.

4.2. Destabilising shocks: temporary

Let us first deal with a monetary shock. What happens during the ensuing period of adjustment? In the case of an over-issue, for example, the rise in prices 'being confined to this country alone [...] would check exportation and encourage importation' (Ricardo to Malthus, VI: 74). But the phenomenon is temporary because, as a consequence, there would be 'a demand for bills and a fall in the exchange' which restore the previous flows of foreign trade. 'This rise of prices and fall of the exchange, [...] would not be temporary [...] unless it were corrected by a reduction of the amount of the currency here' (VI: 74:), which is the case in a regime of convertibility.

The story is not essentially different in a regime of inconvertible paper money. While the over-issue cannot be corrected automatically, the effect on foreign trade is the same. The exchange rate deviates from par 'in the same proportion as [...] money might be multiplied beyond that quantity which would have been allotted' to the country 'by general commerce, if the trade in money had been free, and the precious metals had been used, either for money, or for the standard of money' (I: 230). As before, foreign trade is only affected temporarily because 'the effect on the exchange would counterbalance the effect of high prices' (I: 232). Suppose, Ricardo writes, that the circulation of gold pound sterling is replaced by paper money, and this paper money is doubled in quantity. What will happen?

> [E]very commodity in England would be raised to double its former price, and the exchange would be 50 per cent against England; but this would occasion no disturbance in foreign commerce, nor discourage the manufacture of any one commodity. If, for example, cloth rose in England from 20*l.* to 40*l.* per piece, we should just as freely export it after as before the rise, for a compensation of 50 per cent would be made to the foreign purchaser in the exchange; so that with 20*l.* of his money, he could purchase a bill which would enable him to pay a debt of 40*l.* in England. (I: 231)

4.3. Destabilising shocks: permanent

In the case of a technological shock, Ricardo supposes that England can now produce wine in a very economical way. Before the innovation, the prices of one unit of wine or cloth were, respectively, £50 and £45 in England, and £45 and £50 in Portugal. After the innovation, wine would fall to £45 in England 'while cloth continued at its former price, and in Portugal no alteration would take place in the price of either commodity' (I: 137). This would progressively modify the flows of exchange between the two countries. England, the innovating country, stops importing wine from Portugal. Portugal continues to import cloth from England but exports bullion instead of wine since gold will then be the cheapest commodity.[12]

As a consequence, a quantity of gold leaves Portugal and flows into England. Prices change accordingly: the products of the innovating country, England, become dearer, and those of Portugal cheaper. Consequently the price of cloth rises 'to 46*l.* or 47*l.*' in England and falls 'to 49*l.* or 48*l.*' in Portugal (I: 140). The flows of gold and the induced movements in prices will continue for a while, as long as cloth is exported to Portugal 'because its price would continue to be higher in Portugal than here'. But this exportation will eventually stop when 'the accumulation of money [gold] here, and its diminution abroad, should so operate on the relative value of cloth in the two countries, that it would cease to be profitable to export it' (I: 137). In the end, England stops importing wine and Portugal stops importing cloth.

But it is even possible, Ricardo states, that with an important technological shock, the alteration in the flows of trade may be so strong as to reverse the initial flows of trade. In this case, England could end up by exporting wine and importing cloth, and Portugal by exporting cloth and importing wine. 'If the improvement in making wine were of a very important description, it might become profitable for the two countries to exchange employments; for England to make all the wine, and Portugal all the cloth consumed by them' (I: 137–38).

Ricardo was however aware of the limits of the simple model which overrates the magnitude and the consequences of the international movements of gold. Changes in gold flows, prices and flows of foreign trade appear so clear-cut because a very small number of commodities are taken into account. If, he writes, we consider the many commodities that can be the objects of trade between the two nations – 'the thousands of commodities which may be exported' (VI: 55) – the price movements generated in these countries by a technical innovation will seriously be dampened because the inflows and outflows of gold will be less important.

Portuguese merchants, for example, no longer being able to export wine, could export another commodity instead of gold.

> By the abstraction of money [gold] from one country, and the accumulation of it in another, all commodities are affected in price, and consequently encouragement is given to the exportation of many more commodities besides money [gold], which will therefore prevent so great an effect from taking place on the value of money [gold] in the two countries as might otherwise be expected. (I: 141)

The previous pages show that we should be cautious in our interpretations of Ricardo, and be well aware of the complexity of his texts – 'too much compressed', it is true. There is no doubt that they present many difficulties and ambiguities, but despite these obstacles Ricardo's coherent approach can be restated. It is simply not legitimate to isolate some two-country two-commodity examples, or just a few paragraphs, from the rest of his works. Each part of his writings is a piece in a kind of jigsaw puzzle – it cannot be contemplated separately and only finds its relevance when all the pieces of the picture are put together again. And sometimes, one seemingly predominant piece simply fades away when put in proper perspective: this is what happens to the 'principle of comparative advantage'.

Notes

1 Chapter 6 in the first edition, 1817, Chapter 7 in the subsequent ones, 1819 and 1821. The content, however, remained unchanged. All references to Ricardo's writings are to the 1951–73 Sraffa edition in the following format: volume: page.

2 This chapter is based on Faccarello (2015a, 2015b, 2022). The literature on Ricardo and international trade is immense: I only focus here on some basic points.

3 An example of an exchange of cloth and wine between England and Portugal can already be found in Ricardo's 'Notes on Bentham's "Sur les prix"' (1810–11, III: 330).

4 For a qualification of this appellation, see Faccarello (2015a: 758n).

5 For Ricardo, there is no fundamental difference between domestic and international trade. See Faccarello (2015a: Section 3).

6 On some aspects of this history see, for example, Viner (1937), Maneschi (1998), King (2013: Ch. 4), Gehrke (2017). The attribution to Ricardo of the 'principle of comparative advantage' was contested and authorship was sometimes granted to Robert Torrens or James Mill himself – see, for example, Thweatt (1976), Maneschi (1998), Aldrich (2004) and Ruffin (2005). While the traditional *interpretation* of the so-called principle can without doubt be attributed to J. Mill (Faccarello 2022), the question of authorship fades away once a more accurate interpretation of Ricardo's paragraphs is made – the 'principle' itself vanishes.

7 On Yukizawa, whose contributions are still not translated, see Tabuchi (2017); on Ruffin's account, see Gehrke (2015).

8 The theoretical approach also involves a version of the quantity theory of money and a specie-flow mechanism (the existence of bounties, taxes, etc. is disregarded at this point). It must be noted that, in the texts, the use of the term 'money' is in places ambiguous: Ricardo refers sometimes to gold (the standard) and sometimes to the currency, thus provoking possible misinterpretations.

9 The phrase 'purchasing power of gold', sometimes used by commentators in this context, is anachronistic and rejected in advance by Ricardo. 'When we speak of the high or low value of gold, silver, or any other commodity in different countries, we should always mention some medium in which we are estimating them, or no idea can be attached to the proposition. Thus, when gold is said to be dearer in England than in Spain, if no commodity is mentioned, what notion does the assertion convey? If corn, olives […] be at a cheaper price in Spain than in England; estimated in those commodities, gold is dearer in Spain. If, again, hardware, sugar […] be at a lower price in England than in Spain, then, estimated in those commodities, gold is dearer in England. Thus gold appears dearer or cheaper in Spain, as the fancy of the observer may fix on the medium by which he estimates its value' (I: 376–77; see also IV: 59–60).

10 We know that Ricardo struggled with his theories of value and prices and significantly modified his presentation thereof from the first (1817) to the third (1821) editions of his *Principles* – he was still dealing with this question a few months before his death in the 1823 manuscripts 'Absolute value and exchangeable value' (Sraffa 1951). For a recent restatement see Faccarello (2015c).

11 The hypothesis of an international immobility of capital seems instead to be necessary to some traditional approaches to Ricardo's texts. On this point, and for the refutation of other possible objections to the present developments, see Faccarello (2015a: 764, 767–68).

12 For Ricardo, bullion is a commodity like any other: it is in fact the third commodity behind the usual two-commodity model. 'There does not appear to me to be any substantial difference between bullion and any other commodity, as far as regards the regulation of its value, and the laws which determine its exportation or importation. It is true that bullion, besides being a commodity useful in the arts, has been adopted universally as a measure of value, and a medium of exchange; but it has not on that account been taken out of the list of commodities' (to Malthus, VI: 24).

References

Aldrich, John. 2004. 'The Discovery of Comparative Advantage'. *Journal of the History of Economic Thought* 26, no. 3: 379–99.

Faccarello, Gilbert. 2015a. 'A Calm Investigation into Mr Ricardo's Principles of International trade'. *The European Journal of the History of Economic Thought* 22, no. 5: 754–90.

Faccarello, Gilbert. 2015b. 'Comparative advantage'. In *The Elgar Companion to David Ricardo*, edited by Heinz D. Kurz and Neri Salvadori, 69–77. Cheltenham: Edward Elgar.

Faccarello, Gilbert. 2015c. 'Labour Theory of Value'. In *The Elgar Companion to David Ricardo*, edited by Heinz D. Kurz and Neri Salvadori, 245–55. Cheltenham: Edward Elgar.

Faccarello, Gilbert. 2022. '"I Profess to Have Made No Discovery". James Mill on Comparative Advantage'. *The European Journal of the History of Economic Thought* 29, no. 1: 61–81.

Gehrke, Christian. 2015. 'Ricardo's discovery of comparative advantage revisited. A critique of Ruffin's account'. *The European Journal of the History of Economic Thought* 22, no. 5: 791–817.

Gehrke, Christian. 2017. 'Foreign trade, international values, and gains from trade: Ricardo, Pennington, Whewell, and John Stuart Mill'. In *Ricardo and International Trade*, edited by Shigeyoshi Senga, Masatomi Fujimoto and Taichi Tabuchi, 139–63. New York: Routledge.

King, John E. 2013. *David Ricardo*. London: Palgrave Macmillan.

Maneschi, Andrea. 1998. *Comparative Advantage in International Trade. A Historical Perspective*. Cheltenham: Edward Elgar.

Maneschi, Andrea. 2004. 'The true meaning of Ricardo's four magic numbers'. *Journal of International Economics* 62, no. 2: 433–43.

McCulloch, John Ramsay. 1824. *A Discourse on the Rise, Progress, Peculiar Objects and Importance of Political Economy*. Edinburgh: Archibald Constable and Co.

Mill, James. 1821. *Elements of Political Economy*. London: Baldwin, Cradock and Joy.

Mill, James. 1824. *Elements of Political Economy*. Second edition. London: Baldwin, Cradock and Joy.

Mill, James. 1826. *Elements of Political Economy*. Third edition. London: Baldwin, Cradock and Joy.

Mill, John Stuart. 1829–30. 'Of the Laws of Interchange between Nations, and the Distribution of the Gains of Commerce among the Countries of the Commercial World'. In *Essays on Some Unsettled Questions of Political Economy*, 1–46. London: John W. Parker, 1844. As in *Collected Works of John Stuart Mill*, vol. IV: *Essays on Economics and Society, 1824-1845*, 232–61. Toronto: The University of Toronto Press, 1967.

Ricardo, David. 1951–73. *The Works and Correspondence of David Ricardo*, edited by Piero Sraffa with the collaboration of Maurice Herbert Dobb. Cambridge: Cambridge University Press.

Ripley, George and Charles A. Dana (eds). 1861. *The New American Cyclopaedia. A Popular Dictionary of General Knowledge*, vol. XI, New York: D. Appleton and Company.

Ruffin, Roy. 2002. 'David Ricardo's Discovery of Comparative Advantage'. *History of Political Economy* 34, no. 4: 727–48.

Ruffin, Roy. 2005. 'Debunking a Myth: Torrens on Comparative Advantage'. *History of Political Economy* 37, no. 4: 711–22.

Samuelson, Paul Anthony. 1969. 'Presidential Address. The Ways of an Economist'. In *International Economic Relations. Proceedings of the Third Congress of the International Economic Association*, edited by P. A. Samuelson, 1–11. London: Palgrave Macmillan.

Smith, Adam. 1776. *An Inquiry into the Nature and Causes of the Wealth of Nations*. Oxford: Oxford University Press, 1976.

Sraffa, Piero. 1930. 'An Alleged Correction of Ricardo'. *The Quarterly Journal of Economics* 44, no. 3: 539–45.

Sraffa, Piero. 1951. 'Introduction' to *The Works and Correspondence of David Ricardo*, edited by Piero Sraffa with the collaboration of Maurice Herbert Dobb. Cambridge: Cambridge University Press, vol. I: xiii–xliv.

Tabuchi, Taichi. 2017. 'Yukizawa's Interpretation of Ricardo's Theory of Comparative Costs'. In *Ricardo and International Trade*, edited by Shigeyoshi Senga, Masatomi Fujimoto and Taichi Tabuchi, 48–59. New York: Routledge.

Thweatt, William O. 1976. 'James Mill and the Early Development of Comparative Advantage'. *History of Political Economy* 8, no. 2: 207–34.

Torrens, Robert. 1826. *Essay on the External Corn Trade.* 3rd ed. London: Longman, Rees, Orme, Brown and Green.

Torrens, Robert. 1827. *Essay on the External Corn Trade.* 4th ed. London: Longman, Rees, Orme, Brown and Green.

Viner, Jacob. 1937. *Studies in the Theory of International Trade.* New York: Harper & Brothers.

Yukizawa, Kenzo. 1974. 'The Original Meaning and the Deformed Interpretation of Ricardo's Theory of Comparative Costs' (in Japanese). *Shogaku Ronsan* 15, no. 6: 25–51.

Yukizawa, Kenzo. 1978. 'Formation of the Classical Theory of International Trade: Ricardo and James and John Stuart Mill' (in Japanese). In *On Method and History of Social Science*, edited by K. Yukizawa, M. Tanaka, T. Hirai and K. Yamaguchi, 203–24. Kyoto: Minerva Shobo.

Chapter 4

'A TOLERABLY CORRECT LAW RESPECTING PROPORTIONS': RICARDO ON INCOME DISTRIBUTION

Christian Gehrke

1. Introduction

It seems apposite, even if rather conventional, to open this essay by quoting Ricardo's famous statement in the Preface of his *Principles*:

> The produce of the earth – all that is derived from its surface by the united application of labour, machinery, and capital, is divided among the three classes of the community; namely, the proprietor of the land, the owner of the stock or capital necessary for its cultivation, and the labourers by whose industry it is cultivated. But in different stages of society, the proportions of the whole produce of the earth which will be allotted to each of these classes, under the names of rent, profits, and wages, will be essentially different; depending mainly on the actual fertility of the soil, on the accumulation of capital and population, and on the skill, ingenuity, and instruments employed in agriculture. To determine the laws which regulate this distribution, is the principal problem in Political Economy. (Ricardo, 1951–73, I: 5)

Ricardo's statement elicits three – perhaps more unconventional – remarks. Firstly, it must be noted that it implied a significant change, in relation to the foundational definition proposed by Adam Smith, with regard to what is seen as the 'principal problem' or the 'true objects' of the science of Political Economy. Ricardo motivated this shift, away from the *production* of wealth to its *distribution*, not only by the unsatisfactory treatment of this problem by his precursor (I: 5), but also, and more importantly, by referring to the theoretical difficulties involved in ascertaining the absolute size of the social product and its development over time (in a letter to Malthus of 9 October 1820):

> Political Economy you think is an enquiry into the nature and causes of wealth – I think it should be called an enquiry into the laws which determine the division of the produce of industry amongst the classes who concur in its formation. No law can be laid down respecting the quantity, but a tolerably correct one can be laid down respecting proportions. Every day I am more satisfied that the former enquiry is vain and the latter only the true objects of the science. (VIII: 278–79)

A second remark concerns the fact that Ricardo's focus on income shares or 'proportions' gave rise to a novel wage concept that he first presented in the *Principles*: the notion of the 'real value of wages'. In Ricardo's understanding, this new share concept of wages held the key to a proper analysis of the dynamics of the capitalist economic system, because it allowed him to assert, or so he thought, that the level of the general rate of profits was determined exclusively by the 'real value of wages': the two distributive variables, Ricardo contended, must *always* be inversely related. He indeed considered this 'fundamental proposition' on distribution to hold true also with regard to an evolving economic system, in which the technological production conditions of each and every commodity, and thus also the values of individual commodities as well as the value of the total social product, and even the types of commodities produced as well as the commodity content of the workers' consumption basket, may change over time.

The third remark is that Ricardo's attempt 'to determine the laws which regulate this distribution' was not fully successful, and that he failed to lay down even a 'tolerably correct one [...] respecting proportions'. For he had to admit, in one of his *Notes on Malthus*, that rent 'is not a proportion of the produce obtained – it is not governed like wages or profits by proportions' (II: 196–97, note 1), so that the development of the rent share remained indeterminate. Moreover, he also committed a serious mistake in his famous demonstration of the inverse wage–profit relationship, because he based his argument on the simplifying assumption that the advanced capital consists only of wages, overlooking thereby that in circular production systems the means of production cannot be reduced to advanced wages in a finite number of steps. Nevertheless, Ricardo's analysis of income distribution, in spite of these shortcomings, is full of important theoretical insights, and must be considered a major analytical achievement.

Ricardo's distribution analysis is often presented by confounding elements from his earlier analysis in the *Essay on Profits* with his later exposition in the *Principles*, thus disregarding the fact that his thinking about income distribution evolved considerably over time. The present chapter attempts to provide instead a brief chronological account that emphasizes those differences between his earlier and later analysis, without denying, however, the clearly also existing elements of continuity. The structure of the chapter is the following: Section 2 provides a summary account of Ricardo's analysis of the wage–profit–rent relationship before the publication of his *Principles*. In Section 3, Ricardo's novel share concept of wages is explicated, and related to the more conventional notions of 'money wages' and 'real wages.' It is then shown that Ricardo's demonstration of the inverse wage–profit relationship was erroneous. Section 4 turns to Ricardo's admission of the indeterminacy of the rent share in the total product, and also comments briefly on some interpretations of his theory of income distribution. Section 5 concludes.

2. Ricardo's Analysis of Wages, Profits, and Rents before the *Principles*

Although his interest in Political Economy had been aroused by his reading of Adam Smith's *Wealth of Nations*, Ricardo's first economic publications were confined exclusively to monetary and currency problems. It was only later, in his correspondence of 1813 and 1814 with Malthus and others, that he first turned his attention to the problem of income distribution.

Profits. In February 1814 Ricardo had written 'some papers on the profits of Capital', which however have not survived. From a summary of their contents, contained in a letter to Trower of March 1814, we know however that the theory of profits, which Ricardo was to present in his *Essay on Profits* in the following year, was already fully developed (IV: 3–4). In this letter Ricardo maintained that

> it is the profits of the farmer which regulate the profits of all other trades, – and as the profits of the farmer must necessarily decrease with every augmentation of Capital employed on the land, provided no improvements be made at the same time in husbandry, all other profits must diminish and therefore the rate of interest must fall. (VI: 104)

At this time, Ricardo clearly was familiar with the idea of diminishing returns in agriculture, but he nowhere in his correspondence entered into the theory of rent. According to Sraffa, 'the rational foundation of the principle of the determining role of the profits of agriculture [...] is that in agriculture the same commodity, namely corn, forms both the capital (conceived as composed of the subsistence necessary for workers) and the product; so that the determination of profit by the difference between total product and capital advanced, and also the determination of the ratio of this profit to the capital, is done directly between quantities of corn without any question of valuation' (1951: xxxi). In the special case contemplated by Ricardo a price change in the agricultural sector would affect both the product and the capital, and thus could not alter its rate of profit. Therefore, it is the prices of the products of the other industries that must adapt so as to generate a uniform rate of profits across all industries. The numerical examples in the *Essay on Profits*, published in February 1815, in which both the net product and the capital are expressed in units of corn, reflect this earlier 'corn model' reasoning as the underlying principle for the determination of the general rate of profits.

Rents. From an analytical point of view, the main novelty of the *Essay on Profits* was the incorporation of the Malthusian differential rent theory into Ricardo's already existing theory of profits. While Ricardo fully acknowledged Malthus's priority in having first stated this theory in print (VI: 172), it appears not to have been regarded by him as a major theoretical novelty that called for a thorough reconsideration of his economic doctrines but, rather, as a piece that fitted nicely into his already established system of thought (see Signorino (2015: 128)).

Ricardo's lucid exposition of the theory of differential rent, in both the extensive and the intensive form, has led to the popular belief that this theory actually originates with him, although he himself noted that it had been adopted from Malthus's *Inquiry into Rent* (IV: 10). As Sraffa pointed out, one of 'the further consequences of the mistaken notion that Ricardo actually invented the theory of rent' is that he is widely regarded 'as the originator of the whole marginal theory' (IV: 6). Since the theory of intensive rent can indeed be regarded as 'the thin end of the wedge by which the marginalist approach to economic theory has been introduced and generalized' (Bharadwaj [1978] 1986: 41n), it needs to be emphasized that Ricardo's general approach to income distribution is fundamentally different from the later, and now dominant, marginalist approach. Ricardo, consistently throughout his writings, explained profits and rents as shares in the *surplus* product, which remains after deducting from the annual total product the annual capital advances, including also the advanced wages. In this analysis, Ricardo typically started from *given* real wages (specified differently in the *Essay on Profits* and in the *Principles*, as will be explained below) and from a given state of technology, that is, in a first step of the analysis he set aside technical progress, and in particular 'improvements […] in agriculture, or in the implements of husbandry' (IV: 11). Moreover, Ricardo expounded the theory of extensive and intensive rent by starting from a given (finite) set of methods from which cost-minimizing producers can choose, that is, without assuming continuity with regard to the available agricultural production technology.

Supposing the demand for corn to increase with the size of the population, Ricardo then depicted the growth process as a sequence of states of income distribution at different stages of capital accumulation. In the first stage of the growth process, due to the abundance of fertile land, profits absorb the whole surplus product:

> In the first settling of a country rich in fertile land, and which may be had by any one who chooses to take it, the whole produce, after deducting the outgoings belonging to cultivation, will be the profits of capital, and will belong to the owner of such capital, without any deduction whatever for rent. (IV: 10)

An increase in population and hence demand for corn and the extension of tillage to less fertile or less favourably situated plots of land decreases the rate of profits and gives rise to the emergence of differential rent on the more fertile or better situated plots of land. The same result also follows from the intensification of land use through increasing the capital advances on the types of land of better quality, because '[t]he general profits of stock depend wholly on the profits of the last portion of capital employed on the land' (IV: 21). Because farmers in competitive conditions must earn the same rate of profits, irrespective of the quality of land they cultivate, the income gains which derive from the emerging cost differentials in the production of corn on the better qualities of land can be pocketed by the landowners as rents. This implies, as Ricardo pointed out, that 'rent [...] is in all cases a portion of the profits previously obtained on the land. It is never a new creation of revenue, but always part of a revenue already created' (IV: 18). It also implies that if the landowners 'were to relinquish the whole of their rents, they would neither raise the general profits of stock, nor lower the price of corn to the consumer. It would have no other effect [...] than to enable those farmers, whose lands now pay a rent, to live like gentlemen' (IV: 21–22).

It should be noted that Ricardo's attention in the *Essay on Profits* focused mainly on the *rates* of profits and rent, both defined as a percentage of the advanced capital – although profit and rent *shares* were of course also considered. While the rate of profits is a familiar and well-established concept in economic analysis, the 'rate of rent', as the ratio between the corn rent and the corn capital, is a rather unusual concept that is almost unique to Ricardo. But it is the development of these two rates at different levels of capital advances, and not the course of the shares, that Ricardo chose to depict in the famous 'Table, shewing the Progress of Rent and Profit under an assumed Augmentation of Capital':

> It will be seen by the table, that, in a progressive country, rent is not only absolutely increasing, but is also increasing in its ratio to the capital employed on the land; [...] the landlord not only obtains a greater produce, but a larger share. (IV: 17–18)

It is easy, of course, to calculate from the figures in the table also the profit and rent shares, and thereby to confirm Ricardo's statement that 'for a certain time that part of the produce which belongs to the profits of stock, as well as that part which belongs to rent will increase; but [...] at a later period, every accumulation of capital will be attended with an absolute, as well as a proportionate diminution of profits,– though rents will uniformly increase' (IV: 16). Ricardo considered this finding to be both original and important: 'This is a view of the effects of accumulation which is exceedingly curious, and has, I believe, never before been noticed' (IV: 16). It must be carefully noted, however, so as to avoid confusion with his later distribution analysis in the *Principles*, that Ricardo here refers to the changing proportions of profits and rents in the *net* or *surplus* product (and not to the shares of profits, rents, *and wages* in the *value* of the *total* product). In order to ascertain the income shares in the total social product from the figures in Ricardo's table additional assumptions have to be introduced (see King (2013: 62–65)), unless it is assumed that the advanced capital consists only of the wages bill.[1]

Wages. In the *Essay on Profits*, Ricardo's attention focuses mainly on the rates and shares of profits and rents; the discussion of wages is brief. The course of real wages is said to depend on the rate of capital accumulation relative to the growth rate of the population, and it is noted that 'a fall of the real wages of labour' may lead to an increase in the rate of profits (IV: 22). Obviously, the term 'real wages' is used here in the sense of 'corn wages' (with 'corn' serving as a short-hand expression for all the necessaries of life). However, as 'experience demonstrates that capital and population alternately take the lead, and wages in consequence are liberal or scanty, nothing can be positively laid down, respecting profits, as far as wages are concerned' (IV: 23). Ricardo therefore conducts his analysis on the assumption that 'capital and population advance in the proper proportion, so that the real wages of labour continue uniformly the same' (IV: 12). Clearly, Ricardo's aim in the *Essay on Profits* was to bring out the effects of diminishing returns in agriculture on the general rate of profits, and for this purpose it was convenient to assume a constant real wage rate.

Ricardo's analysis draws attention to the existence of a distributional conflict between capitalists and workers, in the sense that a higher corn wage implies a lower rate of profits, and vice versa. But Ricardo also asserted a conflict over the distribution of the surplus product between the capitalists and the landlords, because the latter benefit, and the former suffer, from high corn prices and a high demand for domestically produced corn. The landowning class therefore gains from corn import restrictions, at the expense of the class of the capitalists in both the agricultural and the manufacturing sector. With his pamphlet, Ricardo intended to influence the debates on the Corn Laws in the House of Commons, and he therefore particularly stressed the rent–profit antagonism with reference to the shares in the surplus product: 'High rent and low profits [...] invariably accompany each other.' (IV: 21).[2] He also pointed out, however, that in regard to the effects of the Corn Laws the workers share common interests with their employers:

> The interest of the landlord is always opposed to the interest of any other class in the community. His situation is never so prosperous, as when food is scarce and dear: whereas, all other persons are greatly benefited by procuring cheap food. (IV: 21)

3. Ricardo's Novel Conceptualization of Income Distribution in the *Principles*

In the *Principles*, with the adoption of the labour theory of value, Ricardo could show the determination of the rate of profits in society as a whole instead of in a single sector with hypothesized special characteristics only. And he could also dispense with the simplifying assumption that the workers' wage basket consists only of corn, which had been under frequent attack from Malthus, and could allow for both agricultural and manufactured commodities entering into the labourers' subsistence. It was now labour instead of corn, in which both the product and the advanced capital were expressed; accordingly, 'the rate of profits was no longer determined by the ratio of the corn produced to the corn used up in production, but, instead, by the ratio of the total labour of the country to the labour required to produce the necessaries for that labour' (Sraffa 1951: xxxii). As regards income shares, Ricardo now referred to the proportions received by each class of the *value* of the *total* social product (inclusive of wages).

3.1. Ricardo's concept of the 'real value of wages'[3]

When Ricardo had first exposed the fallacy of Adam Smith's 'adding-up-of-components' theory of value in his *Essay on Profits* and had shown that the wage rate and the general rate of profits are inversely related, his argument had been conducted in terms of corn wages. Moreover, the inverse relationship between the two distributive variables was derived by assuming a given technical environment, that is, by explicitly setting aside improvements in the methods of production (see Ricardo (IV: 12)). Prompted by objections that were raised by Malthus in subsequent debates, Ricardo then developed a new conceptualization of wages, and in edition 1 of the *Principles* he presented the proposition that the general rate of profits must always vary inversely with the 'real value of wages', that is, with the share of wages in the *value* of the (total) social product.[4] Ricardo seems to have forged this new concept because he believed – wrongly, as it later turned out – that it would enable him to demonstrate an inverse relationship between the general rate of profits and the share of wages even in a technologically evolving world. For Ricardo had conceded, in discussions with Malthus in 1815 and 1816, that the inverse wage–profit relationship need not necessarily hold if real wages are specified in corn (or in terms of a consumption basket composed of given amounts of commodities): with an improvement in the production of wage goods, both the rate of profits and the quantities of the commodities received by the workers as 'real wages' could well rise together. This is, indeed, precisely what happens also in the numerical example by means of which Ricardo illustrated his novel concept of the 'real value of wages':

> It is not by the absolute quantity of produce obtained by either class, that we can correctly judge of the rate of profit, rent, and wages, but by the quantity of labour required to obtain that produce. By improvements in machinery and agriculture, the whole produce may be doubled; but if wages, rent, and profit be also doubled, the three will bear the same proportions to one another as before, and neither could be said to have relatively varied. But if wages partook not of the whole of this increase; if they, instead of being doubled, were only increased one-half; if rent, instead of being doubled, were only increased three-fourths, and the remaining increase went to profit, it would, I apprehend, be correct for me to say, that rent and wages had fallen while profits had risen; for if we had an invariable standard by which to measure the value of this produce, we should find that a less value had fallen to the class of labourers and landlords, and a greater to the class of capitalists, than had been given before. We might find, for example, that though the absolute quantity of commodities had been doubled, they were the produce of precisely the former quantity of labour. Of every hundred hats, coats, and quarters of corn produced, if
>
> | | |
> |---|---|
> | The labourers had before … | 25 |
> | The landlords … | 25 |
> | And the capitalists … | 50 |
> | | 100: |
>
> And if, after these commodities were double the quantity, of every 100
>
> | | |
> |---|---|
> | The labourers had only … | 22 |
> | The landlords … | 22 |
> | And the capitalists … | 56 |
> | | 100: |
>
> In that case I should say, that wage and rent had fallen and profits risen; though, in consequence of the abundance of commodities, the quantity paid

> to the labourer and landlord would have increased in the proportion of 25 to 44. Wages are to be estimated by their real value, viz. by the quantity of labour and capital employed in producing them, and not by their nominal value either in coats, hats, money, or corn. (I: 49–50)

The device of measuring the rise or fall in the real value of wages by the change in 'the proportion of the value of the total product received by the workers', or by 'the proportion of the total annual labour which is necessary to support the labourers',[5] rather than by an increase or decrease in the amounts of commodities received by the workers, was not merely another way of expressing the relative distribution of income. Ricardo rather conceived of it as an analytical device that allowed him to assert, or so he thought, what may be called his 'fundamental proposition' on distribution: that the *rate* of profits depends on *proportional wages*, and on nothing else.[6] An explicit statement of this proposition can be found, for instance, in one of Ricardo's notes on Malthus's *Principles*: 'Profits in fact depend on high or low wages, and on nothing else. The greater the proportion of the value of the whole produce necessary to support the labourer, the higher will be wages' (II: 252). And in his own *Principles*, Ricardo stressed: 'It has been my endeavour to shew throughout this work, that the rate of profits can never be increased but by a fall in wages' (I: 132).

Incidentally, it may be noted that the three-commodities-example ('hats, coats, and quarters of corn'), in terms of which Ricardo illustrated his argument, can also be considered as a generalization of the 'corn model', in the sense that it allows for a determination of the rate of profits in physical terms, without a need to have recourse to values. This is because in the special case contemplated by Ricardo both the product and the advanced capital are supposed to consist of a 'composite commodity' into which the same three goods enter in the same proportions. When, as Ricardo tended to assume in much of his argument on the wage–profit relationship, the advanced capital is supposed to consist only of the wages bill, the rate of profits amounts to 50/25 = 200% before, and 56/22 ≈ 255% after the improvement (see Kurz (2015: 828)).

In the *Principles*, the inverse wage–profit relationship was expressed in labour value terms,[7] and although it was no longer maintained that the rate of profits is determined in agriculture alone, it was still suggested that the agricultural sector obtained a special relevance in the determination of the general rate of profits. With his new share concept of wages Ricardo now felt confident that he could state,

> that in all countries, and all times, profits depend on the quantity of labour requisite to provide necessaries for the labourers, on that land or with that capital which yields no rent. (I: 126)

Ricardo's analysis of the long-term development of the economic system is substantially the same as in the *Essay on Profits*. He again considers the 'natural course' of economic development, characterized by capital accumulation and population growth in the absence of technical progress and without corn (or food) imports. Due to decreasing returns in agriculture, and notwithstanding constant or increasing returns in manufacturing, the 'natural tendency' of the rate of profits then 'is to fall; for, in the progress of society and wealth, the additional quantity of food required is obtained by the sacrifice of more and more labour' (I: 120). Food or corn is thus still considered as the most essential input, because it enters directly into the production of all commodities due to its role as the principal wage good in the workers' consumption basket. The declining rate of profits tends to slow down the pace of capital accumulation, and must eventually bring the growth of the economic system to a halt. But already 'long before' it has fallen to zero, Ricardo contended, 'the very low rate of profits will have arrested all accumulation, and almost the whole produce of the country, after paying the labourers, will be the property of the owners of the land and the receivers of tithes and taxes' (I: 120–21). Note that Ricardo here seems to refer, again, to the rise of the rent share in the *surplus* product, exclusive of wages. In fact, throughout the *Principles* Ricardo sometimes stresses the rent–profit antagonism and refers to *surplus* product shares, while in other passages his argument clearly relates to the rent and profit shares in the *value* of the *total* product.

3.2. Money wages and commodity wages

Side by side with his newly developed share concept of wages, which he employed in the investigation of the inverse wage–profit relationship, Ricardo in the *Principles* also used the more conventional concepts of 'money wages' and 'real (or commodity) wages'. To these two concepts he also applied a distinction which is similar to the Smithian distinction between 'natural prices' and 'market prices'. Ricardo thus defined the 'natural price of labour' as 'that price which is necessary to enable the labourers, one with another, to subsist and to perpetuate their race, without either increase or diminution'. Its level, he maintained, 'depends on the price of the food, necessaries and conveniences required for the support of the labourer and his family' (I: 93). He stressed that the 'natural wage' is not to be considered as given once and for all, and that, though set at the 'subsistence level', it is not meant to consist only of the commodities that are strictly necessary for the physiological preservation of the worker and his family:

> It is not to be understood that the natural price of labour, estimated even in food and necessaries, is absolutely fixed and constant. It varies at different times in the same country, and very materially differs in different countries. It essentially depends on the habits and customs of the people … Many of the conveniences now enjoyed in an English cottage, would have been thought luxuries at an earlier period of our history. (I: 96–97)

The 'market price of labour' is regulated by 'the proportion of the supply to the demand; labour is dear when it is scarce, and cheap when it is plentiful. However much the market price may deviate from its natural price, it has, like commodities, a tendency to conform to it' (I: 94). However, this statement receives an important qualification. In spite of the continuous operation of this tendency, the 'market price' of labour may very well deviate from the 'natural price' also for prolonged periods of time:

> Notwithstanding the tendency of wages to conform to their natural rate, their market rate may, in an improving society, for an indefinite period, be constantly above it; for no sooner may the impulse, which an increased capital gives to new demand for labour be obeyed, then another increase of capital may produce the same effect; and thus, if the increase of capital be gradual and constant, the demand for labour may give a continued stimulus to an increase of people. (I: 94–95)

The labour supply is thus considered to adapt *endogenously* to a continuously increasing labour demand, but only with a delay. In the reverse case, when the labour demand falls short of the supply, the delayed response in the labour supply may lead to persistent unemployment. Ricardo thus clearly endorsed some elements of the Malthusian population theory, and in particular the idea of an impact of the level of real wages on the population growth rate. However, he firmly rejected Malthus's 'wages fund reasoning', which made the wage level (or, alternatively, the employment level) dependent on the available amount of food. As opposed to Malthus, Ricardo maintained that a higher demand for corn and other necessaries provides a sufficient stimulus for encouraging the application of additional capital in the production of those goods. Accordingly, in his view workers' (or trade union) demands for higher money wages, if successful, could well be effective in raising real wages. Similarly, he also argued, against Malthus, that the adaptation of the food supply to the existing demand could be achieved by indexing the poor relief to the bread scale. In view of the conventional elements in the determination of the subsistence wage level, Ricardo thought it desirable that more and more commodities that formerly were considered luxuries should enter into the workers' customary consumption basket:

> The friends of humanity cannot but wish that in all countries the labouring classes should have a taste for comforts and enjoyments. […] There cannot be a better security against a superabundant population. (I: 100)

Rent. The chapter 'On rent' in the *Principles* is noteworthy mainly for its lucid exposition of the differential rent theory and for its detailed analysis of different forms of agricultural improvements. In the *Essay on Profits*, Ricardo had mentioned agricultural improvements only briefly, as one of three possible causes for an increase in the general rate of profits, but referred to them mainly in connection with an *argumentum ad absurdum*:

> If the interests of the landlord be of sufficient consequence, to determine us not to avail ourselves of all the benefits which would follow from importing corn at a cheap price, they should also influence us in rejecting all improvements in agriculture, and in the implements of husbandry; for it is as certain that corn is rendered cheap, rents are lowered, and the ability of the landlord to pay taxes, is for a time, at least, as much impaired by such improvements, as by the importation of corn. To be consistent then, let us by the same act arrest improvement, and prohibit importation. (IV: 41)

In the *Principles*, Ricardo distinguished between land-saving or capital-saving improvements and showed by means of numerical examples that the impact on rents depends on how the existing cost differentials and the marginal method of cultivation are affected by them. Unlike Malthus, who contended that improvements in agriculture must lead to rising real incomes and an increased demand for agricultural products, and thus ultimately to rising rents, Ricardo concentrated on the more immediate impact of improvements and conducted his analysis on the assumption that the demand for agricultural produce is unchanged. The general principle then is 'that whatever diminishes the inequality in the produce obtained from successive portions of capital employed on the same or on new land, tends to lower rent; and that whatever increases that inequality, necessarily produces an opposite effect, and tends to raise it' (I: 83).[8]

3.3. Ricardo's blunder in his statement of the 'fundamental proposition'

That in the *Principles* Ricardo had introduced a novel concept of real wages was duly noticed, and sharply criticized, by Malthus, who in his own

Principles protested against Ricardo's adoption of 'new and unusual language' in connection with wages (II: 194).[9] As Ricardo put it in a letter to James Mill:

> Malthus thinks it monstrous that I should say labour had fallen in value, when perhaps the quantity of necessaries allotted to the labourer may be really increased. (VII: 378)

The peculiarity of Ricardo's proportional wage concept was noticed also by several other commentators, but its meaning and purpose was not always correctly understood. Alfred Marshall (1920 [1890]: 550n), for instance, completely missed its proper meaning by applying it at the level of individual firms, and Edwin Cannan (1967 [1893]: 267–76), who praised Ricardo for having analysed 'proper distribution' (which refers to the proportional division of the produce between wages, profits, and rents – instead of 'pseudo-distribution', which is concerned with 'wages per head, profits per cent, and rent per acre'), departed from Ricardo's conceptualization by simply supposing that product shares can be ascertained without any problems of valuation also outside of a one-commodity world (such as the 'corn model', on which Ricardo had relied in his early analysis).[10]

The significance and analytical importance of Ricardo's concept of proportional wages was clearly perceived by Ladislaus von Bortkiewicz, who observed with regard to Ricardo's proposition on the wage–profit antagonism:

> It must not be overlooked that in Ricardo's oft-repeated phrase that every rise in wages must necessarily be accompanied by a fall in profits, and *vice-versa*, one must understand by wages neither money wages, nor real wages, but that amount of labour which is needed to produce the complex of goods forming real wages. [...] Furthermore, it is noteworthy that, although Ricardo does not speak of *rate* of profit, but simply of profit, and although he often measures the level of profit by the capitalist's share in the value or the price of the product, yet he nevertheless intends his assertion of the antagonism between wages and profit to be extended specifically to the rate of profit. ([1906–7] 1952: 47–48)

Bortkiewicz then proceeded to warn also of another common misunderstanding of Ricardo's proposition on the inverse wage–profit relationship:

> We cannot, finally, stress sufficiently strongly that there is no mention in Ricardo of this antagonism prevailing only insofar as there is no change in the value or the price of the product. Such a qualification, which has been proposed as a correction by various people, not only contradicts Ricardo's own words; it deprives his thesis – that high wages *always* go with low profits, and high profits with low wages – of its point and reduces it to triviality. ([1906/07] 1952: 48)

Bortkiewicz thus grasped correctly the meaning and purpose of Ricardo's 'proportional wage' concept. He failed to notice, however, that a close follower and critic of Ricardo, Karl Marx, had detected an important error in Ricardo's analysis of the wage–profit relationship. As Marx pointed out, Ricardo had overlooked the existence of a maximum rate of profits, which obtains if wages are (hypothetically) reduced to zero (or, as Marx put it, if the workers 'could live on air and hence did not have to work for themselves at all' (1959 [1894]: 247).[11]

Marx approved of Ricardo's new conceptualization of real wages, and in his manuscripts of *Theories of Surplus Value* he observed: 'It is one of Ricardo's great merits that he examined relative or proportionate wages, and established them as a definite category.' (1989 [1861–63]: 419) Moreover, he pointed out:

> The concept of *relative* wages is one of Ricardo's greatest contributions. It consists in this – that the *value of the wages* (and consequently of the *profit*) depends absolutely on the proportion of that part of the working day during which the *worker works for himself* (producing or reproducing his wage) to that part of his time which belongs to the capitalist. This is important economically, *in fact* it is only another way of expressing the real theory of surplus value. (1989 [1861–63]: 226–67)

In Marxian terms, Ricardo's concept of the 'real value of wages' is indeed merely another way of expressing the relation between the value of the social surplus (S) and the value of the social variable capital (V). Accordingly, his 'fundamental proposition', according to which the general rate of profits falls (rises) if and only if proportional wages rise (fall) is equivalent to the statement that its fall (rise) is conditional on a decrease (increase) in the aggregate rate of surplus value. As against this, Marx put forward the following objection:[12]

> In his observations on profit and wages, Ricardo [...] treats the matter as though the entire capital were laid out directly in wages. (1989 [1861–63]: 10)

What he meant by this was that Ricardo, for simplicity, had envisaged the production process as a uni-directional process of finite duration, leading from a series of dated labour inputs to a final output: the advanced capital can then be reduced to advanced wages in a finite number of steps. But when the advanced capital consists only of advanced wages, and wages are hypothetically reduced to zero, the rate of profits goes to infinity. With his simplifying assumption, Ricardo had overlooked that with circular production relations some 'constant capital' is needed in each line and at each stage of the production process, which implies that the rate of profits has an upper limit (R), which is given by the inverse of the 'organic composition of capital' of the system as a whole. In Marx's terms, the latter is equal to the ratio of 'dead' (C) to 'living' labour ($L = V + S$), that is, it is given by $C/L = 1/R$. Since in a technologically changing economic system the 'organic composition of capital' is bound to change over time, the maximum rate of profit, R, is bound to change as well. But this implies that the proportional wage and the general rate of profits need not always be inversely related, but may also rise (or fall) simultaneously. It was perhaps one of Marx's most important analytical achievements to have demonstrated this error of Ricardo.[13]

Finally, it should be noted that Ricardo's concept of 'proportional wages' was adopted more recently also by Piero Sraffa (1960: 10–11). By normalizing to one both the total annual amount of labour and the value of the national income, w denotes the proportional wage, which for a *given* system of production is inversely related to the rate of profits. However, as Sraffa also demonstrated, Ricardo's proposition does not carry over to a system with changing technical conditions, since the maximum rate of profits will in general not remain constant with technical changes.

4. Ricardo's Correction of His Views on the Rent Share

In a (deleted) passage of one of his *Notes on Malthus*, composed in the autumn of 1820, Ricardo observed that

> Rent is not a proportion of the produce obtained – it is not governed like wages or profits by proportions – depending as it does on the difference between the quantity of produce obtained by two equal capitals. (II: 196–97, note 1)

A number of small textual alterations, which Ricardo then introduced in the third edition of his *Principles* (see Ricardo (I: 49, 83, 402–403)), reflect this note (Sraffa 1951: lvi). These textual changes, however, have not been successful in preventing many of his readers from misunderstanding Ricardo's mature views on the development of the rent share, and on the wage–profit–rent relationship more generally. This is because commentators on Ricardo's analysis of income distribution have often indiscriminately confounded his statements in the *Essay on Profits* with those in the different editions of the *Principles*.

In order to disentangle the prevailing confusion, let us turn again to Ricardo's statements on the rent share in the *Essay on Profits* and in the first two editions of the *Principles*, before turning to note 115 in Malthus's *Principles*, in which he tried to clarify his meaning. In the *Essay on Profits*, as was noted above, Ricardo had asserted that in a progressive country with a rising demand for food and raw produce, 'rent is [...] increasing in its ratio to the capital employed on the land';

it had also been suggested there, clearly with regard to the *net* social product (exclusive of wages and measured in corn), that 'the landlord not only obtains a greater produce, but a larger share' (IV: 16 and 18). It is difficult to see, then, how a reader of the *Essay* could not have formed the view that for Ricardo the natural course of economic development was bound up with a rising share (and rate) of rent, and a falling share (and rate) of profits – where the two shares together make up, of course, the entire *surplus* or *net* social product (which, of course, is itself changing in size in the natural course of economic development).

With the adoption of the labour theory of value in the first edition of his *Principles* Ricardo had then maintained, in Section VII of Chapter 1, that 'the division *of the whole produce of the land and labour of the country* between the three classes of landlords, capitalists, and labourers' must be judged in terms of 'the proportion of the product of the annual labour of the country that is received by each class as rents, profits, and wages' (I: 49, note 1; emphasis added) – with the value of the product being measured, of course, by the total amount of labour annually expended in its production. The division of the value of the annual product in terms of proportions was thus applied explicitly to wages, profits, *and rents*. And in the first two editions of the *Principles* rent was also explicitly conceptualized as 'the proportion of the whole produce' in the chapter 'On Rent' (I: 83, note 1). Instead of referring to shares in the *surplus* product, measured in corn, Ricardo now referred to shares in the *value* of the *total* social product, measured in labour.

As Sraffa (1951: lvi) pointed out, the small textual changes that were introduced in edition 3 of the *Principles* can be explained by the fact that 'Malthus in his *Principles* had [...] criticised Ricardo for having applied to rent his measure by "*proportions* or cost in labour", and having suggested as a result that with the extension of cultivation the proportion of rent to the total produce of land would increase' (1951: lvi).[14] Malthus's criticism in fact prompted Ricardo to a restatement of his position in his *Notes on Malthus*, and to explain 'in effect that rent would take up an increased proportion of the produce of the *old* lands, or, if additional capitals be employed on the same lands, an increased proportion "of each quantity before obtained"' (1951: lvi).

In order to better grasp this important point, let us take a closer look at Ricardo's reply to Malthus in note 115. In the opening paragraph Ricardo conceded that 'my language about proportions may not have been so clear as it ought to have been' (II: 196), and he therefore set out to explain anew his novel concept of proportional wages with the help of a numerical example, in which he illustrates his analytical device for a hypothetical case, in which only a single commodity, corn, is produced:

> Suppose the last land now in cultivation yields 180 qrs. of corn with the employment of a given quantity of labour, and in consequence of the rise

> in the price of corn a still inferior quantity of land shall be cultivated next year which shall yield only 170 qrs. If this year the labourer shall have one third of the 180 quarters, and next year he shall have one third of the 170 quarters, I say his wages will be of the same value next year, as this, because the whole 170 quarters next year will be of the same value as the 180 quarters are this year, and consequently , a fourth, or a third of either of these quantities will be also of the same value. (II: 196)

Ricardo's explication of his novel conceptualization of wages in the context of a one-commodity model only served him to demonstrate in simpler terms what he had previously already set out in more general terms, in Section VII of Chapter 1 of the *Principles*, with reference to the three-commodities example: that his conceptualization of the proportional distribution of income refers, not to the proportion of the total *quantity* of produce received by each class, but to the proportion of the *value* of the total produce received by each class. In the next paragraph, however, he then stressed that 'this division by proportions' must only be applied, and should only have been applied by him, to wages and profits at the agricultural margin, but not to rents:

> When I speak of this division by proportions, I always apply it, or ought to apply it, (and if I have done otherwise, it has been from inadvertence), to the produce obtained with the last capital employed on the land, and for which no rent is paid. (II: 196)

The significance of Ricardo's clarifying remark consists not so much in the fact that it disposes of the common misunderstanding that Ricardo had predicted an increasing rent share in the *total* product in the 'natural course' of economic development. More importantly, the remark shows that in Ricardo's understanding infra-marginal production conditions are not involved in the determination of the value of the social product, which can be shared out among workers, capitalists, and landlords. This value is rather determined, with regard to agricultural products, by the amount of labour that must be expended at the agricultural margin. It also disposes of the idea, which could easily (but wrongly) be inferred from the *Essay on Profits*, namely that Ricardo had envisaged an inverse relationship between the rates of profits and rent, each defined as a percentage of the advanced capital, in the 'natural course' of economic development.[15]

Ricardo's attempt to clarify his position on the determination of the rent share and its development over time did not meet with much success. Commentators have typically discussed his views by referring to *product* rather than *value* shares, and they often based their argument on diminishing returns aggregate production functions in order to show that the rent share in the total product need not necessarily rise. Cannan, for instance, approved of Ricardo's share concept, but then applied it to total product shares, not noticing that outside of a one-commodity world (including a one-composite-commodity world) this is generally not possible. He then criticized Ricardo for his failure to notice that in his 'natural course' scenario the rent share in the total product need not necessarily rise, and that it 'happens to do so only in special cases' ([1893] 1967: 278). Davidson (1959) set out to demonstrate on the basis of a neoclassical aggregate production function that the course of the rent share in the total product need not be strictly increasing, and showed that it is determined by the shape of the average and marginal product curves. Barkai (1966), in his discussion of Ricardo's 'volte face' on rent, suggested that Ricardo had originally predicted a rising rent share in the total product, but that the writing of his *Notes on Malthus* had convinced him that rent need not necessarily rise as a relative share, without himself noticing that his reasoning in the *Notes* was implicitly based on 'a renunciation of diminishing returns as a property of the aggregate production function' (1966: 291).

5. Concluding Remarks

In a letter to McCulloch of 13 June 1820 Ricardo observed:

> After all, the great questions of Rent, Wages and Profits must be explained by the proportions in which the whole produce is divided between landlords, capitalists, and labourers, and which are not essentially connected with the doctrine of value. (VIII: 194)

As we saw above, Ricardo up to at least 1815 had indeed sought to analyse those 'great questions' without finding it necessary to enter into the theory of value. He did so by employing the simplifying device of the 'corn model', which allowed him to demonstrate the inverse relationship between the level of the real wage rate and the general rate of profits in purely physical terms. It also enabled him to show how the agricultural surplus is distributed as profits and rent in different stages of the process of capital accumulation and population growth.

However, he was then groping his way towards a more general theory, and came up with the ingenious device of measuring the 'real value of wages' by 'the proportion of the total annual amount of labour that is necessary to support the labourers'. This made it possible to study the development of income distribution in an evolving and complex economic system, in which a great variety of commodities is produced, and also to assert, or so he thought, his fundamental proposition on the wage–profit relationship for such a system. He at first overlooked, however, that the rent share in the *value* of the total social product was not governed by proportions, and he omitted to clarify his position on the rent share sufficiently clearly in the third edition of his *Principles*. He also overlooked that in his demonstration of the inverse wage–profit relationship he had committed a serious mistake by disregarding the circularity of the social production process.

Nevertheless, in the short period from 1813 to 1823, Ricardo's analysis of income distribution increased substantially in both theoretical sophistication and the achieved level of generality. In a more or less continuous process of elaboration and clarification, Ricardo sought to vindicate the basic insights he had gained from the simple corn model also for the case of a complex, evolving economic system with ongoing technical change, continuous changes in relative prices, and the emergence of new and hitherto unknown products. It would therefore be quite wrong to assess his analysis by over-emphasizing its omissions and shortcomings, as perhaps was the case in this chapter, but it would be even more wrong to present and criticize his analysis by employing a simple diminishing returns aggregate production function, and thus by supposing only a one-commodity world.

Notes

1 As Ricardo refers explicitly to 'fixed capital, such as buildings, implements, &c.' (IV: 10), this interpretation clearly seems too narrow.

2 Because in his table he showed, side by side, the increasing rent rate and the declining profit rate with an assumed augmentation of capital, Ricardo also seemed to suggest an inverse relationship between the *rates* of profits and rents.

3 On the following, see also Gehrke (2011).

4 A first allusion to the new concept can perhaps be found in a letter to Malthus of 14 October 1816; see Ricardo (VII: 81).

5 It is important to recall that Ricaredo's argument in the *Principles* – except in chapter 1 – was based on the simplifying assumption that prices are invariant with regard to changes in distribution because commodities exchange according to the amounts of labour embodied in them. Due to this assumption, a greater (smaller) proportion of the value of the total product received by the workers as wages also means that a greater (smaller) proportion of the total annual labour is devoted to the reproduction of their wages (De Vivo 1984: 46–50).

6 For a similar statement, see also (I: 411).

7 See also Ricardo's statement in a letter to McCulloch of 13 June 1820: 'The greater the portion of the result of labour that is given to the labourer, the smaller must be the rate of profits, and vice versa' (VIII: 194).

8 For a discussion of Ricardo's analysis of improvements in agriculture, see Gehrke, Kurz, and Salvadori (2003).

9 See also Malthus (1986 [1827]: 23–36). For a similar criticism, see also Senior (1965a [1826]: 238, and 1965b [1836]: 5 and 142–48).

10 Cannan avoided the problem of valuation in his numerical examples by supposing that the shares are percentages of a composite commodity, similar to Ricardo's three-commodities example in chapter 1 of the *Principles*.

11 On the following, see also Gehrke and Kurz (2006).

12 Unfortunately, Marx did not succeed in expressing his correct criticism accurately so that he has often been misunderstood as asserting that Ricardo had generally omitted to consider non-wage capital – a charge which can easily be shown to be quite wrong. What Marx insisted on was that Ricardo had omitted to take into account non-wage capital *in his analysis of the wage–profit relationship*.

13 John Stuart Mill, in his *Essays on Some Unsettled Questions*, also pointed out that 'Mr. Ricardo's theory is defective: that the rate of profits does *not* exclusively depend upon the value of wages' (1968 [1844]: 101). However, Mill's attempt to remedy Ricardo's erroneous proposition was a failure. According to Mill, 'it is strictly true, that the rate of profits varies inversely as the *cost of production of wages*' (ibid.: 103; emphasis added), where by 'cost of production of wages' he means the wages of the labour employed, directly and indirectly, in the production of wage goods, plus 'the *profits* of those who, in any antecedent stage of the production, have advanced any portion of those wages' (ibid.: 102). It is clear that Mill's concept of the 'cost of production of wages' is not a useful device for ascertaining the rate of profits, because it depends on it.

14 Sraffa's interpretation has been contested by Peach, who suggested that the textual alterations under consideration should rather be interpreted as 'the substitution of a "micro" method of treating distribution for the one previously framed at the level of social aggregates' (1993: 221; see also 290–91). This reading seems to overlook that in order to determine the functional distribution of income in the presence of land scarcity, the demand for agricultural products in the economic system as a whole must be known: What possible analytical meaning can be given, then, to the phrase 'a "micro" method of treating distribution'?

15 Marx, in particular, appears to have entertained this idea: He made a great effort to show, against Ricardo, that the rates of profit and rent (as a percentage of the advanced capital) need not necessarily be inversely related. For a discussion of Marx's reading of Ricardo's views on the profit–rent relationship, see Gehrke (2012).

References

Bharadwaj, K. 1989. *Themes in Value and Distribution – Classical Theory Reappraised*, London: Unwin Hyman.

Bortkiewicz, L. 1906/7. Wertrechnung und Preisrechnung im Marxschen System (Value Calculation and Price Calculation in the Marxian System), in three parts, *Archiv für Sozialwissenschaft und Sozialpolitik*, 23, 1–50, 25, 10–51, 445–88.

Bortkiewicz, L. 1952 [1906/7]. 'Value and Price in the Marxian System' (English trans. of parts 2 and 3 of L. von Bortkiewicz (1906–07), 'Wertrechnung und Preisrechnung im Marxschen System'). *International Economic Papers* 2, 5–60.

Cannan, E. 1967 [1893]. *A History of the Theories of Production and Distribution in English Political Economy from 1776–1848*, London: P. S. King.

Davidson, P. 1959. 'A Clarification of the Ricardian Rent Share'. *Canadian Journal of Economics and Political Science* 25, no. 2: 190-95.

De Vivo, G. 1984. *Ricardo and his Critics. A Study of Classical Theories of Value and Distribution*, Università degli studi di Modena, Studi e ricerche dell'Istituto Economico n. 23, Modena.

Gehrke, C. 2011. 'Price of Wages: A Curious Phrase'. In *Sraffa and Modern Economics*, Volume 1, edited by Roberto Ciccone, Christian Gehrke and Gary Mongiovi, 405–22. London: Routledge.

Gehrke, C. 2012. 'Marx's Critique of Ricardo's Theory of Rent: A Re-assessment'. In *Classical Political Economy and Modern Theory. Essays in Honour of Heinz D. Kurz*, edited by Christian Gehrke, Neri Salvadori, Ian Steedman and Richard Sturn, 51–84. London: Routledge.

Gehrke, C. 2014. 'Rent, as share of produce, not governed by proportions'. In *Sraffa and the Reconstruction of Economic Theory*, Volume 3: *Sraffa's Legacy. Interpretations and Historical Perspectives*, edited by Enrico Sergio Levrero, Antonella Palumbo, and Antonella Stirati (2012), 261–80. London: Palgrave Macmillan.

Gehrke, C. and Kurz, H. D. 2006. 'Sraffa on von Bortkiewicz: Reconstructing the Classical Theory of Value and Distribution'. *History of Political Economy* 38, no. 1: 91–149.

Gehrke, C., Kurz, H. D., and Salvadori, N. 2003. 'Ricardo on Agricultural Improvements: A Note'. *Scottish Journal of Political Economy* 50, no. 3: 291–96.

King, J. E. 2013. *David Ricardo, (Great Thinkers in Economics Series)*, London: Palgrave Macmillan.

Kurz, H. D. 2015. 'David Ricardo: On the Art of "Elucidating Economic Principles" in the Face of a "Labyrinth of Difficulties"'. *The European Journal of the History of Economic Thought* 22, no. 5: 818–51.

Malthus, T. R. 1989 [1820]. *Principles of Political Economy*, 1st edn 1820, Variorum edition, edited by J. Pullen, Cambridge: Cambridge University Press.

Malthus, T. R. 1986 [1827]. *Definitions in Political Economy*, 1st ed. 1827, London: John Murray. Reprint 1986, Fairfield, NJ: A. M. Kelley.

Marshall, A. 1920 [1890]. *Principles of Economics*. 1st ed. 1890. Reprint of the 8th ed. (1920) with new setting of 1949, London: Macmillan.

Marx, K. 1989 [1861–63]. *Economic Manuscript of 1861–63. A Contribution to the Critique of Political Economy ["Theories of Surplus Value"]*. Vol. 31 of Karl Marx, Frederick Engels: *Collected Works*. New York: International Publishers.

Marx, K. 1959 [1894]. *Capital*, Vol. III. Moscow: Progress Publishers. English translation of *Das Kapital*, Vol. III, Hamburg 1894: Meissner.

Mill, J. 1844 [1826]. *Elements of Political Economy*. 1st ed. 1821; 3rd ed. 1826; Reprint 1844. London: Henry G. Bohn.

Ricardo, D. 1951–73. *The Works and Correspondence of David Ricardo*, edited by Piero Sraffa with the collaboration of M. H. Dobb, 11 vols, Cambridge: Cambridge University Press. (Cited as *Works*, volume number, page number)

Signorino, R. 2015. 'Essay on Profits'. In *The Elgar Companion to David Ricardo*, edited by Heinz D. Kurz and Neri Salvadori, 128–35. Cheltenham and Northampton: Edward Elgar.

Sraffa, P. 1951. 'Introduction'. In vol. I of *The Works and Correspondence of David Ricardo*, edited by Piero Sraffa with the collaboration of M. H. Dobb, xiii–lxii. Cambridge: Cambridge University Press.

Sraffa, P. (1960), *Production of Commodities by Means of Commodities*, Cambridge: Cambridge University Press.

Chapter 5

RICARDO ON ECONOMIC POLICY

John E. King

There is absolutely no doubt that David Ricardo was one of political economy's greatest theorists. Nicholas Kaldor suggested many years ago that his *Principles of Political Economy and Taxation* should be rated as one of the discipline's five great texts, preceded by Adam Smith's *Wealth of Nations* and followed by Karl Marx's *Capital*, Alfred Marshall's *Principles of Economics* and John Maynard Keynes's *General Theory* (Kaldor 1982: 259). But, like these four authors, Ricardo was no armchair theorist. His interest in political economy was first aroused by his concern with the important policy question of the causes of the high price of bullion, which led in 1809–11 to his first publications, and in the *Principles* he devotes 15 of its 32 chapters to policy issues. To explain both Ricardo's concern with questions of economic policy and the positions that he took on these matters, I begin this chapter by describing the society that he lived in and his understanding of the problems that were posed by the nature of its economic and political systems. I then outline Ricardo's own political beliefs, before examining his position on four crucial issues: monetary policy, fiscal policy, social welfare and international trade. I conclude the chapter with something related yet very different, the views of the so-called Ricardian Socialists, who accepted the truth of the labour theory of value but took a very different position from that of Ricardo on many of these questions.

1. Ricardo's England

Ricardo's England had three essential characteristics. First, it was a very complex society, which had changed very substantially since the ending of feudalism several centuries earlier. Second, it was continuing to change very rapidly. Third, and despite these two important features, it contained a very simple core that formed the basis of Ricardo's policy prescriptions: there were three social classes, landlords, capitalists and workers, who faced very different circumstances and so behaved in very different ways (King 2013: chapter 1).

According to the 1771 census, the England into which Ricardo was born in the following year had 6.6 million people. Half a century later, two years before his death in 1823, it had increased to 11.5 million. By the 1820s the English population was growing at 1.5 per cent per annum, faster than ever before and unparalleled anywhere in the world. The rapid population growth was due largely to the increased fertility permitted by secure food supplies and an absence of plagues and other health catastrophes, with a much smaller contribution coming from reduced mortality rates. England was now the most highly-urbanised country in Western Europe, with one-third of the population living in towns of more than 5,000 people and London alone accounting for 11 per cent of the nation's population in 1801. The next largest city was Manchester, with 80,000 people, and the capital had a larger population than Manchester and the next 25 towns combined (Rule 1992a, 1992b; Wrigley 2004). The sharpness of the urban-rural divide should not be exaggerated. The active urban population was not confined to manufacturing, while the countryside 'was as concerned with services, commerce and "proto industries" as with agriculture' (Mann 1993: 93). Taking England as a whole, as late as 1831 manufacturing was 'dwarfed by employment in retail trade and handicrafts', the biggest occupations being shoemakers, carpenters, tailors, publicans, shopkeepers, blacksmiths, masons, butchers, bricklayers and bakers (Wrigley 2004: 91–92).

While Ricardo's England was easily the richest country in Europe, it was still very poor by twenty-first century standards. In 1760 Britain as a whole was 'marginally richer than India or Bolivia [were] in 2000, but a little poorer than Armenia or Indonesia'; as late as 1850, income per head was less than that of Lebanon or the Philippines in 2000 (Voth 2004: 269). However, the increase in per capita income in Ricardo's lifetime was quite substantial, with labour productivity growing in all sectors of the economy, including agriculture, where output per acre rose faster than output per worker. Malthusian fears about the prospects for agriculture in England were widely shared, and they seemed to be confirmed by the heavy and increasing reliance on imports of food and raw materials (Mokyr 2010).

The benefits of economic growth were not evenly shared. Real wages rose by only 4 per cent between 1760 and 1820, while real consumption per head was stagnant for most of Ricardo's lifetime although hours of work were long and increasing. Thus, the share of non-wage income (rent and profit) grew rapidly, while for the great mass of the population life expectancy increased very little and literacy rates improved hardly at all. The distribution of wealth was even more unequal than the distribution of income, with the richest 5 per cent of individuals in Britain in 1810 owning no less than 85.3 per cent of total wealth, compared with 21 per cent in the United States (Schneider 2004:

20–21, 28–29). More than half of this wealthy elite (which included Ricardo) were landowners, so that an 'observer entering a room full of Britain's 200 wealthiest men in 1825 might be forgiven for thinking that the Industrial Revolution had not occurred' (Rubinstein 1981: 60–61).

Ricardo's analytical simplification of the socio-economic reality of the England of his day flowed directly from his awareness of these huge inequalities. The workers were assumed to be too poor to save, and their low and stagnant real wages also held down the incomes of self-employed traders and craftsmen, making it impossible also for them to save. Since the landlords were too prodigal to make significant savings, it followed that only the capitalists could be relied upon to consume less than their total incomes. This social reality carried a crucial implication. Since for Ricardo it was saving that drove investment, and not (as for Keynes) the other way round, protecting the incomes of capitalists was critical for continued economic progress. Economic policy must not under any circumstances threaten the rate of profit on capital.

The profound social and economic inequalities were inevitably reflected in the operation of the political system. In Ricardo's England the landlords enjoyed considerable political power, which had been consolidated by the 'Glorious Revolution' of 1688 that restricted the power of the Crown and consolidated the influence of aristocratic values and the perceived legitimacy of aristocratic leadership. Slightly more than 1,000 men – hereditary peers, their heirs and younger sons, along with hereditary knights or baronets – controlled the House of Lords and a large part of the House of Commons, through direct membership and the extensive use of patronage (Mann 1993; Rule 1992a).

2. Ricardo's Politics

This highly limited representative system brought with it very substantial opportunities for what would today be described as rent-seeking behaviour, but in Ricardo's day was known (and denounced) as 'Old Corruption': the use of political influence to advance private vested interests, often at the considerable expense of society as a whole. David Ricardo's opposition to Old Corruption especially (but not only) when it operated in the interests of the landlords helps to explain why he became a convinced free-market liberal, advocating a small government and very limited state intervention in market activities.

While the mature David Ricardo was a classic Enlightenment liberal, his early life had not made it at all easy for him to reach this position. The Ricardo family were devout Sephardic Jews, and the young David grew up in an obscurantist, authoritarian and claustrophobic milieu in which all contact with non-Jews was strongly discouraged. As the novelist Maria Edgeworth later recalled him telling her:

> My father gave me but little education. He thought reading, writing and arithmetic sufficient because he doomed me to be nothing but a man of business, he sent me at eleven to Amsterdam to learn Dutch, French and Spanish. But I was so unhappy at being separated from my brothers and sisters and family that I learned nothing in two years but Dutch which I could not help learning. (cited by Heertje 2004: 286)

Thus he was of necessity very largely self-taught, not least on questions of economic and social policy.

But Ricardo eventually abandoned the Sephardic community and became a Unitarian. As Piero Sraffa noted, in Ricardo's day the Unitarians constituted 'the most liberal section of that "Wide Dissent", as it was called, which was accused of paving the way to irreligion pure and simple; and during the French Revolution they came to be regarded as a centre of rationalism and republicanism' (X: 39). Like many Unitarians, Ricardo was agnostic on matters of religion. 'On these difficult points I keep my mind in a state of doubt', as he told James Mill, 'from which in this world I can never be relieved. To account for evil in a world governed by a Being of unbounded benevolence and power is or appears to be impossible' (VII: 206). At this time Unitarianism was indeed 'the Enlightenment religion par excellence', encouraging a firm belief in 'the possibility of progress […] a distrust of the old, landed elite and the established Church, Whig if not radical politics, and a disposition towards commerce or its encouragement' (Jacob 2000: 279).

Ricardo's attachment to the radical liberal views of writers like Jeremy Bentham and James Mill was almost certainly welcomed by his Unitarian friends. 'My motto, after Mr. Bentham, is "the greatest happiness of the greatest number"', as he told Maria Edgeworth (IX: 239). He was also familiar with the writings of George Berkeley, David Hume and John Locke. But too much should not be made of all this, as most of Ricardo's reactions to philosophical questions came after the publication of the *Principles* in 1817, when his ideas on the political system and on matters of economics and economic policy were already firmly established.

The traditional view of Ricardo's political ideas is that they were largely unoriginal, reflecting the rational, secular Enlightenment liberalism that Élie Halévy once described as 'Philosophical Radicalism', making him both an enemy of all forms of Old Corruption and a proponent of a gradual, peaceful but far-reaching reform of the political system. Despite the contention of

Murray Milgate and Shannon Stimson (1991) that he was in fact a much stronger supporter of democracy and the political rights of the working class, the majority opinion remains that Ricardo was indeed a political moderate (King 2013: 42–49), endorsing the introduction of the secret ballot and more frequent Parliamentary elections but always rejecting the case for universal suffrage (let alone votes for women!).

For Ricardo the underlying principle was always the need to ensure social stability and continued economic progress by protecting private property, keeping taxes low and reducing the opportunities for rent-seeking behaviour that were offered by Old Corruption. And all this was underpinned by the basic principles that governed his views on economic policy: the entrepreneurial capitalist class was not only responsible for economic progress but also the only source of the savings that were required to implement it. Thus, the protection of profitability was the crucial priority, which determined Ricardo's position on all aspects of economic policy.

3. Ricardo's Views on Economic and Social Policy

There were four distinct areas of economic policy that concerned Ricardo: monetary policy, fiscal policy, social policy and international trade. I shall begin with his views on monetary policy, since this was the area that first aroused his interest in questions of political economy.

3.1. Monetary Policy

When the Napoleonic Wars began, the stock of money in England consisted of gold coins and of bank notes issued in London by the privately owned Bank of England, which functioned as the country's central bank, and elsewhere by the country banks. By 1797, as several years of massive government military spending put the public finances under increasing strain, there was a run on the banks and convertibility of bank notes into gold was suspended. This removed any legal constraint on the quantity of notes that the Bank of England could issue, and soon the price level was rising steadily and the pound sterling was depreciating against its competitors. What was to be done?

The ensuing 'Bullion Controversy' prompted Ricardo's first public involvement in questions of political economy. The so-called 'Anti-Bullionists' had claimed that the rising price level could not be blamed on over-issuing of paper money by the Bank of England, which was simply discounting 'real bills' in order to maintain private investment expenditure. They believed that an increase in the quantity of money might well have beneficial consequences for aggregate output and employment. For their part the 'Bullionists' argued that this would be 'a recipe for unlimited inflation and exchange depreciation', problems which by 1809–1810 had become especially dangerous (Laidler 1987: 281–82).

David Ricardo was one of the so-called 'rigid' or 'extreme' Bullionists, who saw the Bank of England's over-issue of paper currency as the only cause of renewed inflation and a falling exchange rate, and denied that there might be other causes, for example harvest failure. The 'moderate' Bullionists, for their part, denied that over-issue was the only possible cause of inflation and did not rule out increasing the quantity of Bank of England notes under all circumstances. A Parliamentary Select Committee was appointed to investigate the question, which rejected the 'real bills' doctrine and urged a rapid return of convertibility. Ricardo became the most prominent public defender of this position.

There is an important sense in which his position on these questions was inescapable, given his support for the labour theory of value (and similar considerations would determine the attitude of the great Marxian economist Rudolf Hilferding to the theory of money, a full century later). A quantity of gold bullion embodies a significant quantity of human labour and thus has a clear and in principle a measurable labour value. Paper notes, however, require little or no labour for their production, so that their value depends on the quantity of them that has been produced per unit (per ounce or kilogram) of gold. This leads the labour value theorist inevitably to what would later be described as the 'quantity theory of money', according to which the price level depends entirely on the quantity of paper tokens that have been issued, a rising price level is the only consequence of printing more money, and the only cause of price inflation is an increase in the quantity of tokens that has been produced.

For this reason Ricardo was a consistent supporter of the Bullion School, and he drew the necessary implications for monetary policy. An increase in the supply of paper money would increase the price level but would have no effect on real macroeconomic variables like output and employment. In the late twentieth century this would become the platform of the very influential 'rational expectations' school of macroeconomists under the leadership of Robert Lucas.

3.2. Fiscal Policy

If monetary policy could not be used to secure full employment, what were the prospects for fiscal policy? Here, too, Ricardo was profoundly sceptical. Rather surprisingly he wrote nothing on this question until October-November 1816, when he was already at work on the *Principles*. He came to devote no less than twelve chapters to taxation (I: chapters 8–18, 29), and two more to the closely related question of government subsidies (I: chapters 22–23). The context, of course, was the same as that which had provoked his writings on monetary policy six or seven years earlier: the Napoleonic Wars. The British war effort had at first been financed by massive borrowing, but the huge increase in government debt soon led to an increased reliance on tax revenues, with the introduction of an income tax in 1799 that shifted the burden of taxation to the wealthy (Bordo and White 1991).

As a 'small government, low tax' man Ricardo found this to be no less alarming. In the *Principles* he wrote at some length on the adverse effects of high taxation on the savings of the capitalists, and hence on the rate of capital accumulation. 'Aside from a tax on pure land rent', he maintained, 'it makes very little difference, except in the short period, what major tax is imposed. Wealthy consumers of luxury products may pay a small amount of the total tax bill; the rest will come out of profits' (Shoup 1960: 250). This concern was reinforced by his opposition to Old Corruption, since he believed it to be inevitable that increased tax receipts would encourage powerful vested interests to lobby for increased government spending as part of their continuing rent-seeking activities.

For these reasons Ricardo opposed the government's Sinking Fund, which was intended to be used to pay off the public debt but was in fact more likely to encourage yet further wasteful spending. Instead he proposed a one-off wealth tax, the so-called 'capital levy', to pay off the debt once and for all. He did not, however, campaign for a 'single tax' on land, as would later be proposed by Henry George. Ricardo's belief in the sanctity of private property was at issue here; a tax confined to the income from land would have struck him as tantamount to confiscation.

In chapter 17 of the *Principles* Ricardo compared the two methods of financing a war, government borrowing and increased taxation. From a theoretical perspective, he argued, the consequences were the same. In practice, however, government borrowing 'tends to make us less thrifty – to blind us to our real situation' (I: 247). As he wrote to his friend Sir John Sinclair, three years later: 'Men do not like to make an immediate sacrifice for a future good; and they please themselves with imaginary riches, from which they really derive no advantage' (VIII: 187). Thus, Ricardo 'recognized that taxpayers suffer from what we now call "fiscal illusion"', since 'he believed that the existence of the debt issue would deceive the wealth holder-taxpayer into believing that he was richer than he was in fact' (O'Driscoll 1977: 208, 209). This was enough to prevent him from giving unqualified endorsement to what late twentieth-century New Classical macroeconomists sometimes described as the principle of 'Ricardian equivalence', according to which deficit-financed government spending would simply reduce private expenditure by an equivalent amount and have no net effect on output or employment (Barro 1974). Ricardian equivalence requires taxpayer rationality, which is inconsistent with fiscal illusion.

Not that Ricardo was in any sense a supporter of proto-Keynesian measures of counter-cyclical fiscal policy. His negative conclusion on this important question was derived from the proposition asserted by the contemporary French economist Jean-Baptiste Say that later came to be known as 'Say's Law'. Ricardo himself stated it very clearly in chapter 21 of the *Principles*:

> Mr. Say has, however, most satisfactorily shewn, that there is no amount of capital which may not be employed in a country, because demand is only limited by production. No man produces, but with a view to consume or sell, and he never sells, but with an intention to purchase some other commodity, which may be immediately useful to him, or which may contribute to future production. By producing, then, he necessarily becomes either the consumer of his own goods, or the purchaser and consumer of the goods of some other person. (I: 290)

This led Ricardo to disagree strongly on this issue with his friend Robert Malthus, who had rejected Say's Law. As he wrote in his *Notes on Malthus*:

> Mr. Malthus's error is in supposing that cheap corn, and cheap commodities, necessarily imply a glut of corn and commodities. We agree that a glut is an evil… It arises *always* I think from a bad selection in the object produced, but cheapness from facility of production, which I think is the only legitimate cheapness, never fails of being attended with the happiest effects, and is as different from a glut, as light is from darkness. (II: 412–13; added stress)

This is about as clear a statement as we might wish of the possibility of *partial* over-production and the impossibility of *general* over-production, and Ricardo's position on this question was supported by the great majority of the political economists of his generation. On this crucial issue, as Keynes famously wrote, 'Ricardo conquered England as completely as the Holy Inquisition conquered Spain' (Keynes 1936: 32).

3.3. Social Policy

As we have seen, Ricardo was very definitely a 'small government' man. There were macroeconomic reasons for this, which came out of his support for Say's Law and his negative assessment of the prospects for expansionary fiscal policy. As he told Malthus in January 1817:

> I am not one of those who think that the raising of funds for the purpose of employing the poor is a very efficacious mode of relief, as it diverts those funds from other employments which would be equally if not more productive to the community. That part of the capital which employs the poor on the roads for example cannot fail to employ men somewhere and I believe every interference is prejudicial. (VII: 116)

But there was also an important element of microeconomics involved. Ricardo firmly believed that free markets worked best, with government intervention almost always reducing the efficiency of resource allocation, not least because of the encouragement that it gave to rent-seeking behaviour (especially by landlords).

On questions of social policy he was therefore a firm opponent of both government interference in the labour market and of efforts to provide what today would be described as social security through the provision of what was then known as 'poor relief'. For centuries the English state had set minimum wages and regulated the apprenticeship system, supposedly in the interests of the working man. When Ricardo entered Parliament the last vestiges of these controls were under attack, and he agreed wholeheartedly that they should go. As he told the Commons in 1823, in a debate on the Silk Manufacture Bill, 'the question was, whether labour should or should not be free'. For Ricardo, for whom 'the principles of true political economy never changed', it was entirely 'improper that those wages should be artificially kept up by the interference of a magistrate' (V: 296, 307):

> Why should this particular trade come under the cognisance of the magistrates more than any other? Why should he interfere with this particular branch of the trade when many other branches of it were not under his control? […] Why should he have the power to fix the price of labour, more than the price of bread, meat or beer? (V: 296)

Similar considerations applied to government controls over technical progress. He admitted that new machinery might

> […] operate prejudicially to the working classes. But he still would not tolerate any law to prevent the use of machinery. The question was, – if they gave up a system which enabled them to undersell in the foreign market, would other nations refrain from pursuing it? Certainly not. They were therefore bound, for their own interest, to continue it. (V: 303)

As for wages, he told the Commons, they were invariably and quite rightly determined by the supply and demand for labour.

On questions of broader social policy Ricardo was also a firm opponent of government efforts to offer what would today be called social security through the provision of poor relief. Again there were both macroeconomic and microeconomic reasons for his hostility. On these questions Ricardo was a strong Malthusian, believing that any system of poor relief would encourage excessive population growth. As he asked Hutches Trower in January 1817: 'Is it not desirable that the poor laws should be done away [with], and the labouring classes should receive the recompense for their labour rather in the shape of wages than of bounty? (VI: 124). This, he maintained, would reduce the rate of growth of the population, since '[t]he population can only be repressed by diminishing the encouragement to its *excessive* increase, – by leaving contracts between the poor and their employers perfectly free, which would limit the quantity of labour in the market to the effective demand for it (VII: 125; original stress).

In the *Principles* he was even more emphatic on this question:

> It is a truth which admits not a doubt, that the comforts and well-being of the poor cannot be permanently secured without some regard on their part, or some effort on the part of the legislature, to regulate the increase of their numbers, and to render less frequent the increase of their numbers, and to render less frequent among them early and improvident marriages. The operation of the system of poor laws has been directly contrary to this. They have rendered restraint superfluous, and have invited imprudence, by offering a portion of the wages of prudence and industry. (I: 106–7).

Ricardo also believed that the provision of poor relief had served to degrade and demoralise the working population. As he told Trower in January 1818:

> The great object should be to teach the labouring classes that they must themselves provide for those casualties to which they are exposed from occasional variations in the demand for particular manufactured goods, and which should not be the subject of legislation. A man's wages should, and would on a really good system, be sufficient not only to maintain himself and his family when he is in full work, but also to enable him to lay up a provision in a Savings Bank for those extraordinary calls. (VII: 248)

He was even opposed to the provision of private charity, which he thought to be no better than tax-financed poor relief: 'To relieve the poor by an *extended* system of private charity would hardly be less objectionable than the evil of which we now complain' (VII: 248; original stress). In all of this Ricardo saw himself as a defender of the self-reliance and independence of the working people. To his credit he opposed the introduction of the Combination Acts, which criminalised trade union activity and which he regarded as 'unjust to labour' (Grampp 1979: 506, citing VIII: 316). Thus he placed the 'freedom to organize and cooperate with others' above his 'strong anti-guild and anti-monopolist sentiments' (Mokyr 2010: 355).

3.4. International Trade

The classic statement by Ricardo of the universal benefits that can be expected from global free trade comes in chapter 7 of the *Principles*:

> Under a system of perfectly free commerce, each country naturally devotes its capital and labour to such employments as are most beneficial to each. This pursuit of individual advantage is admirably connected with the universal good of the whole. By stimulating industry, by rewarding ingenuity, and by using most efficaciously the peculiar powers bestowed by nature, it distributes labour most effectively and most economically; while, by increasing the general mass of productions, it diffuses general benefit, and binds together by one common tie of interest and intercourse, the universal society of nations throughout the civilized world. It is this principle which determines that wine should be made in France and Portugal, that corn should be grown in America and Poland, and that hardware and other goods should be manufactured in England. (I: 133–34)

Crucially, he believed that free trade would raise the rate of profit, stimulating the accumulation of capital and the growth of output. As he wrote in 1815, in his *Essay on the External Corn Trade*, free trade in corn would have 'a decided tendency to raise the real wages of labour' and, as rents declined, 'all capitalists whatever, whether they be farmers, manufacturers, or merchants, will have a great augmentation of profits' (IV, p. 35). He did make one small qualification:

> That the farmers of the poorer lands would be losers, there can be no doubt, but the public would gain many times the amount of their losses; and, after the exchange of capital from land to manufactures had been effected, the farmers themselves, as well as every other class of the community, except the landholders, would very considerably increase their profits. (IV: 33)

Ricardo concluded from this that there was a case for continuing to protect farmers until new, low-rent leases could be negotiated, and in chapter 19 of the *Principles* he made a similar argument for a temporary (and steadily declining) tax on corn imports at the end of a protracted war in which domestic agriculture had expanded to replace imports (I: 266–68, 272). In chapter 11, he even endorsed a permanent tax on imports to compensate farmers for their obligation to pay tithes, the tax levied on agricultural output by the Church of England (I: 179).

In chapter 25, Ricardo recognised that there were additional problems where trade was carried out between a colonial power and its dependent territories:

> It is evident, then, that the trade with a colony may be so regulated, that it shall at the same time be less beneficial to the colony, and more beneficial to the mother country, than a perfectly free trade. As it is disadvantageous to a single customer to be restricted in his dealings to one particular shop, so it is disadvantageous for a nation of consumers to be obliged to purchase of one particular country. (I: 343)

This seems to imply that the supposedly universal benefits of free trade in fact require a world of independent and equally powerful nations. Controversy on this question has continued down to the present day (King 2013: 100–6).

If Ricardo was not an unreasonably dogmatic supporter of free trade under all circumstances and regardless of all transitional issues, he certainly was a committed free trader. Just because there were tariffs on many manufactured goods, he argued in chapter 22 of the *Principles*, there was no good reason to protect agriculture: 'It would be much wiser to acknowledge the errors which a mistaken policy has induced us to adopt, and immediately to commence a gradual recurrence to the sound principles of an universally free trade' (I: 317–18). On this question, as on several others, Ricardo displays 'a kind of hard-right, libertarian radicalism' (Hutchison 1993: 16 n11) which is only slightly qualified by his use of the term 'gradual'.

4. And Now for Something Completely Different

Well, almost. The radical writers who were described by Herbert Foxwell in 1899 as the 'Ricardian Socialists' drew on the same sources as Ricardo (in particular on John Locke and Adam Smith) and were enthusiastic supporters of the labour theory of value. But they disagreed with Ricardo on almost everything else. In particular, the Ricardian Socialists maintained that the distribution of income and wealth in early nineteenth century England was profoundly unjust, argued that the serious material problems facing working people were the product of economic and social contradictions rather than the 'niggardliness of nature', and campaigned for the replacement of the capitalist mode of production by a fundamentally more egalitarian system.

The four most prominent Ricardian Socialists were John Francis Bray (1809–97), John Gray (1799–1883), Thomas Hodgskin (1787–1869) and William Thompson (1775–1833). Significant contributions came also from a forerunner, Charles Hall (c.1738–c.1825), from the pseudonymous Piercy Ravenstone, and from the author of an anonymous 1821 pamphlet on *The Source and Remedy of the National Difficulties*. Four of the six whose biographical details are known were English, while Thompson was Irish and Bray was born and died in the United States but lived in England from 1822 to 1842. They have attracted a considerable academic literature (King 1983, 2015; N. Thompson 1988).

These radical critics were operating in a lively milieu where several different but broadly consistent intellectual sources came together. The influence of the French Revolution was one of them, with Jacobin thinking spreading widely on the northern side of the Channel. Owenite socialism was another important element, not least in the work of John Gray. Radical monetary reformers also conducted sharp criticism of the prevailing economic and social order, while there were many radical critics of Old Corruption. Early advocates of the People's Charter campaigned for thoroughgoing democratic reform, which they saw as a necessary (if not also a sufficient) condition for wide-ranging social and economic reform. All these currents of radical opinion came together in the thinking of Ricardo's personal enemy, William Cobbett, who was part conservative, part radical and part rabble-rouser (N. Thompson 1998: chapter 2). As we have seen, these agitators were operating in an environment characterised by great economic and political discontent, which was itself the product of stagnant real wages, massive and increasing inequality in income and wealth, and blatant political and social injustice.

First and foremost, the Ricardian Socialists asserted the workers' 'right to the whole produce of labour', which Anton Menger (cousin of the Austrian neoclassical economist Carl Menger) used as the title of his book-length critique of their thinking (Menger 1899). The existing system of property rights, they insisted, was artificial and unjust and had resulted in working people receiving very much less than their ethical entitlement. 'All the advantages of our improvements go to the capitalist and the landlord', in Hodgskin's words, even though capital is nothing more than the 'co-existing labour' of other workers and the 'instruments and tools' that are termed 'fixed capital' are 'merely the result of *previous* labour' (Hodgskin 1825 [1969]: 23, 45, 54; original stress). Instead he endorsed 'the admirable maxim that "he who sows shall reap"', ending his short book with a call 'to do justice, and allow labour to possess and enjoy the whole of its produce' (ibid.: 104, 109). In a later book Hodgskin drew on Locke to argue that the individual's right to property was always derived from labour, while contemporary society 'severs the natural connection between labour and its rewards', encouraging idleness, luxury and crime (Hodgskin 1832 [1973]: 155).

The anonymous pamphleteer concurred, in a passage later quoted by Karl Marx: 'Whatever may be *due* to the capitalist, he *can only receive the surplus labour* of the labourer [...] the interest paid to the capitalists, whether in the nature of rents, interests of money, or profits of trade, is paid out of the *labour of others*' (Anon., 1821: 23; original stress). 'Wealth is produced by labour', Thompson wrote. 'Labour is the sole universal measure, as well as the characteristic distinction of wealth [...] All the products of labour ought to be secured to the producers of them' (W. Thompson 1824 [1963]: 4–6). Gray agreed, arguing that the payment of interest and rent was fundamentally unjust: 'Every unproductive member of society is a DIRECT TAX on the productive classes' (Gray 1825 [1971]: 11). For Bray, too, only labour creates wealth, but a 'most unequal system of exchanges' had 'benefitted the capitalist at the expense of the labourer', so that the interests of 'the capitalists and the employers' are deeply opposed to those of 'the producers at large' (Bray 1839 [1968]: 48, 61).

The second fundamental criticism made by the Ricardian Socialists followed on directly from this. They claimed that the capitalist system was not only unjust but also highly inefficient, since the periodic industrial crises that brought about the destitution of millions of working people and led the economy to operate well below capacity were themselves due to the highly unequal distribution of income. This powerful criticism originated with Hall, who estimated that the typical working man and his family were able to consume no more than one-eighth of the produce of their labour. Deficient effective demand was thus inescapable (Dinwiddy 1992). Twenty years later Gray made a similar criticism. 'In the present state of society', he wrote, 'production is limited by *demand*', which was itself limited by competition, especially by 'the increased struggle to obtain employment' (Gray 1825 [1971]: 47, 51; original stress).

Ravenstone, too, was convinced that mass poverty in England was not a natural phenomenon. It was due not to 'Providence' but rather to 'our own institutions'. Population had increased everywhere other than England without 'any inconvenience', and this alone was enough to refute Malthus: 'What is peculiar to one country cannot have arisen from causes common to all' (Ravenstone 1821 [1966]: 77, 150). In similar vein Hodgskin attacked the law of diminishing returns, which he regarded as both factually incorrect and inconsistent with 'the progress of society'. The 'Political Economists' were quite wrong in seeing poverty as something natural and inevitable. 'All the arguments they have urged in justification of their views', he argued, 'seem to be founded on the effects of some social institutions, which they assume to be natural laws' (Hodgskin 1827 [1966]: 226, 268).

In his powerful attack on Say's Law, Bray came to the same conclusion:

> Thousands now starve in unproductive inaction because the capitalist cannot employ them – the capitalist cannot give them work because he cannot find a market for his produce – there is no market for the produce because those who want to produce have nothing but their labour to give in exchange for it – and their labour is unemployed because the capitalist does not know how to set them to work – and thus the evils of the present system run round in a circle, one connected with and dependent upon another, and every one individually incurable. (Bray 1839 [1968]: 156)

The crucial point was that these evils emanated from the operation of 'the present system', and were not the outcome of laws of nature. Gray's understanding of the nature of deficiencies in effective demand would later be taken up, and endorsed, by Karl Marx.

This crucial point led the Ricardian Socialists to the third component of their critique: the need to replace capitalism with a different system, one that would combine social justice with economic efficiency. Bray himself advocated 'the subversion of the present system' and its replacement by a 'system of communities' in which production would be carried out by worker-owned joint-stock companies according to plans drawn up by 'general and local boards of trade' (ibid.: 107, 162). Thompson also called for the establishment of socialist communities, while Gray set out a draft constitution for a 'Friendly Association for Mutual Interests' along Owenite lines. Only Hodgskin took a more liberal position, arguing instead for free competition between self-employed workers in essentially unregulated markets. In effect he was proposing the introduction of what Marx and his disciples would later term 'simple commodity production', while Bray, Gray and Thompson were advocating slightly different versions of a post-capitalist (socialist or communist) social order. Even John Stuart Mill, in the third edition of his *Principles*, declared his support for a system of self-managed workers' cooperatives.

While the single principle that united the Ricardian Socialists was their unqualified hostility to Malthus on every important issue other than under-consumption, the parallels with Marx are not really surprising. As we have seen, Hall made use of the quintessentially Marxian notion of surplus labour, he also anticipated Marx's critique of the fetishism of commodities, maintaining that in capitalist production 'the exploitative nature of the whole process was not transparent. Rather, "money covers and conceals the action, as the case of a watch does the motion"' (Cunliffe 1994: 541, citing Hall

1805 [1965]: 103). Edmonds foreshadowed the Marxian concept of surplus value and set out a three-stage typology of human history in which the 'slave system has been succeeded by the money system, and the money system will be succeeded by the social system, one system following the other, perhaps in a necessary order' (Edmonds 1828 [1969]: 58). A very similar approach had been taken by Thompson, who distinguished three 'modes of human labour […] first, labour by force, or compulsion direct or indirect; second, labour by unrestricted individual competition; third, labour by mutual cooperation' (Thompson 1824 [1963]: xviii).

So, how Ricardian were they in reality? This is debatable. Other than Hall, who wrote well before the publication of the *Principles*, they would all have had some knowledge of Ricardo's ideas. But the references to him in their published works were relatively few and not especially complementary (King 2015: 461–62). Indeed, Noel Thompson concludes that 'Marx was the only Ricardian socialist. Hodgskin, Gray, Thompson and Bray may be more appropriately designated "Smithian"' than Ricardian (Thompson 1984: 105).

5. Conclusion

Ricardo himself, of course, was an economist of the highest quality. As a rigorous theorist he ensured that his conclusions on matters of economic policy dovetailed with both his formal analysis and his commitment to the fundamental principles of liberalism. In the early nineteenth century, this was a considerable achievement, and the issues on which he focused have remained central to economists ever since. The deficiencies in his policy proposals arose from the assumptions that he made, especially regarding population growth and technical change, but these were widely believed to be true at the time and the contemporary empirical evidence was insufficient to provide a conclusive refutation. As a consequence it is not surprising that Ricardo's writings on economic policy have earned the respect of later generations of economists, whatever their own school of thought.

References

Anon. 1821. *The Source and Remedy of the National Difficulties, deduced from Principles of Political Economy, in a Letter to Lord John Russell.* London: publisher not stated (cited by K. Marx, *Theories of Surplus Value, Part III.* London: Lawrence & Wishart, 1972: 587).

Barro, R. J. 1974. 'Are government bonds net wealth?' *Journal of Political Economy* 82, no. 6, November–December: 1095–1117.

Bordo, M. D. and White, E. N. 1991. 'A Tale of Two Currencies: British and French Finance during the Napoleonic Wars'. *Journal of Economic History* 51, no. 2, June: 303–16.

Bray, J. F. 1839 [1968]. *Labour's Wrongs and Labour's Remedy.* New York: A. M. Kelley.

Cunliffe, J. 1994. 'Charles Hall: Exploitation, Commercial Society and Political Economy'. *History of Political Thought* 15, no. 4, Winter: 535–53.

Dinwiddy, J. R. 1976 [1992], 'Charles Hall, Early English Socialist'. *International Review of Social History* 21, no. 2: 256–76. Cited from J. R. Dinwiddy, *Radicalism and Reform in Britain 1780–1850*. London: Hambledon Press: 87–107.

Edmonds, T. R. 1828 [1969]. *Practical, Moral and Political Economy*. New York: A. M. Kelley.

Grampp, W.D. 1979. 'The Economists and the Combination Laws'. *Quarterly Journal of Economics* 93, no. 4, November: 501–22.

Gray, J. 1825 [1971]. *A Lecture on Human Happiness*. New York: A. M. Kelley.

Hall, C. 1805 [1965]. *The Effects of Civilization on the People in European States*. New York: A. M. Kelley.

Heertje, A. 2004. 'The Dutch and Portuguese-Jewish background of David Ricardo'. *European Journal of the History of Economic Thought* 11, no. 2, Summer: 281–94.

Hodgskin, T. 1825 [1969]. *Labour Defended against the Claims of Capital*. New York: A. M. Kelley.

Hodgskin, T. 1827 [1966]. *Popular Political Economy*. New York: A. M. Kelley.

Hodgskin, T. 1832 [1973]. *The Natural and Artificial Rights of Property Contrasted*. New York: A. M. Kelley.

Hutchison, T. W. 1993. '"Ricardian Politics": Another Version of Ricardian Hagiography'. *History of Economics Review* 19, Winter: 1–17.

Jacob, M. C. 2000. 'Commerce, Industry, and the Laws of Newtonian Science: Weber Revisited and Revived'. *Canadian Journal of History* 25, no. 3: 275–92.

Kaldor, N. 1982. 'Limitations of the *General Theory*', *Proceedings of the British Academy* 68: 259–73.

Keynes, J. M. 1936. *The General Theory of Employment, Money and Interest*. London: Macmillan.

King, J. E. 1983. 'A Reconsideration of the Ricardian Socialists'. *History of Political Economy* 15, no. 3, Fall: 345–73.

King, J. E. 2013. *David Ricardo*. Basingstoke: Palgrave Macmillan.

King, J. E. 2015. 'Ricardian Socialists'. In *The Elgar Companion to David Ricardo*, edited by H. D. Kurz and N. Salvadori, 455–64. Cheltenham, UK and Northampton, MA, USA.

Laidler, D. 1987. 'Bullionist controversy'. In *The New Palgrave: a Dictionary of Economics*, edited by J. Eatwell, M. Milgate and P. Newman, 289–94. Basingstoke: Macmillan.

Mann, M. 1993. *The Sources of Social Power, Volume 2: The Rise of Classes and Nation-States*. Cambridge: Cambridge University Press.

Menger, A. 1899. *The Right to the Whole Produce of Labour*. New York, Kelley, 1970.

Milgate, M. and Stimson, S. 1991. *Ricardian Politics*. Princeton, NJ: Princeton University Press.

Mokyr, J. 2010. *The Enlightened Economy: an Economic History of Britain, 1700–1859*. New Haven, CT: Yale University Press.

O'Driscoll, G.P. Jr. 1977. 'The Ricardian Non-Equivalence Theorem'. *Journal of Political Economy* 85, no. 1, February: 207–10.

Ravenstone, P. 1821 [1966]. *A Few Doubts as to the Correctness of Some Opinions Generally Entertained on the Subjects of Population and Political Economy*. New York: A. M. Kelley.

Rubinstein, W. D. 1981. *Men of Property: the Very Wealthy in Britain since the Industrial Revolution*. London: Croom Helm.

Rule, J. G. 1992a. *Albion's People: English Society 1714–1815*. London: Longman.

Rule, J. G. 1992b. *The Vital Century: England's Developing Economy 1714–1815*. London: Longman.

Schneider, M. P. 2004. *The Distribution of Wealth*. Cheltenham: Edward Elgar.

Shoup, C. S. 1960. *Ricardo on Taxation*. New York: Columbia University Press.

Thompson, N. 1984. *The People's Science: The Popular Political Economy of Exploitation and Class, 1816–1834*. Cambridge, UK: Cambridge University Press.

Thompson, N. 1988. *The Market and Its Critics: Socialist Political Economy in Nineteenth Century Britain*. London: Routledge.

Thompson, N. 1998. *The Real Rights of Man: Political Economies for the Working Class*, 1775–1850. London: Pluto.

Thompson, W. 1824 [1963]. *Inquiry into the Principles of Wealth most Conducive to Human Happiness*. New York: A. M. Kelley.

Thompson, W. 1827 [1969]. *Labour Rewarded: the Claims of Labour and Capital Conciliated*. New York: A. M. Kelley.

Voth, H.-J. 2004. 'Living standards and the urban environment'. In *The Cambridge Economic History of Modern Britain: Volume 1, Industrialisation, 1700–1860*, edited by R. Floud and P. Johnson, 268–94. Cambridge: Cambridge University Press.

Wrigley, E. A. 2004. 'British population during the "long" eighteenth century, 1680–1840'. In *The Cambridge Economic History of Modern Britain: Volume 1, Industrialisation, 1700–1860*, edited by R. Floud and P. Johnson, 57–95. Cambridge: Cambridge University Press.

Chapter 6

(MIS)INTERPRETING RICARDO

Heinz D. Kurz

1. Introduction

Major interpreters of David Ricardo assess his contribution to political economy in vastly different terms. Karl Marx praises Ricardo's 'scientific impartiality and love of truth' (Marx 1954, p. 412) and the 'honesty which so essentially distinguishes him from the vulgar economists' (Marx 1959, p. 555; original emphasis). William Stanley Jevons is one in a row of critics who contended that the doctrine of the classical authors and especially Ricardo 'is radically fallacious; it involves the attempt to determine two unknown quantities from one equation' (Jevons [1871] 1965, p. 258; see also 258–59): profits and the level of output, given the real wage rate. Léon Walras reiterates the criticism: 'In the language of mathematics one equation cannot be used to determine two unknowns' (Walras [1874–77] 1954, §368), while Joseph A. Schumpeter stokes it up: according to him Ricardo's 'fundamental problem' was that he 'wanted to solve in terms of an equation between four variables: net output equals rent plus profits plus wages' (Schumpeter 1954, p. 569). Schumpeter also accuses Ricardo of 'piling a heavy load of practical conclusions upon a tenuous groundwork' (1954, p. 1171). The 'Ricardian vice' is said to consist in drawing bold policy conclusions from oversimplified and arbitrarily closed models of the economy. Knut Wicksell instead defends Ricardo against this kind of criticism: 'the way in which Ricardo develops his argument [...] is a model of strictly logical reasoning about a subject which seems, at first glance, to admit of so little precision'. And: 'Ricardo's theory of value is, one finds, developed with a high degree of consistency and strictness' (Wicksell [1893] 1954, pp. 34 and 40). He adds

> Since, according to Ricardo, wages represent a magnitude fixed from the beginning, and since – as he later shows – the level of rent is also determined by independent causes, the cause of capital profit is already settled. It is neither possible nor necessary to explain capital profit in other ways, if the other assumptions are sound. (ibid., pp. 36–37)[1]

Interestingly, a few years earlier Alfred Marshall dubs Ricardo the head of the 'brilliant school of deductive reasoning' (Marshall 1890, p. 629), and explains: 'His strong constructive originality is the mark of the highest genius in all nations. […] Ricardo's power of threading his way without slip through intricate paths to new and unexpected results has never been surpassed' (ibid, p. 629, n. 1). On Ricardo's approach to the theory of relative prices, Marshall in Chapter XV of Book V, 'General Relations of Demand, Supply, and Value', writes: 'Ricardo's theory of cost of production in relation to value occupies so important a place in the history of economics that any misunderstanding as to its real character must necessarily be very mischievous'. Contrary to a widespread opinion Marshall insists 'that the foundations of the theory as they were left by Ricardo remain intact' (ibid., pp. 416–17).[2]

John Maynard Keynes is mainly concerned about the 'realism' of Ricardo's theory. To him 'Ricardo was the abstract and *a priori* theorist' – a man 'with his head in the clouds' (Keynes *CW* X, pp. 95 and 98).[3] Ricardo's failure to understand the *Principle of Effective Demand*, which according to Keynes Thomas Robert Malthus had established, and which governs output as a whole and employment, rendered his analysis not only analytically largely useless but also socially harmful. Keynes sighs: 'If only Malthus, instead of Ricardo, had been the parent stem from which nineteenth century economics proceeded, what a much wiser and richer place the world would be to-day!' (Keynes *CW* X, pp. 100–101)

Why is there such a diversity of opinions on Ricardo? Why does the discussion of his doctrines not converge on a widely shared point of view? Put differently: Why is your Ricardo different from mine?

In this paper I put forward what in my opinion are some of the main reasons for what I consider to be essentially misunderstandings and misinterpretations of Ricardo. I thus side with Wicksell and other commentators who hold Ricardo in high esteem and praise his analytical capabilities, his originality and his sense of realism. Ricardo's writings are not easy to understand. They may much more easily be misunderstood, as several examples dealt with below show. Ricardo was not given the time to elaborate his ideas in a fully coherent and comprehensive way. His analysis, for the elaboration of which he had only a few years, remained in *statu nascendi*. Many of his insights he never managed to work out fully. A lack of conceptual clarity is reflected in the formulation of ideas, which increases for readers the barriers to entry in Ricardo's analysis. It also leaves somewhat in the dark how various ideas are interconnected, how the parts make up the whole of Ricardo's economics. One thing the attentive reader will swiftly understand: he cannot expect to learn all that is to be known about a particular theme by turning just to the chapter in the *Principles* that refers to the theme in its title. To come to grips with Ricardo's position on exhaustible resources, for example, it is not good enough to focus attention only on Chapter III, 'On the Rent of Mines', just as it is not good enough to read only Chapter VII, 'On Foreign Trade', in order to get a comprehensive picture of his views on international trade. Major obstacles in the way to a better understanding of Ricardo's views appear to be a lack of awareness of his method of reasoning. He typically begins his reasoning by first contemplating a situation in which capital accumulates and the population grows, but in which there is no technical progress. It is only in a second step that he investigates how various types of 'improvement' modify the results obtained. Also, the numerical examples Ricardo constructs in order to illustrate what in his view is the main principle at work in a given case have frequently been misunderstood. The paper seeks to clear up some of the misconceptions encountered in the secondary literature on Ricardo. The emphasis is on the theory of value and distribution, the role of scarce natural resources, various types of technical change and on foreign trade. It will be argued that while the form in which Ricardo presents his argument is frequently less than optimal and a source of misinterpretation, its content is generally remarkable and rich with insights, several of which have not been fully recovered as yet.[4]

The composition of the chapter is the following. Section 2 scrutinises the claim that Ricardo was a purely abstract theorist. Section 3 summarises his method of analysis and the role of numerical examples in it. Section 4 deals with his approach to the theory of value and distribution and the intuition that guided his consecutive attempts at solving the problem. Section 5 touches briefly upon the contention that his analysis of different forms of technical progress in Chapter II, 'On Rent', is hopelessly muddled; it is shown that this is not so. Section 6 then turns to the case of exhaustible resources and argues that his treatment in terms of differential rent is perfectly sensible: while different from the analysis of Harold Hotelling, it is not inferior to, but compatible with it. Section 7 turns to his discussion of machinery and clears up some misunderstandings in the literature on it. Finally, Section 8 addresses the Theorem of comparative cost and argues that it cannot be properly understood without a reference to arbitrageurs, that is merchants, and the role of money in trade. Section 9 concludes.[5]

2. Ricardo – the Man 'with His Head in the Clouds'?

Ricardo has been chastised for his 'abstract reasoning', which allegedly lacked any realism and was not practically applicable. Its barrenness is well expressed, his critics contend, by the purely hypothetical numerical examples he constructs for illustrative purposes, which are said to have little or nothing to do with the 'real world'. Comparing Ricardo and Malthus, Keynes opines: 'In economic discussions Ricardo was the abstract and a priori theorist, Malthus the inductive and intuitive investigator who hated to stray too far from what he could test by reference to the facts and his own intuitions' (Keynes *CW* X, p. 95). Keynes adds with reference to the correspondence between the two authors dealing with the determination of output, income distribution and relative prices:

> One cannot rise from a perusal of this correspondence without a feeling that the almost total obliteration of Malthus's line of approach and the complete domination of Ricardo's for a period of a hundred years has been a disaster to the progress of economics. Time after time in these letters Malthus is talking plain sense, the force of which *Ricardo with his head in the clouds* wholly fails to comprehend. Time after time a crushing refutation by Malthus is met by a mind so completely closed that Ricardo does not even see what Malthus is saying. (Keynes *CW* X, p. 98; emphasis added)

This verdict clearly does not apply to Ricardo, the stock jobber, whose knowledge about money, finance and banking probably came second to none in his time. Keynes admits: 'when it came to practical finance, the rôles of the Jewish stockbroker and the aristocratic clergyman were, as they should be, reversed' (Keynes *CW* X, p. 95). Ricardo knew even minute technical and organisational details of the banking business of his time and he knew financial mathematics – compound interest, annuities, etc. – a knowledge the majority of contemporary economists lacked. But what about the real side of the economy, production processes in agriculture and manufacturing, the organisation of commerce and trade, the export and import of commodities, technical progress? Was Ricardo really the man 'with his head in the clouds'?

Timothy Davis (2002, 2005) had already shown that Ricardo's theoretical views and economic policy advice were typically based on a thorough knowledge of the available macroeconomic empirical data. Mary Morgan provides further compelling evidence that Ricardo 'was no less informed, or less able to judge, the agricultural realities of his day than Malthus, who was for many years the parson of a rural parish' (Morgan 2012, p. 48). As a matter of fact, Ricardo appears to have known a great deal more about the importance of drainage, new crops and crop rotation and the gradual beginning of mechanisation in agriculture than most of his contemporaries. Morgan focuses attention on

> the common ground and unexpected connection between the two practical domains of political economy and experimental agriculture, and in particular the fundamental importance of these links in Ricardo's works. His account of distribution depended on substantive elements from practical and experimental farming.

She goes on: 'His political arithmetic, or as I shall suggest, his model and modelling, mirror the numerical expression and content of agricultural experimental work'. And: 'Ricardo knew about all this. He was familiar with the experimental farming activities of his day' (Morgan 2012, pp. 53 and 55). It was only on the basis of such practical knowledge that he could develop his 'law of distribution', that is, his analysis of changes in the sharing out of the products as wages, rents and profits as capital accumulates, the population grows and technical progress transforms the methods of production.

As regards the manufacturing sector, Ricardo was one of the first to investigate the sector's mechanisation, especially in Chapter XXXI, 'On Machinery', added to the third edition of the *Principles* (1821). He did so partly as a response to the activities of the Luddites, who took machines to be the source of workers' distress and therefore sought to destroy them. Contrary to Adam Smith, Ricardo may be said to have glimpsed the tremendous rise in importance of the manufacturing sector in general and of the machine producing industry in particular for the development of the economic system as a whole. And while he did not yet grasp the sector's elevation to the 'engine of growth' of industrialising economies, he sensed that something important was happening that affected also the production of 'necessaries' – the gradual industrialisation of agriculture. As an end state of this development he even contemplated a situation in which machine power had completely replaced labour power, with machines producing machines – a fully automated economic system. This had important consequences with respect to income distribution, as he wrote in a letter to McCulloch of 30 June 1821: 'If machinery could do all the work that labour now does, there would be no demand for labour. Nobody would be entitled to consume any thing who was not a capitalist, and who could not buy or hire a machine' (*Works* VIII, pp. 399–400).

We may conclude by saying that Ricardo was not the proverbial man with his head in the clouds. When his adversaries in Parliament denounced him as a 'visionary on commercial subjects' (*Works* VIII, p. 197) and as someone who has 'just descended from some other planet' (*Works* V, p. 85), this was not because he lacked practical knowledge and analytical judgement on these matters. It was rather because his proposals were seen to harm his adversaries' interests and to be possessed of a compelling logic. Ricardo understood the financial world of his days better than most of his contemporaries. He was also familiar with some of the technical and organisational revolutions that took place before his eyes in the various sectors of the economy and analysed the consequences of different types of technical progress on development and growth, income distribution and relative prices. A careful scrutiny of his works and correspondence shows that his thinking was not overwhelmed, as is frequently contended, by a concern with diminishing returns in agriculture in combination with Malthus's law of population. This brings us to our next theme: Ricardo's method of analysis and the role of numerical examples in it. These appear to have frequently been misapprehended and have led to assessments of Ricardo that are difficult to sustain.

3. Ricardo's Method and Numerical Illustrations

The theory Ricardo sought to elaborate shared with Smith's at least three important features. First, the theory had to be *general*: it had to deal with the economic system as a whole and with the interdependence between its different parts. Second, it had to come to grips with the modern economy's *inherent dynamism*, a system that is continually changing from within due to the accumulation of capital, the growth of population, the scarcity of renewable (land) and exhaustible (mines) resources, technical change in all sectors of the economy, a growing social division of labour both domestically and internationally, an expansion of outputs and an increasing heterogeneity and diversity of commodities. What are the laws governing the system and, especially, what are the laws governing the *distribution* of a growing product amongst the different classes of society, workers, capitalists and landlords? Third, the analytical method Smith and Ricardo employed in order to investigate the system is known as the *long-period method*. It focuses attention on situations in which, in the ideal case of *free competition*, a uniform rate of profits and uniform rates of wages and of rents for each particular quality of labour or of land obtain. Competitive forces are taken to let 'market prices' and the distributive variables gravitate towards (or oscillate around) their 'natural' levels. The latter were the theoretical magnitudes on whose explanation, and determination, the classical authors focused attention.

In a *first step* of the analysis Ricardo typically studied in abstract terms the situation of an economy *in a given place and time*. In a *second step* he then studied the path the economy would take in the case in which it followed the 'natural course of things'. By this he meant a course of events in which capital accumulates, the population grows, etc., but in which there is no further technical progress – there are no further 'improvements'' in the methods of production. The order according to which lands of different 'fertility' will be cultivated upon the first settling of a country and the subsequent gradual increase of effectual demand for corn, as discussed in Chapter II, 'On Rent', reflects well this course and Ricardo's *method of counterfactual reasoning*: the system expands, but technical knowledge is taken to be frozen in. It is only in a *third step* that he takes technical progress into account and expounds the different effects different types of it have.

The focus of much of Ricardo's analysis is on steps one and two. Understandably, he was keen to get the foundations of his analysis right.

Setting aside technical progress was also motivated by the fact that little can be known today about future technical breakthroughs. What could at most be done was to assess the impact of different well-specified forms of improvements on the economic system. Alas, his stance in this regard appears to have led some commentators to see in Ricardo a technical pessimist, who expected the stationary state to lurk around the corner (see Kurz 2010, pp. 1184 and 1195). This misinterpretation could only have been amplified by the fact that in his discussions with Malthus Ricardo variously had recourse to the former's law of population. Since Ricardo repeatedly expressed scepticism as to the validity of this alleged 'law' (see Kurz and Salvadori 2009), the question is why he nevertheless accepted it in some of his debates with his friend. He appears to have invoked it in order to get a firm ground to stand on in his controversy with Malthus about the determinants of the general rate of profits. With a real wage rate that is given and constant thanks to the population mechanism, an explanation of the rate of profits in terms of the surplus product left after the necessary means of production and means of sustenance of workers have been deducted from the social product is straightforward and clear, which it is not in the case in which the real wage rate is not fixed.

Ricardo had the habit of illustrating his reasoning in terms of numerical examples; see especially his *Essay on Profits* (*Works* IV), in which the argument is developed around an elaborate numerical example. He was in fact one of the first economists to do so, and to good purpose. The simplicity of several of the numerical illustrations and the derivation of economic policy conclusions from some of them has earned him Schumpeter's accusation of 'Ricardian vice'; and the difficulties besetting some of the examples has prompted critics to call his respective analysis 'a complete and hopeless failure' (Cannan [1893] 1967, p. 260). While there can be no doubt that some of Ricardo's illustrations are somewhat misconstrued, how can this be explained in view of Ricardo's untiring effort to get his argument right? There is no need to speculate in this regard, because Ricardo told the reader how he proceeded. His main concern was with the general thrust of the argument, the basic principle he saw at work in the particular situation under consideration. He left it to the reader to think through any further ramifications the argument might have and also the implications of a change in its setting. He emphasised:

> In all these calculations I have been desirous only to *elucidate the principle*, and it is scarcely necessary to observe, that my whole basis is assumed at random, and merely for the purpose of exemplification. The results though different in degree, would have been the same in principle, however accurately I might have stated the [details]. My object has been to simplify the subject [...] (*Works* I, pp. 121–22; emphasis added)

What mattered to him were the economic principles he wished to establish; the numerical examples were simple illustrations, chosen *ad hoc*. To point out slips in the illustrations does not imply that the underlying argument is erroneous. Yet this is what some critics of Ricardo have argued. Below a few examples will be given, with regard to which they tended to throw out the baby with the bathwater. It will be argued that several of Ricardo's examples can easily be rectified and brought into harmony with the economic principle he was desirous to elucidate.

4. Ricardo's Approach to the Theory of Value and Distribution

The theory of value and distribution forms the backbone of all other economic theory in Ricardo: the theory of capital accumulation and economic development, of scarce natural resources, of foreign trade, of taxation and public debt and so on. This explains why it was at the centre of debates ever since it saw the light of the day. The comprehension of Ricardo and the classical authors has dramatically improved with the publication of *The Works and Correspondence of David Ricardo* (Ricardo 1951–1973), Piero Sraffa's introductions, especially to Volume I of the Edition, and Sraffa's 1960 resumption of and elaboration on the 'standpoint of the old classical economists from Adam Smith to Ricardo' (Sraffa 1960, p. v). Sraffa's introductions, Luigi Pasinetti (2012, p. 1310) stressed, 'have opened up the way to a clearer and deeper understanding than has ever been the case before of classical economic theory'. In this state of affairs, it suffices to resume important aspects of Ricardo's approach and dispel some misinterpretations in the literature.

Relating to what we called the first step in Ricardo's analysis, Sraffa pointed out that the investigation 'is concerned exclusively with such properties of an economic system as do not depend on changes in the scale of production or in the proportions of "factors"' (Sraffa 1960, p. v). The given *system of production* whose (mathematical) properties were to be studied is characterised in terms of (i) given gross output levels of the various commodities and (ii) given methods of production to produce these outputs.[6] Are the givens (or independent variables) (i) and (ii) both necessary and sufficient to ascertain the range within which the magnitudes can vary in which the classical economists were most interested – the wage rate(s), the rent(s) of land, the general rate of profits and relative prices?

Sraffa (1960) demonstrated that the answer to this question is yes.[7] More specifically (and setting aside the problem of scarce natural resources, such as land) he showed that the givens (i) and (ii) suffice to determine the competitive rate of profits and relative prices if *real wages* are given and form a part of the physical real costs of production. This case regards 'wages as consisting of the necessary subsistence of the workers and thus entering the system on the same footing as the fuel for the engine or the feed for the cattle' (1960, p. 9). In the simple case of single-product industries and thus circulating capital only, and normalising gross output levels of the different industries as unity, the price equations of classical derivation can be written as

$$\mathbf{p} = (1+r)\ (\mathbf{M}+\mathbf{S})\mathbf{p} \quad or \quad \mathbf{p} = (1+r)\mathbf{A}\mathbf{p}, \tag{1}$$

where $\mathbf{p}$ is the n-dimensional price vector $(p_1, p_2, \ldots, p_n)^T$, r is the general rate of profits, $\mathbf{M}$ is the $n \times n$ matrix of material means of production, $\mathbf{S}$ is the matrix of the necessary subsistence of workers and $\mathbf{A} = \mathbf{M} + \mathbf{S}$. On the simplifying assumption of a uniform real wage per unit of labour employed in production, given by vector $\mathbf{c} = (c_1, c_2, \ldots, c_n)$, and denoting the quantities of (direct) labour needed per unit of output in the different industries by $\mathbf{l} = (l_1, l_2, \ldots, l_n)^T$, $\mathbf{S} = \mathbf{l}\mathbf{c}^T$. With $\mathbf{M}$, $\mathbf{l}$ and $\mathbf{c}$ given, and taking a bundle of non-negative quantities of the different commodities $\mathbf{d} = (d_1, d_2, \ldots, d_m)^T$ as the standard of value, that is setting its value equal to unity,

$$\mathbf{d}^T\mathbf{p} = 1, \tag{2}$$

the general rate of profits r and the prices in terms of the standard $\mathbf{d}$ can be ascertained; see, for example, Kurz and Salvadori (1995, chap. 4). No other data or known variables (and especially no demand and supply functions) are needed to determine the unknowns. Hence, the contention put forward by Jevons, Walras and Schumpeter that Ricardo tried to determine two (or several) unknowns from a single equation is false.

What applies to the case of a particular level of the real wage rate applies to all levels of the real wage compatible with a non-negative rate of profits. This leads to Ricardo's so-called *fundamental law of distribution* – the inverse relationship between the rate of profits (r) and wages (w), or w–r relationship or wage curve, which was arguably one of his most important analytical discoveries. The argument applies also to the case in which 'proportional wages' are given. By this Ricardo meant a given share of wages (see Gehrke 2011). Also, in this regard Sraffa proved Ricardo's intuition to be correct.[8]

Ricardo stressed that 'Profits come out of the surplus produce' (*Works* II, p. 128). The *surplus product* consists of the quantities of commodities that are left over after all the necessary means of production and means of subsistence in the support of (productive) workers have been deducted from the quantities actually produced of the various commodities during a year; it is a vector of commodities. Setting aside the rents of land, the surplus product constitutes the commodity content of profits. The *capital advanced* on the other hand consists of the means of production and the means of subsistence employed and (partly) used up; this is another vector of commodities. Physically, the *general rate of profits* is the ratio of the two vectors, with the surplus product (profits) in the numerator and the necessary inputs (capital) in the denominator.

Apparently the two magnitudes can only be compared, if the various commodities are rendered commensurable with one another. It is here that the theory of value enters the stage of the classical surplus-based approach to income distribution, as Garegnani (1984) stressed. It actually seems to be irrefutable that the general rate of profits can only be ascertained in terms of, or simultaneously with, the prices of commodities. It therefore cannot but come as a surprise that Ricardo was *not* of this opinion: he was convinced that the problem of distribution could be dealt with independently of the problem of value. In a letter to McCulloch of 13 June 1820 reflecting upon his previous efforts to elaborate a consistent theory of profits he insisted:

> After all the great questions of Rent, Wages, and Profits must be explained by the proportions in which the whole produce is divided between landlords, capitalists, and labourers, and *which are not essentially connected with the doctrine of value*. (*Works* VIII, p. 194; emphasis added)

He was clear that he had not yet managed to establish the validity of this bold claim in sufficiently general terms, but he was confident that it could be done: 'The truth of this doctrine I deem to be absolutely demonstrable' (*Works* VIII, p. 195).

These are remarkable statements. How could the laws of distribution not be essentially connected with the doctrine of value vis-à-vis the heterogeneity of the bundles of commodities that form the surplus product and social capital? And how could Ricardo hope to be able to convince a Malthus and other contemporaries of the truth of his apparently extravagant doctrine?[9]

Ricardo's view applies, of course, in the case of what became known as the "corn model" subsequent to the publication of Volume I of the Ricardo edition. In his Introduction to it, Sraffa famously put forward the 'corn-ratio' interpretation of Ricardo's theory of profits (Sraffa 1951, pp. xxxi-xxxii). Here we need not dwell on this interpretation and the occasionally heated controversy it triggered. It suffices to point out the following. First, Ricardo was not the only author keen to exemplify his basic intuition as regards the problem under consideration. He was well aware of the fact that he was confronted with a myriad of complex relationships, whose precise form neither he nor anyone else (including Malthus) knew at the time (and for a long time thereafter). In a letter to

Malthus of 17 April 1815 he spoke of his 'simple doctrine', designed to 'account for all the phenomena in an easy, natural manner', thus staying away from 'a labyrinth of difficulties' (*Works* VI, p. 214). The corn model in the *Essay on Profits* of 1815 was designed to accomplish this.

As is well known, in the *Principles* Ricardo suggested to render heterogeneous commodities commensurate in terms of the amounts of labour bestowed upon them in their production. The labour theory of value was the device by means of which he intended to overcome as best as he could the impasse in which he found himself, lacking a consistent and general theory of value.[10] However, this did not make him entirely abandon his vision that the question of income distribution could be discussed independently of the theory of value. Interestingly, in all three editions of the *Principles* we encounter a numerical example, which satisfies the *homogeneity condition* of output and capital, but now no longer with regard to a single industry (corn production) only, but with regard to the *aggregate* of several industries taken together; see *Works* I, pp. 50 and 64–66. As in other parts of his theory of profits, in the example under consideration, Ricardo for simplicity takes capital to consist only of wages advanced at the beginning of the year.[11]

In the example there are three commodities: in addition to corn there are also hats and coats. All three commodities enter the real wage rate and thus are 'necessaries' or capital goods needed in the production of the three commodities themselves (and also in that of other commodities, about which Ricardo does not speak in the context under consideration). If of 100 units produced of each of them, workers and landlords get 25 (or 22) units each, profits consist of 50 (or 56) units of each of them. If capital consists only of the real wages bill, the rate of profits can be ascertained independently of values and amounts to $\frac{50}{25}=2$ (or $\frac{56}{22}=\frac{28}{11}$). The inverse relationship between the rate of profits and real wages (and rents) is alluded to: if wages fell from 25 to 22 units, profits would increase from 50 to 56 units, and the rate of profits would rise from 200 per cent to approximately 254.55 per cent.

Taking into account a multiplicity of wage (or capital) goods, as Malthus had requested in his debate with Ricardo, does not spell trouble for the latter's grand vision of the factors affecting the general rate of profits and the possibility of conceiving of it in physical terms. The rate depends on the conditions of production in all industries that directly or indirectly contribute to the production of wage goods, while it does not depend on the conditions of production of 'luxuries'. Ricardo's above example thus could be said to elevate the corn-ratio theory from its previous single (and only implicitly composite) commodity conceptualisation to an explicitly multi-commodity one.

We may conclude by pointing out how Sraffa in terms of the concept of the 'Standard system' and 'Standard commodity' succeeded in corroborating

Ricardo's basic intuition under consideration within a framework in which commodities are produced by means of commodities (and wages are paid *post factum*). Starting from any actual economy (with single production) a hypothetical system may be constructed by reproportioning the industries of the actual economy until the requested *homogeneity condition* of output and capital is met. As Sraffa (1960, p. 23) emphasised, the particular proportions of the Standard system 'give transparency to a system and render visible what was hidden, but they cannot alter its mathematical properties'. Sraffa (1960, p. 22) thus succeeded in demonstrating the truth of Ricardo's doctrine that 'the rate of profits [can be understood] as a ratio between quantities of commodities irrespective of their prices.' The particular perspective from which one looks at an object – here the system of production in use – allows one to see things which one would not see or see only vaguely, if another perspective was taken.

In the following we deal with a number of propositions contained in the *Principles*, which met with reactions ranging from incomprehension to misinterpretation, criticism and rejection. It will be shown, however, that in each case the substance of Ricardo's argument is perfectly sound and only the form in which it is presented leaves something to be desired. For the most part we follow Ricardo in assuming that natural prices or 'prices of production' are approximated with sufficient precision by labour values. We begin with his discussion of different forms of improvements in agriculture and their implications for the distribution of the product between workers, capitalists and landlords in the latter part of Chapter II, 'On Rent'.

5. Different Forms of Technical Progress in Agriculture

Ricardo's respective discussion was scrutinised by major economists, including John Stuart Mill, Karl Marx, Alfred Marshall, Knut Wicksell and Paul Samuelson. The numerical examples Ricardo put forward to illustrate the cases of land saving and capital (alias labour saving) improvements were generally rejected by commentators. Edwin Cannan ([1893] 1967, pp. 259–60) formulated perhaps the strongest verdict by calling Ricardo's argument 'absolutely and almost obviously wrong' and ending 'in complete and hopeless failure'. Similar judgments came from Harry Johnson (1948, p. 792), Mark Blaug ([1967] 1997, p. 113), Denis O'Brien (1975, pp. 128–29) and Samuelson (1977, p. 521).

A critical examination of Ricardo's argument shows, however, that the verdict cannot be sustained.[12] Ricardo was not wrong in any substantive sense and can only be criticised for having changed the timing at which rents are paid by passing from one numerical example (*Works* I, pp. 81–82) to the other one

(*Works* I, pp. 82–83). While he at first assumed rents to be paid *post factum*, which conforms to his definition of rent as 'the difference between the produce obtained by the employment of two equal quantities of capital and labour' (*Work* I, 71; emphasis added), he then assumed them to be paid *ante factum* (see Works I, pp. 82–83), assuming that additional amounts of product of equal size are obtained by increasing amounts of capital. This has understandably irritated readers, but it does not render his analysis 'wrong' or worthless. This can be shown with the help of a simple formalisation.

As regards the first case, assume with Ricardo that equal amounts of capital *K* are employed on *n* different qualities of land and obtain decreasing amounts of product $Q_j (j = 1, 2, \ldots, n; Q_1 > Q_2 > \ldots > Q_n)$. With rents paid *post factum*, we have

$$(1+r)K + R_j = Q_j \qquad (j = 1, 2, \ldots, n)$$

with r as the general rate of profits and R_j as the rent obtained on land of quality j. Since the last portion of capital n (on marginal land) pays no rent, $R_n = 0$, and therefore

$$(1+r)K = Q_n$$
$$r = (Q_n / K) - 1$$
$$R_j = Q_j - Q_n$$

As regards the second case, assume that additional *equal* amounts of product Q are obtained by increasing amounts of capital $K_j (j = 1, 2, \ldots, n; K_1 < K_2 < \ldots < K_n)$. If rents are paid ante factum, we have

$$(1+r)(K_j + R_j) = Q \qquad (j = 1, 2, \ldots, n)$$

With rent on marginal land being equal to zero, $R_n = 0$, we obtain

$$(1+r)K_n = Q$$
$$r = (Q / K_{n)} - 1$$
$$R_j = K_n - K_j$$

Confronting the two sets of equations on the one hand with Ricardo's numerical examples on the other shows that the former express precisely what Ricardo does in the latter. There is a remarkable symmetry between differences in outputs produced by the same capital, and differences in capital producing the same output. We may in this context recall Ricardo's statement that when desirous to 'elucidate a principle', he was keen 'to simplify the subject' in terms of illustrations chosen 'at random'.

We may conclude by saying that the substance of Ricardo's argument is perfectly sound and the criticism levelled at it is out of proportion with the venial sin he committed by not informing the reader that he changed the definition of rent as he carried on. It might at most be said that Ricardo was not almost obviously right.[13]

6. Exhaustible Resources in Ricardo and in More Recent Economic Theory

Ricardo analysed not only renewable natural resources, such as lands of different fertilities, but also exhaustible resources, such as coal or metals. 'Nature, indeed produces them; but it is the labour of man which extracts them from the bowels of the earth, and prepares them for our service' (*Works* I, p. 85). However, one must not expect to find Ricardo's respective analysis in the barely three pages of Chapter III, 'Of the Rent of Mines', in the *Principles*, but rather has to turn to Chapter XXIV, 'Doctrine of Adam Smith Concerning the Rent of Land'.[14] He criticised Smith for confounding profits and rents, which, he insisted, ought to be carefully distinguished, because in the course of the development of a country, and setting aside technical progress, they typically move in *opposite* directions: while the rents of land tend to rise, the rate of profits tends to fall.

Here we are not concerned with Ricardo's criticism of Smith. We rather ask ourselves whether vis-à-vis modern resource economics, which is based on Hotelling's Rule (see Hotelling 1931), Ricardo's analysis is inferior and therefore should be abandoned. This is at least the implication one might draw from the fact that Ricardo's analysis is hardly ever mentioned any longer, as if what was right in it has been absorbed in the modern literature, and what was wrong has rightly been jettisoned. However, things are different and vastly more difficult. Ricardo's approach to the problem is not defective and inferior to Hotelling's, the two approaches rather deal with very different worlds contemplated by the theorist and can be integrated into a single analysis.[15]

Let us first be clear about what is meant by the Hotelling Rule. In competitive conditions, and assuming the usual long-period framework of the analysis, all extraction, production and conservation processes yield a uniform rate of profits. This means that the *in situ* price of a scarce exhaustible resource will rise from one period to another at the profit rate obtaining in the period. With p designating the price of the resource, we thus have

$$p_{t+1} = (1 + r_t)p_t$$

Hotelling derived this result within a partial equilibrium framework with an exogenously given and constant rate of interest (profit), in which the following two conditions are met:

(i) The resource is available in homogeneous quality and in an overall quantity that at any moment of time is known with certainty, and what is known at the beginning of a period is just the amount of the resource inherited from the previous one.
(ii) In a single period of time the entire amount of the resource can be extracted, that is, there is no capacity constraint limiting the output per unit of time in the extraction industry.

The Hotelling Rule thus contemplates the highly special case of a resource, whose exhaustion is actually foreseeable with certainty.

The situation contemplated by Ricardo (and Smith) is very different. While Ricardo was aware of the principal exhaustibility of certain resources, he did not think that the problem was imminent: first, because 'new and more productive mines may be discovered, in which, with the same labour, more metal may be obtained'; second, because 'Improvements may be made in the implements and machinery used in mining, which may considerably abridge labour'; and third, because 'the facilities of bringing [the resource] to the market may be increased' (*Works* I, p. 86). While these factors tend to reduce the value of the metal, 'the increasing difficulty of obtaining [it], occasioned by the greater depth at which the mine must be worked [etc.]' (ibid.), tend to increase it. Ricardo added: 'By the discovery of America and the rich mines in which it abounds, a very great effect was produced on the natural price of the precious materials' (ibid.).

All things considered, Ricardo felt entitled to approach the problem of exhaustible resources in terms of his theory of differential rent.[16] Setting aside technical progress in exploration, extraction and other methods, we may for the sake of the argument define Ricardo's approach in terms of the following two assumptions:

(i) For each exhausted deposit of the resource another one with the same characteristic features will be discovered and the cost of the search in terms of labour and capital will always be the same.
(ii) The working of each deposit is subject to a capacity constraint that limits the amount of the resource that can be extracted per unit of time.

Since there will generally be deposits of different quality or fertility, each of which is subject to such a constraint, effectual demand will typically be met by working *several* deposits *simultaneously*. As in the theory of the rent of land, there will be a marginal, no-rent, deposit worked together with several other, intramarginal deposits that will yield their proprietors differential rents, which are higher, the lower are the costs of extraction of one unit of the resource.

In this way, deposits of resources may be dealt with like fixed capital goods, such as machines or other tools of production: whenever one item is worn out a freshly produced one steps in and replaces it (see Kurz and Salvadori 1995, chap. 7). A world that can broadly be characterised in such terms reflects crucial elements of Ricardo's and, more generally, the classical economists' vision of the issue at hand and is very different from the world contemplated by the Hotelling model. Therefore we do not encounter in the former the concept of royalties, which are a special form of profits – the profits obtained in conservation processes. As regards 'realism', Ricardo's approach may perhaps be said to fare better than the Hotelling model. However, both approaches can be integrated into a single one and combine Ricardo's rent perspective with Hotelling's Rule (see Kurz and Salvadori 2009, 2011).

7. On Machinery and Its Effects

We now turn to another Chapter in Ricardo's *Principles*, which had a considerable impact on the subsequent discussion of the problem under consideration and frequently met with a lack of understanding or even severe misunderstanding: the chapter 'On Machinery' added to the third edition of Ricardo's magnum opus.[17] The chapter came as a surprise to his contemporaries, especially his follower John Ramsay McCulloch, because in it Ricardo recanted his previous position according to which any displacement of workers would be swiftly compensated by new employment possibilities, either in the same or in some other industries. He wrote: 'I am convinced, that the substitution of machinery for human labour, is often very injurious to the interests of the class of labourers' (*Works* I, p. 388).

Here we focus attention exclusively on the particular case of *induced innovation*. Whenever new technical knowledge becomes available, cost-minimising producers will have to decide whether or not to adopt the newly available knowledge in terms of new methods of production or new products, such as new machines. It may then turn out that a new method of production or new machine, while it incorporates new technical knowledge, may not be profitable. This is the case when at the real wage rate and prices ruling in the economy at a given place and time, the employment of the new method or machine exhibits extra costs and thus yields its proprietor a lower rate of profit. The new method or machine may, however, be cost minimising at other levels of the real wage rate and prices of commodities. If such levels happen to be brought about by the endogenous dynamics of the system, the new method of production or machine will be adopted and we face what John R. Hicks (1932) called an 'induced innovation'. The question then is, did Ricardo discuss already the case of induced innovations, and if yes, what did he achieve in this regard?

According to no lesser an authority than Joseph A. Schumpeter, Ricardo nowhere analysed induced innovations. With explicit reference to the machinery chapter, Schumpeter (1954, p. 679, n. 94) contends that Ricardo was unaware of the possibility of machines being introduced 'that are no novelties to producers and, so far as technological knowledge is concerned, could have been introduced but were not introduced before, because it would not have been profitable to do so'. This dictum comes as a surprise, because in Ricardo's chapter it is stated explicitly: 'Machinery and labour are in constant competition and the former can frequently not be employed until labour rises' (*Works* I, p. 395). Hence, there can be little doubt that Ricardo was perfectly aware of the fact that the introduction and diffusion of certain technical novelties (inventions) into the economic system may at first be prevented and then retarded, because the economic environment into which they are born is not conducive to their adoption (innovation). It is only when the environment changes that they will be employed.

Which changes did Ricardo have in mind? He wrote: 'The same cause that raises labour, does not raise the value of machines, and, therefore with every augmentation of capital, a greater proportion of it is employed on machinery' (*Works* I, p. 395). Interpreting this passage, C. E. Ferguson contended: 'one *must* interpret "labour rises" as meaning an increase in the *real* wage rate' (Ferguson 1973, p. 6; emphases added). In his interpretation an increase in the real wage rate would lead to the adoption of a technique that uses less of the factor that has become relatively more expensive, labour, and more of the factor that has become relatively less expensive, machinery. Ferguson interpreted Ricardo's argument as if it concerned a discussion of a choice of technique problem within a static marginalist framework. However, there are clear indications that this is not what Ricardo (could have) had in mind. He rather referred to a process of development in which capital accumulates and the population grows, but there are no new technical inventions, that is, the 'natural course of things'. In such a dynamic framework the bundle of wage goods constituting the real wage tends to become more expensive relative to machines invented in the past, but not yet introduced. Because of diminishing returns in agriculture, the prices of some necessaries, especially corn, will rise relatively to commodities produced in the manufacturing sector, such as machines. In order for workers to be able to afford a *given and constant real wage bundle, money wages must increase.* This is what Ricardo speaks of when he refers to 'the *same* cause that raises labour, [but] does not raise the value of machines'. In terms of the analytical concept of the *w–r* relationship, or wage curve: the reference is not to a movement *along* a given curve, but a movement *across* a set of such curves parallel to the abscissa, where each of these curves represents a different quality of land when that land happens to be the marginal (no-rent bearing) quality. This movement reflects the growing scarcity of the best qualities of land, which is accompanied by a rise in the price of corn and thus the price of the real wages bundle relative to the price of a machine that has some time ago been invented. Eventually the change in the relative price under consideration will be such that the machine can profitably be employed. Its employment is thus *induced by price and money wage dynamics, given the real wage rate.*

We may illustrate Ricardo's case of induced mechanisation with the help of Figure 6.1. Techniques T_0 and T_3 refer to the *w–r* relationships belonging to two techniques corresponding to two different stages in the development of the economy in the purely hypothetical case in which the accumulation of capital is carried out without any further improvements in the methods of production. Obviously, T_0 relates to an early stage, T_3 to a later one, in which the no-rent quality of land is of lower fertility than at stage 0. This is reflected, among other things, in a lower rate of profits: with a given and constant real wage rate, $w = w^*$, measured along the ordinate, the rate of profits will fall from $r = r_{T0}$ to $r = r_{T3}$, measured along the abscissa. This fall will be accompanied by a rise in rents on intramarginal lands and in the money wage rate that is just sufficient to counterbalance the corresponding rise in the money prices of wage goods.

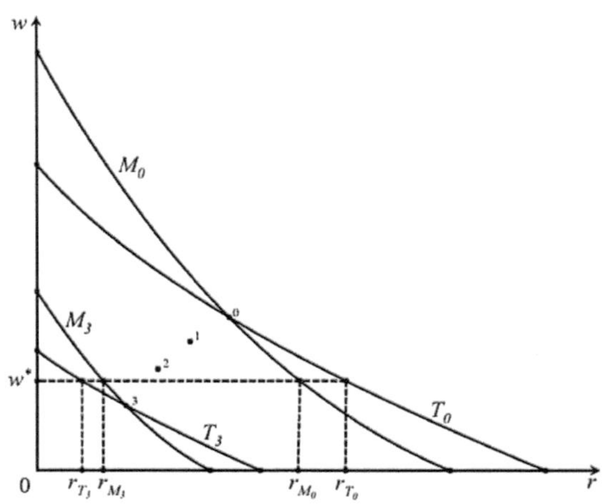

Figure 6.1 Induced mechanisation in Ricardo

If we now take into consideration that at any moment of this process cost-minimising producers will have to ask themselves, whether it would be profitable to shift to a technique employing the machine, the picture changes in the following way. The machine using technique can be represented at any moment of time by a *w–r* relationship that is alternative to the technique that does not use it. In Figure 6.1, M_0 is the corresponding wage curve in the initial situation (i.e. when using the machine became an option). However, at the given real wage rate w^* it was not profitable to adopt the new machine-using method of production and abandon the old one, because whoever would have done so would have incurred extra costs and thus obtained an individual rate of profit lower than the current general rate, r_{T0}. (The inferiority of the new method at the initially prevailing prices (given the real wage rate) is also reflected in a lower level of the general rate of profits associated with M_0 compared with that of T_0: $r_{T0} > r_{M0}$.)

Apparently the new machine will be introduced into the economic system as soon as the 'switch-point' between the *w–r* relationships corresponding to the with-machine and the without-machine techniques, M_i and T_i ($i = 0, 1, 2, \ldots$), across the various stages of economic development, crosses the line that is parallel to the abscissa at the level of the given real wage rate w^*. In Figure 6.1 each stage is characterised, in descending order, by a different quality of land that is marginal and different relative prices, and so forth; points 0, 1, 2 and 3 give such switch-points. Through each such point pass two wage curves, one that represents the with-machine system and the other that represents the without-machine system of production. Points 0, 1 and 2 lie above the line and thus correspond to situations in which the machine will not be adopted. However, point 3, the switch-point of techniques M_3 and T_3 lies below the line. In the then prevailing economic conditions, the machine using technique is superior to its alternative and will be adopted by cost-minimising producers. The general rate of profits in the with-machine situation will be r_{M3}, which is larger than the rate that would be obtained in the without-machine alternative, r_{T3}.

The 'rise in labour', that is *money* wages, is an endogenous mechanism Ricardo contemplated that induces the further mechanisation of production and decelerates the falling tendency of the actual rate of profits. It is worth noting that the introduction of improved machinery is accompanied by a reduction in the maximum rate of profits, which obtains at wages that are hypothetically equal to zero. (See the points of intersection of the with-machine *w–r* relationships with the abscissa.) It deserves to be noted that this type of technical progress Marx thought to dominate the development of capitalist economies: a rise in the 'organic composition of capital' implies a falling maximum rate of profits and in the end, Marx was convinced, also a falling actual rate.[18]

8. Foreign Trade and Comparative Advantage

According to Samuelson, Ricardo's theory of comparative advantage is one of the few, if not the only, proposition in economics that is both true and not trivial. That it is not trivial, Samuelson added, 'is attested by the thousands of important and intelligent men who have never been able to grasp the doctrine for themselves or to believe it after it was explained to them' (Samuelson 1969, p. 683). Textbook presentations of the theory are a case in point: they frequently misapprehend or distort Ricardo's argument beyond recognition. This is partly due to the fact that Chapter VII, 'On Foreign Trade', is a hard nut to crack, because in it all major threads of which the fabric of Ricardo's theory is made meet and basically all problems that come to one's mind in the context under consideration are being discussed in quick succession on just a few pages: the causes and effects of foreign trade with respect to production, income distribution, different monetary regimes, the production of specie, technical change, etc.

Here is not the place to discuss the bewildering richness of the chapter or the gross misunderstandings of it encountered in the literature in any detail. I shall rather focus attention on aspects of the problem under consideration that are perhaps helpful in clarifying what appears to me to be the gist of Ricardo's argument.

I am aware of the fact that what I say in the following differs from other presentations of it, which I consider to be faithful to what Ricardo wrote (and it differs, of course, from the usual textbook presentations of what is called the 'Ricardian model', which distorts his argument beyond recognition).[19]

In the chapter on foreign trade merchants and money play important roles. In fact, without taking them into account, Ricardo's argument is difficult to understand and will almost inevitably be misinterpreted. Alas, in much of the literature devoted to the principle of comparative advantage both merchants and money are surprisingly entirely absent. This neglect is probably due to the numerical example in terms of which Ricardo illustrates the principle at work (see *Works* I, p. 135–36). Its assumptions may be tabulated as in Table 6.1.

Table 6.1 Ricardo's example in labour terms

Number of men whose labour is required for one year in order to produce a given quantity of	**Cloth**	**Wine**
In Portugal	90	80
In England	100	120

Ricardo concludes from this that it would be advantageous for England to export cloth in exchange for wine imported from Portugal, and for Portugal to export wine in exchange for cloth from England. Under these circumstances 'England would give the produce of the labour of 100 men, for the produce of the labour of 80' (*Works* I, p. 135).[20] This may easily be misinterpreted as if Ricardo was of the opinion that countries rather than agents (merchants, etc.) trade with one another, and that their direct concern is with quantities of labour (or employment), and not profits and prices. However, as will be seen, what the example illustrates is just the macroeconomic outcome of the micro-behaviour of self-interested agents, with merchants in the front row. In terms of a recently much abused concept we might say that Ricardo cared of course for the micro-foundations of his analysis.

Before we begin with the main argument, a few observations are apposite. Ricardo's argument must be seen against the background of the rest of his analysis in the *Principles*. Without an understanding of this fact it is difficult to come to grips with his trade doctrine. We have discussed in Section 3 the salient features of the method and the content of Ricardo's general analysis. Here it suffices to recall that Ricardo in a first step typically leaves technical progress out of the picture and assumes that capital accumulates and the population grows vis-à-vis given quantities and qualities of natural resources: only well-known methods of production can be used. In a second step he then every so often investigates how different forms of technical progress, that is, new methods of producing goods, modify the analysis.[21] This method he also applies in the chapter on foreign trade, which exposes readers to a situation that may take them by surprise, but which is perfectly understandable when seen against the background of Ricardo's approach. Setting aside technical progress, more advanced economies are typically characterised by higher (direct and indirect labour) costs of production of agricultural products (on the quality of land that pays no rent); and since these enter as means of subsistence (via the wages of labour) and raw materials into manufactures therefore also by higher (labour) costs of manufactured products. This is reflected in the four numbers of the numerical example above: England, the more developed economy, exhibits higher unit costs (in terms of labour) of both commodities.

Further important (implicit) features of the numerical example are the following. First, production typically needs labour of various skills, capital goods of various kinds and lands of different qualities. Heterogeneous labours are rendered commensurable in terms of given wage differentials. Capital goods are taken to transmit the labour they embody entirely (circulating capital) or partly (fixed capital) to the product. What matters as regards the domestic value of a given commodity in whose production land is needed is the sum total of labour in its production on that quality of land that pays no rent (later called 'marginal land'). The interpretation of Ricardo's example in much of the textbook literature (and even in scholarly articles) on foreign trade as involving only a single factor of production, homogenous labour, amounts to a travesty of facts.

Secondly, the two products under consideration, cloth and wine, stand for two types of commodities that perform different roles in the economic system: while cloth is a 'necessary' or wage good, wine is a 'luxury' – the former enters the real wage and thus the production of each and every commodity produced in the economy, whereas the latter does not. The general rate of profits, Ricardo stresses repeatedly, depends only on the conditions of production of wage goods and of commodities that directly or indirectly enter in the production of wage goods. Hence, if due to technical progress in these sectors or due to the opening of trade wage goods become cheaper in a country, a given and constant real wage rate will be reflected in a lower money wage rate and a higher general domestic rate of profits. Ricardo explains:

> It has been my endeavour to shew throughout this work, that the rate of profits can never be increased but by a fall in wages, and that there can be no permanent fall of wages but in consequence of a fall [in the price] of the necessaries on which wages are expended. If, therefore, by the extension of foreign trade, or by improvements in machinery, the food and necessaries of the labourer can be brought to market at a reduced price, profits will rise. If, instead of growing our own corn, or manufacturing the clothing and other necessaries of the labourer, we discover a new market from which we can supply ourselves with these commodities at a cheaper price, [nominal] wages will fall and profits rise; but if the commodities obtained at a cheaper rate, by the extension of foreign commerce, or by the improvement of machinery, be exclusively the commodities consumed by the rich [e.g. wine], no alteration will take place in the rate of profits. The rate of wages would not be affected, although wine, velvets, silks, and other expensive commodities should fall 50 per cent., and consequently profits would continue unaltered. (*Works* I, p. 132; see also p. 143)

Ricardo thus sees an analogy between the extension of foreign trade and technical progress as regards their impact on the general rate of profits, given the real wage rate. He concludes: 'Foreign trade [...] has no tendency to raise the profits of stock, unless the commodities imported be of that description on which the wages of labour are expended' (*Works* I, p. 133).

Third, as has already been indicated, the two commodities differ in the following important respect from one another: while wine is produced in agriculture, which is subject to diminishing returns, cloth is produced in manufacturing, which exhibits constant (or increasing) returns.[22] Since the manufacturing sector uses as inputs commodities (raw materials and means of subsistence) produced in the primary sector (which includes agriculture), the costs per unit of manufactures may nevertheless increase in the course of economic development and international specialisation. This is the case when rising prices of primary products more than balance falling amounts of inputs per unit of output in manufacturing.

Fourth, Ricardo stresses repeatedly that being bound together by 'commercial connexion' does not imply that there will be a tendency towards a uniform rate of profits across all countries involved: 'In one and the same country, profits are, generally speaking, always on the same level; or differ only as the employment of capital may be more or less secure and agreeable. *It is not so between different countries*' (*Works* I, p. 134: emphasis added). While capital can be considered to be freely mobile within a country, this is typically not so between countries. Ricardo traces this back to 'the fancied or real insecurity of capital, when not under the immediate control of its owner, together with the natural disinclination which every man has to quit the country of his birth and connexion, and intrust himself with all his habits fixed, to a strange government and new laws' (*Works* I, p. 136). For these reasons 'men of property [are] satisfied with a low rate of profits in their own country, rather than seek a more advantageous employment of their wealth in foreign nations' (*Works* I, p. 137).[23]

Let us now turn to Ricardo's theory of comparative advantage. The numerical example expresses the basic idea in labour terms, which appears to have distracted attention away from the mechanism which, according to Ricardo, gives rise to the specialisation indicated. It seems to have escaped the majority of commentators that the first type of agent that enters the stage on the very first page of the chapter on foreign trade is the merchant (see *Works* I, p. 128). He is on the lookout for profitable opportunities, and he is the first beneficiary of foreign trade. We may contemplate with Ricardo two cases, one in which the currencies of the two countries are non-convertible, the other in which money in both consists of gold. In the former case, while there are imports and exports, there are by assumption no money flows between the countries, whereas in the second case there are.

8.1. *Trade in the case of non-convertible currencies*

Assume that Portugal has the Portuguese Real (R) and England the Pound (£), which are non-convertible. Following Ricardo's labour-based approach to value, the money prices of the quantities of cloth and wine in the two countries are proportional to the quantities of labour spent in producing them. Assume for simplicity that the numbers are the same (see Table 6.2).

Table 6.2 Ricardo's example in currency terms

Price in Reals (Portugal) and Pounds (England) of a given quantity of	Cloth	Wine
In Portugal (Real)	90	80
In England (Pound)	100	120

A stock jobber like Ricardo, versed in seeking out arbitrage opportunities, could easily see the profitable business to merchants involved in this.[24] (In the following we set aside transportation costs.) Take the case of an English merchant. He may buy for £100 a given quantity of cloth at home, ship it to Portugal and sell it there for 90 R. With this sum of money he may then buy wine from a Portuguese wine grower and get altogether 90/80 = 9/8 units of wine, where one unit costs 80 R. This quantity of wine he then ships to England and sells it for 9/8 × £120 = £135 (or a somewhat lower price). He thus yields a profit of £135 – £100 = £35 (or a little less) or a rate of profit of 35 per cent (or a little less) on an investment of £100 over the time it took to export cloth and import wine. Similarly, a Portuguese merchant who may buy for 80 R wine, ship it to England, sell it there for £120 and buy for this sum 120/100 = 6/5 units of cloth. This quantity of cloth he then ships to Portugal and sells it for 6/5 × 90 R = 108 R (or a somewhat lower price). He thus yields a profit of 28 Real (or a little less) or a rate of profit of 35 per cent (or a little less) on an investment of 80 R. (It deserves to be noted that both the English and the Portuguese merchant can use one and the same ship to export and to import goods.)

This variant of the gains from trade according to the principle of comparative costs shows that after the opening of trade the first beneficiaries are the merchants: paraphrasing Smith, Ricardo speaks of 'the great profits which are sometimes made by particular merchants in foreign trade' (*Works* I, p. 128) by exploiting given arbitrage opportunities. Consumers will benefit if the domestic prices of imported goods are lowered.

The remarkable fact here is that while goods are exported and imported, the currencies of the two countries do not cross borders. As Ricardo stressed with regard to a slightly different case: 'without the necessity of money passing from either country, the exporters in each country will be paid for their goods' (*Works* I, p. 138).

Investigating the situation contemplated more closely shows that the barter terms of trade of the English merchant differ from that of the Portuguese. The former leaves his country with 1 unit of cloth and returns to it with 9/8 = 1,125 units of wine, whereas the latter leaves his country with 1 unit of wine and returns with 6/5 units of cloth, which implies a rate of transformation of 1 unit of cloth for 0,833 [...] units of wine. The argument thus implies that there is no uniform world market price ratio of the two commodities. In fact there is no world market in the proper sense of the word. There are only domestic markets, which however can be supplied also from abroad.

The above numerical example can obviously refer only to a short-run situation, because as a result of foreign trade Portugal's cloth producers will experience a dwindling and her wine producers a rising effectual demand, whereas in England the reverse holds true. In conditions of free competition, capital (and labour) will at home flow out of disadvantageous and into advantageous sectors. The four numbers do not imply a complete specialisation of Portugal in wine production and of England in cloth production. We refrain from entering into a deeper discussion of the adjustment processes and the patterns of specialisation that might emerge.

8.2. Gold as the universal means of exchange

Assume now gold (coins) to be the universal means of exchange and unit of account. The total amount of gold (a producible commodity) in the system (comprising the two countries) is given and fixed. The four numbers are now taken to refer to the gold prices of given quantities of cloth and wine in autarky in Portugal and England. Both commodities are more expensive in England, which again implies profitable business for merchants: goods will be shipped from the country in which they are cheaper (Portugal) to the country in which they are dearer (England). Ships would leave Portugal fully laden, but return to her empty. (We set aside any other goods that might be shipped between England and Portugal.) English producers are bound to stop producing both commodities and Portuguese producers would like to expand production and meet effectual demands in both countries.

Assume that Portugal can do so at constant unit costs. (We thus set aside the market price dynamics that might evolve.) Portugal would then experience a trade surplus and England a trade deficit. This would imply a flow of specie from England to Portugal. The quantity of money in Portugal (England) would increase (decrease) and money prices rise (fall). Foreign trade would thus affect prices and the value of money in the two countries. Ricardo observes:

> But the diminution of money in one country, and its increase in another, do not operate on the price of one commodity only, *but on the prices of all*, and therefore the price of wine and cloth will be both raised in [Portugal], and both lowered in [England]. (*Works* I, pp. 139–40; emphasis added) [25]

This, however, brings about "such a state of prices as would make it no longer profitable to continue these transactions" (*Works* I, p. 139).

This is indeed the case, as the following consideration shows. Assume for simplicity that prices in each country increase or decrease proportionately, leaving relative (domestic) prices unaffected. If α is the increase per cent of all Portuguese prices and β is the decrease per cent of all English prices, and if p_{PC} (p_{EC}) denotes the initial gold price of cloth in Portugal (England), then the gold price in the two countries would be the same, if

$$(1+\alpha^*)p_{PC} = (1-\beta^*)p_{EC}$$

This may be considered a break-even point. If prices rose a little more in Portugal or fell a little more in England, the absolute advantage would be reversed: now English cloth would have become less expensive than Portuguese cloth, and the direction of the cloth trade would be reversed from England to Portugal. With regard to the case described by the numerical example, the equation would be fulfilled by all values of α^* and β^* satisfying

$$\alpha^* = 1/9 - (10/9)\beta^*$$

As regards wine, its increase in price in Portugal by the same β^* per cent and its decrease in England by the same α^* per cent would, on the contrary, not render the two commodities equally expensive in both countries, but would still show an absolute cost advantage of Portugal, since

$$(1+\alpha^*)p_{PW} < 1-\beta^*)p_{EW}$$

where p_{PW} (p_{EW}) denotes the initial gold price of wine in Portugal (England). English wine would still be a good deal more expensive than Portuguese wine, and Portugal would continue to export and England to import wine. But 'a new distribution of the precious metals', Ricardo emphasises,

> would in some degree have changed [the value of money] in the two countries, it would be lowered in [Portugal] and raised in [England]. Estimated in money, the whole revenue of [England] would be diminished; estimated in the same medium, the whole revenue of [Portugal] would be increased. (*Works* I, p. 141)

These considerations show that Portugal's (England's) original absolute advantages (disadvantages) in the production of both commodities will not prevail: the specie-flow mechanism will undermine the situation immediately after the opening of trade and will eventually lead to a new pattern of specialisation. The important point to note is this. *The direction of change in absolute cost advantages will bring to the fore the principle of comparative advantage*: as prices rise in Portugal and fall in England, the point will come

Table 6.3 Specie flow and comparative advantage

Price in ounces of gold of a given quantity of	Cloth	Wine
In Portugal	99	88
In England	90	108

where English cloth becomes less expensive than Portuguese cloth, while English wine is still more expensive than Portuguese wine. Portugal will thus end up having both a comparative and absolute advantage in the production of wine and England a comparative advantage in the production of cloth, which is reflected in an absolute one in price terms. Assume, for example, that Portuguese prices rise by 10 per cent and English prices drop by 10 per cent compared with the no-trade situation (see Table 6.3). Cloth is now cheaper in England compared with Portugal, but wine is still dearer. The two countries will specialise according to their comparative advantages, which, however, will only become apparent as a consequence of the redistribution of specie between the two countries and the ensuing change in absolute cost advantages due to changes in the price levels in the two countries.

These considerations show that the theory of comparative advantage cannot be told in a way that is faithful to Ricardo, if it leaves out merchants and money. The conventional textbook illustration of the theory involves a gross distortion of Ricardo's doctrine. Ricardo deserves credit for having provided an analytical framework that allows one to discuss the problem of foreign trade in terms of (i) different agents with different interests (producers, merchants and consumers), (ii) production conceived of as requiring various kinds of labour, capital goods and lands of different quality, and (iii) money as a necessary medium of exchange, including different money regimes. Such a framework, as Ricardo shows, allows also for a discussion of the impact of the scarcity of natural resources and of different forms of technical progress (including progress in the production of the money commodity, bullion) on income distribution, relative prices and the pattern of specialisation.

9. Conclusion

Ricardo variously expressed both his confidence in his theory and at the same time his doubts about being able to express himself convincingly. In a letter to Malthus of 5 October 1816 he stated: 'though I feel strongly the truth of my theory I cannot succeed in stating it clearly' (*Works* VII, p. 71). Ricardo, as is well known, was notorious for his modesty as regards his ability to formulate his ideas in a correct and compelling way. His scepticism had as its deeper reason Ricardo's understanding that there were still numerous open ends in his theory, with new insights contradicting received opinion. Yet, confronted with a 'labyrinth of difficulties', it is truly remarkable how far Ricardo got in his 'most favourite subject' (*Works* VI, p. 263). It is even more remarkable, how often his propositions were misunderstood, misinterpreted and misstated and criticisms levelled at them, which upon closer scrutiny turn out to be untenable. So much for the alleged contention that the market for economic ideas is a perfect selection mechanism that keeps everything that is correct and useful and sorts out everything that is wrong and useless. Ricardo's works are a treasure trove that still contains ideas that are worth excavating and elaborating.

Acknowledgements

I am grateful to Jérôme Boyer des Roches, Christian Gehrke, Gilbert Faccarello, Neri Salvadori, Bertram Schefold, Yoshinori Shiozawa, Ian Steedman, Katsuyoshi Watarai, Takashi Yagi and two anonymous referees for most useful comments and suggestions.

Notes

1 On the relationship between the theories of Walras, Wicksell and Schumpeter, on the one hand, and Ricardo, on the other hand, see Kurz (2000) and Kurz and Salvadori (2002).

2 Marshall's concern with presenting his own theory as a continuation of the objectivist cost-of-production theory of the classical authors, integrated into and amalgamated with the subjectivist marginal-utility theory, made him downplay and even not see fundamental differences between the two.

3 This assessment is foreshadowed in a statement of 1839 by Henry Lord Brougham, who called Ricardo's views often 'abundantly theoretical, sometimes too refined for his audience, occasionally extravagant from his propensity to follow a right principle into all its consequences, without duly taking into account in practice the condition of things to which he was applying it, as if a mechanician were to construct an engine without taking into consideration the resistance of the air in which it was to work, or the strength and the weight and the friction of the parts of which it was to be made' (*Works* V, p. xxxiii). And in a note in his diary about a dinner at Ricardo's on 12 January 1820, J. L. Mallet speaks of Ricardo's 'entire disregard of experience and practice' (*Works* VIII, p. 152 n. 2).

4 It hardly needs to be stressed that Piero Sraffa's edition of *The Works and Correspondence of David Ricardo* (Ricardo 1951–1973) has improved the Ricardo scholarship considerably by making hitherto unknown papers, correspondence etc. available to the reader.

5 In the following I draw partially on earlier works I have written alone or together with Christian Gehrke and Neri Salvadori. All remaining misconceptions are, of course, entirely my responsibility.

6 As one commentator remarked, Ricardo 'meets you upon every subject that he has studied with [...] opinions in the nature of mathematical truths' (*Works* VIII, p. 152 n. 2).

7 While Ricardo typically assumed wages paid *ante factum* (i.e. at the beginning of the uniform period of production), Sraffa assumed wages paid *post factum* (i.e. at its end). However, as can easily be shown this difference does not substantially affect the general argument in the above.

8 Ricardo's basic intuition extended to the cases of fixed capital and scarce land, and also in these respects he can be said to have been on the right scent, deficiencies of his analysis notwithstanding: several of his basic ideas were later given a coherent form by V. K. Dmitriev, Ladislaus von Bortkiewicz, Paul A. Samuelson, Luigi Pasinetti and especially Piero Sraffa.

9 For the following, see also Kurz (2011).

10 Paul Samuelson once asked Sraffa, whether Ricardo held a labour theory of value. Sraffa is reported to have answered: 'He did and he didn't'. What might at first sight be considered a sibylline response turns out to reflect properly Ricardo's point of view, which, for example, in the third edition of the *Principles* comes to the fore when Ricardo speaks 'of labour as being the *foundation of all value*, and the relative quantity of labour as *almost exclusively* determining the relative value of commodities' (*Works* I, p. 20; emphasis added). The following note Sraffa wrote in November 1927 may be read as a comment on Ricardo's statement: 'It is the *whole* process of production that must be called "human labour", and thus causes all product and all values. Marx and Ricardo used "labour" in two different senses: the above, and that of *one* of the factors of production ("hours of labour" or "quantity of labour" has a meaning only in the latter sense). It is by confusing the two senses that they got mixed up and said that value is proportional to quantity of labour (in second sense) whereas they ought to have said that it is due to human labour (in first sense: a non-measurable quantity, or rather not a quantity at all)'. (Sraffa Papers D3/12/11: 64; emphasis in the original) A confusion of the two senses is widespread in the literature on Ricardo. For example, Mary Morgan recently wrote: 'it is *labour alone that creates value*, and [...] there is a direct relationship between labour input and value' (Morgan 2012, p. 60; emphasis added). As we have just seen, Ricardo was decidedly not of this opinion. However, unable to solve the problem of value and distribution to his own satisfaction, Ricardo clung to the labour embodiment hypothesis; see in this regard the rough draft and unfinished manuscript on 'Absolute Value and Exchangeable Value', written in 1823 shortly before he passed away (see *Works* IV).

11 One should recall however that 'corn' in Ricardo's early reasoning was a term designated to encompass all necessaries, like 'bread' in the Bible (a meaning William Petty took up), and thus represented a bundle of heterogeneous commodities.

12 For the following, see Gehrke et al. (2003).

13 It is not difficult to rectify Ricardo's second numerical example and bring it into line with the first one without affecting the substance of what he says; see Gehrke et al. (2003, p. 296).

14 Ricardo himself deplored his problems with 'the difficult art of composition' (*Works* VII, p. 19). Indeed, as several commentators observed, the structure of the *Principles* leaves much to be desired and reflects the hurry in which it has been put together.

15 For the following, see Kurz and Salvadori (2009, 2011).

16 John Stuart Mill reiterated Ricardo's position, but went a step further. He insisted that the working of exhaustible resources is similar to the working of land (a resource that is taken to be inexhaustible); that in both kinds of activities there are two antagonistic forces at work – diminishing returns and technical progress; and that the potential for technical progress is larger in the mining and other extraction processes than in agriculture (see Mill [1848] 1965, p. 495). But then he even opined that 'the almost inevitable progress of human culture and improvement [...] *forbids us to consider [the exhaustion] as probable*' (p. 496; emphasis added). See in this context also Krautkraemer (1998) on the poor empirical performance of the Hotelling Rule. For a discussion of Marx's views on the matter and his indebtedness to Ricardo, see Kurz (2010, section 4).

17 For the following, see Jeck and Kurz (1983) and Kurz (2010, section 3).

18 The following draws on Kurz (2014). Sraffa (1930) corrected a misinterpretation of Ricardo's famous numerical example by John Stuart Mill. This misinterpretation may be said to have triggered readings of Ricardo that eventually led up to the unfortunate modern textbook interpretation. Ruffin (2002) deserves the credit for having rediscovered Sraffa's correction. However, as Gehrke (2015) has shown convincingly, Ruffin had difficulties, in Keynes's words, 'to escape habitual modes of thought and expression'. In interpreting the route via which Ricardo is supposed to have discovered the principle of comparative cost, Ruffin looked at him through the distorting lens of marginalist theory. For a complementary discussion of Ricardo's theory of foreign trade to the one given here, see Faccarello (2015) and Maneschi (2015). For a discussion of Marx's views on the matter and his indebtedness to Ricardo, see Kurz (2010, section 4).

19 The following draws on Kurz (2014). Sraffa (1930) corrected a misinterpretation of Ricardo's famous numerical example by John Stuart Mill. This misinterpretation may be said to have triggered readings of Ricardo that eventually led up to the unfortunate modern textbook interpretation. Ruffin (2002) deserves the credit for having rediscovered Sraffa's correction. However, as Gehrke (2015) has shown convincingly, Ruffin had difficulties, in Keynes's words, 'to escape habitual modes of thought and expression'. In interpreting the route via which Ricardo is supposed to have discovered the principle of comparative cost, Ruffin looked at him through the distorting lens of marginalist theory. For a complementary discussion of Ricardo's theory of foreign trade to the one given here, see Faccarello (2015) and Maneschi (2015).

20 There is no presumption that cloth and wine are the only commodities produced or consumed in the two countries. However, all other commodities remain in the background in Ricardo's analysis and will also do so here.

21 Some commentators took the first step of his analysis (reflecting his research method) wrongly for a factual statement about the unimportance of technical progress; see most recently Piketty (2014, pp. 5–7). (For a criticism of this view, see the argument in previous sections and Kurz 2010.) The fact is that Ricardo was keen to abstain from speculating about future technical improvements, because no reliable knowledge on them was available. He stressed, however, that 'it is no longer questioned' that improved machinery 'has a decided tendency to raise the real wage of labour' (*Works* IV, p. 35; see also VIII, p. 171), without necessitating a fall in the rate of profits, and that there are no indications that capital accumulation will slow down because of a lack of profits.

22 According to Adam Smith's argument about the social division of labour, which Ricardo accepted, it even exhibits dynamically increasing returns. In Smith the invention of improved machines both results from and propels forward the division

of labour (see WN I.i.8). It is therefore interesting to note that when Ricardo discusses the factors counteracting a fall in the general rate of profits he explicitly refers to "the improvements in machinery, by the better division and distribution of labour, and by the increasing skill, both in science and art, of the producers" (*Works* I, p. 94).

23 These considerations echo an argument Smith had invoked in *The Wealth of Nations* in order to describe the socially beneficial working of the 'invisible hand'. By investing at home capitalists promote not only their own interest in profits and security, but also unconsciously the interest of their home country, by giving employment to their fellow-countrymen (see WN IV.ii.5).

24 This is why I find Ruffin's contention (2005, p. 705) that it took Ricardo a 'great and sustained mental effort' to arrive at the principle of comparative advantage dubious. The textual evidence he puts forward does not support his case; see Gehrke (2015).

25 The passage cited actually refers to the effect of technical progress in one line of production in one of the countries on the pattern of specialisation (*Works* I, pp. 137–40). It has been adapted to the case we are concerned with.

References

Blaug, M. 1997. *Economic Theory in Retrospect.* 5th ed. Cambridge: Cambridge University Press.

Cannan, E. [1893] 1967. *A History of the Theories of Production and Distribution in English Political Economy from 1776–1848.* London: P. S. King. Reprint 1967, New York: Augustus M. Kelley.

Davis, T. 2002. 'David Ricardo, Financier and Empirical Economist'. *The European Journal of the History of Economic Thought* 9, no. 1: 1–16.

Davis, T. 2005. *Ricardo's Macroeconomics: Money, Trade Cycles and Growth.* Cambridge: Cambridge University Press.

Faccarello, G. 2015. 'A Calm Investigation into Mr Ricardo's Principles of International Trade'. *The European Journal of the History of Economic Thought* 22, no. 5: 754–90.

Ferguson, C.E. 1973. 'The Specialization Gap: Barton, Ricardo, and Hollander'. *History of Political Economy* 5, no. 1: 1–13.

Garegnani, P. 1984. 'Value and Distribution in the Classical Economists and Marx'. *Oxford Economic Papers* 36, no. 2: 291–325.

Gehrke, C. 2011. 'Price of Wages: A Curious Phrase'. In *Sraffa and modern economics*, edited by R. Ciccone, C. Gehrke, and G. Mongiovi, 405–22. Vol. 1. London: Routledge,.

Gehrke, C. 2015. 'Ricardo's Discovery of Comparative Advantage Revisited: A Critique of Ruffin's Account'. *The European Journal of the History of Economic Thought*, 22, no. 5: 791-817.

Gehrke, C., Kurz, H.D. and Salvadori, N. 2003. 'Ricardo on Agricultural Improvements: A Note'. *Scottish Journal of Political Economy* 50, no. 3: 291–96.

Hicks, J.R. 1932. *The Theory of Wages.* London: Macmillan.

Hotelling, H. 1931. 'The Economics of Exhaustible Resources'. *Journal of Political Economy*, 39, no. 2: 137–75.

Jeck, A. and Kurz, H.D. 1983. 'David Ricardo: Ansichten zur Maschinerie' (David Ricardo: Views on Machinery). In *Technischer Fortschritt und Arbeitslosigkeit*, edited by H. Hagemann and P. Kalmbach, 38–166. Frankfurt am Main: Campus.

Jevons, W.S. [1871] 1965. *The Theory of Political Economy.* London: Macmillan. Reprint (1965) New York: Kelley.

Johnson, H.G. 1948. 'An Error in Ricardo's Exposition of His Theory of Rent'. *Quarterly Journal of Economics* 62, no. 5: 792–93.

Keynes, J.M. 1972. 'Essays in Biography'. In *The collected writings of John Maynard Keynes, Vol. X.*, edited by A. Robinson and D. Moggridge. London: Macmillan (Referred to as CW X), 71–103.

Krautkraemer, JA. 1998. 'Non Renewable Resource Scarcity'. *Journal of Economic Literature* 36, no. 4: 2065–107.

Kurz, H.D. 2000. 'Wicksell and the Problem of the 'Missing' Equation'. *History of Political Economy* 32, no. 4: 765–88.

Kurz, H.D. 2010. 'Technical Progress, Capital Accumulation and Income Distribution in Classical Economics: Adam Smith, David Ricardo and Karl Marx'. *The European Journal of the History of Economic Thought* 17, no. 5: 1183–222.

Kurz, H.D. 2011. 'On David Ricardo's Theory of Profits. The Laws of Distribution are "Not Essentially Connected with the Doctrine of Value"'. *The History of Economic Thought* 53, no. 1: 1–20.

Kurz, H.D. 2014. *Comparative Advantage: Both True and Nontrivial.* Unpublished manuscript. Graz.

Kurz, H.D. and Salvadori, N. 1995. *Theory of Production: A Long-Period Analysis.* Cambridge: Cambridge University Press.

Kurz, H.D. and Salvadori, N. 2002. 'One Theory or Two? Walras's Critique of Ricardo'. *History of Political Economy* 34, no. 2: 365–98.

Kurz, H.D. and Salvadori, N. 2009. 'RICARDO ON EXHAUSTIBLE RESOURCES AND THE HOTELLING RULE'. In *The History of Economic Theory. Festschrift in Honour of Takashi Negishi*, edited by A. Ikeo and H.D. Kurz, 68–79. London: Routledge.

Kurz, H.D. and Salvadori, N. 2011. 'Exhaustible Resources: Rents, Profits, Royalties and Prices'. In *The Evolution of Economic Theory. Essays in Honour of Bertram Schefold*, edited by V. Caspari, 39–52. London: Routledge.

Maneschi, A. 2015. 'Ricardo's Four Magic Numbers. In *The Elgar Companion to David Ricardo*, edited by H.D. Kurz and N. Salvadori, 482–89. Cheltenham: Edward Elgar, 482-89.

Marshall, A. [1890] 1977. *Principles of Economics.* London: Macmillan.

Marx, K. 1954. *Capital.* Vol. I, Moscow: Progress Publishers.

Marx, K. 1959. *Capital.* Vol. III, Moscow: Progress Publishers.

Mill, J. S., [1848] 1965. *Principles of Political Economy with Some of Their Applications to Social Philosophy.* 1st ed. 1848, edited by J. M. Robson. Toronto: University of Toronto Press.

Morgan, M. 2012. *The World in the Model. How Economists Work and Think.* Cambridge: Cambridge University Press.

O'Brien, D. 1975. *The Classical Economists.* Oxford: Oxford University Press.

Pasinetti, L.L. 2012. Piero Sraffa and the Future of Economics. *Cambridge Journal of Economics* 36, no. 6: 1303–14.

Piketty, T. 2014. *Capital in the Twenty-First Century.* Cambridge, MA: Belknap Press.

Ricardo, D., 1951–1973. *The Works and Correspondence of David Ricardo*, 11 vols, edited by P. Sraffa with the collaboration of M. H. Dobb, Cambridge: Cambridge University Press (cited as *Works*, vol. number, page number).

Ruffin, R. 2002. 'David Ricardo's Discovery of Comparative Advantage'. *History of Political Economy* 34, 727–48.

Ruffin, R. 2005. 'Debunking a Myth: Torrens on Comparative Advantage'. *History of Political Economy* 37, no. 4: 711–22.

Samuelson, P.A. 1969. 'The Way of an Economist'. In *International Economic Relations. Proceedings of the Third Congress of the International Economic Association*, edited by Paul Samuelson, 1–11. London: Macmillan.

Samuelson, P.A. 1977. 'Correcting the Ricardo Error Spotted in Harry Johnson's Maiden Paper'. *Quarterly Journal of Economics* 91, no. 4: 519–30.

Schumpeter, J.A. 1954. *History of Economic Analysis*. London: Allen and Unwin.

Smith, A. [1776] 1976. *'An Inquiry into the Nature and Causes of the Wealth of Nations'*. In *The Glasgow edition of the works and correspondence of Adam Smith*, two vols, edited by R. H. Campbell and A. S. Skinner, Oxford: Oxford University Press. (In the text quoted as WN, book number, part number, chapter number etc.)

Sraffa, P. 1930. An Alleged Correction of Ricardo. *Quarterly Journal of Economics* 44, no. 3: 539–44.

Sraffa, P. 1951. 'Introduction'. In D. Ricardo (1971–1973), *The Works and Correspondence of David Ricardo*, xiii–lxii. Vol. I. Cambridge: Cambridge University Press.

Sraffa, P. 1960. *Production of Commodities by Means of Commodities*. Cambridge: Cambridge University Press.

Walras, L. [1874] 1954. *Elements of Pure Economics*. London: Allen and Unwin. English translation of the definitive French edition of Walras (1874) by W. Jaffé.

Wicksell, K. [1893] 1954. *Value, Capital, and Rent*. London: George Allen & Unwin. Translated from the German edition (1893).

Chapter 7

RICARDO'S BUSINESS ACTIVITIES

Wilfried Parys

Nearly every textbook on the history of economic thought singles out David Ricardo as one of the top scholars in economics. When studying his biographical details, however, students are surprised that only in his final eight years Ricardo was able to work like a 'normal' scholar. In all the earlier decades of his career he had to concentrate mainly on his business activities in the noisy and stressful networks of the Stock Exchange in London. In 1786, at the exceptionally early age of fourteen, David Ricardo was already employed there as an assistant to his father Abraham Israel Ricardo. Their collaboration got into difficulties in 1793 when David married Priscilla Ann Wilkinson, a Quaker. David's Jewish parents found this marriage unacceptable and from then on David Ricardo had to continue on the Stock Exchange on his own. In a short time, he became one of the most prosperous and influential dealers there. From 1806 on, his excellent financial standing enabled him to participate in the biddings for the large British loan contracts. Ultimately, he became a co-contractor for seven British loans, the first time in March 1807, and the last time in June 1815, a few days before the Battle of Waterloo.

In 1813 Ricardo had already planned to change his lifestyle, and in 1814 he had bought Gatcombe Park (today the royal estate of Princess Anne), about hundred miles from London. Ricardo's correspondence of 1814 revealed that he preferred the quiet Gatcombe over the noisy Stock Exchange:

> I have not quite given up the Stock Exchange; but for a few months in the year, I mean to enjoy the calm repose of a country life. (VI, 150, letter of 31 October 1814 to John Sinclair)

When he finally gave up his activities at the Stock Exchange, Ricardo's business successes had made him probably the richest economist in history. Sraffa (1955, 102–4) reports that at the end of his life Ricardo owned about £275,000 of landed estates, £200,000 of sums lent on mortgage, £140,000 of French bonds, and various other items. According to Sraffa the total value must have been between £675,000 and £775,000.

Several English archives in London and Cambridge are still very useful when researching some features of Ricardo's business activities. In London the impressive Stock Ledgers of the Bank of England conserve detailed data on Ricardo's sales and purchases of Consols, Reduced Annuities, Navy Fives and other government bonds. The archival material on the London Stock Exchange in Ricardo's time can be found in London too, in the Guildhall Library. The London Metropolitan Archives conserve the Angerstein Family Papers, including a notebook by the prominent financier John Julius Angerstein, which provides useful information on himself, and on Ricardo and other investors, with respect to their role in the contracts for several British loans in the early nineteenth century. The Cambridge University Library holds the Ricardo Papers, which contain a small number of details about Ricardo's activities at the Stock Exchange. The Wren Library (Trinity College) conserves the archives of Piero Sraffa, which include many unpublished notes and letters written by Sraffa when he was working on the sections on 'Ricardo in Business' in Volume X of his edition of *The Works and Correspondence of David Ricardo*. In addition to the editorial notes by Sraffa (1955), several later publications also provide some information on Ricardo's business activities, for example, Weatherall (1976), Henderson and Davis (1997), Samuelson (2009), King (2013), Heertje (2015), Skousen (2016) and Parys (2020, 2021).

1. Ricardo as a Jobber on the Stock Exchange

After the breakdown of the collaboration with his father, David Ricardo started his own career at the London Stock Exchange in 1793, at the age of twenty-one. Until 1815 most of his days were spent on his business activities at the Stock Exchange. Throughout the whole period from 1793 to 1815 Britain was at war with France. This long conflict generated enormous expenses by the British government. At that time, France had a much larger population than Britain, but thanks to its excellent financial credibility, Britain was much more successful in financing the high war costs by means of loans (and increased taxation too, of course). A large part of the transactions on the Stock Exchange in London involved bonds issued by the British government, especially the three per cent Consols, which formed about half of the British National Debt. Another important bond was the three per cent Reduced Annuity. Both these Consols and Reduced Annuities paid three per cent interest every year, but at different dates. They had no fixed day of maturity, but the government had the right to redeem such bonds at par, i.e., by paying their face value. In Ricardo's time, however, three per cent Consols and Reduced Annuities with a face value of £100 could always be bought on the Stock Exchange at a much lower market price. Therefore, the government never organised compulsory redemption at £100, and those Consols and Reduced Annuities were treated by investors as perpetual items.

The low market prices of these bonds were typical of a situation with high market rates of interest, high national debt and expensive war costs. Suppose that the market rate of interest is five per cent; then perpetual bonds with a face value of £100 and yearly interest of £3, normally have a market price of only £60, because at that market price the £3 interest corresponds exactly to the market interest rate of five per cent. Such perpetual bonds were very volatile. In theory, with market rates of interest of three – four – five – six per cent, the market prices of three per cent perpetual bonds will fluctuate around 100 – 75 – 60 – 50. In practice, the exact market prices also depended on expectations, speculation, political and financial events, and in 1793–1815 also on new information (sometimes fake news) about the war against France.

When Ricardo and his contemporaries referred to 'stocks', they usually meant Consols, Reduced Annuities and other similar government bonds. Unlike today, the shares of private firms formed only a very small part of the London Stock Exchange. In the early nineteenth century, both the professional investors (like Ricardo) and the private investors (like Malthus) focused on government bonds.

The transactions on the Stock Exchange involved so-called stock jobbers and brokers. Ricardo was a jobber, which means that he bought and sold on his own account. In other words, he was one of the middlemen who generated a permanent market for the buying and selling of Consols, Reduced Annuities, Navy Fives (five per cent interest), and other bonds. Numerous ordinary citizens invested in such bonds. According to Michie (2006, 53), in 1815 there were an estimated 250,000 holders of the British government securities.

One of them was Jane Austen. She preferred Navy Fives, but I consider a fictive example in which I assume that Jane wanted to buy three per cent Consols with a face value of £100. Normally Jane could not enter the Stock Exchange herself, because outside clients had to use the services of a broker, who then went into the building of the Stock Exchange, contacted a jobber (like Ricardo) and asked for the price, in principle without revealing whether Jane was a buyer or a seller. A typical answer by a jobber was: I buy at £60, and I sell at £60⅛ (normally the jobbers had a margin of ⅛ per face value of 100). Suppose that Jane was a buyer. Then the ownership of the Consols was transferred from the jobber to Jane, and the Bank of England registered the transaction in its Stock Ledgers, which contain numerous large handwritten pages, providing information on all registered sales and purchases.

The new owners could conserve a receipt of the transaction, but they didn't need to panic if they were victims of theft, fire or other causes of losing the receipt. The registration in the well-protected books of the Bank of England was the only legal proof of ownership. The British bonds were not only very liquid, but also physically extremely safe.

Thanks to his integrity and his financial talents, Ricardo attracted an exceptionally large number of customers. Moreover, he also made many clever arbitrage deals. As early as 1795, Ricardo's letters to his brother-in-law Josiah Henry Wilkinson reveal that Ricardo was financially extraordinarily successful. He could afford a wealthy lifestyle already a few years after starting his own business and he did not hesitate to provide financial help to Wilkinson and other relatives when necessary (X, 109–19).

2. Ricardo's First British Loan Contract in 1807

During the war against France, the British government usually launched one new loan each year. The shares of the loan were not sold directly to the public but were distributed with the help of some financially powerful consortia of rich financiers. These consortia could participate in a system of competitive bidding. Often the loan consisted of a basket of three different bonds. For example, on 3 March 1807, the first time that the Barnes-Steers-Ricardo consortium succeeded in making the best bid, the government offered, for every £100 advanced, a basket of bonds, containing the following three items:

- £70 Reduced Annuities (three per cent interest, commencing from 5 April 1807)
- £70 Consols (three per cent from 5 January 1807)
- £ B of Navy Fives (five per cent from 5 January 1807), the value of B to be specified by bidding

The basket of all three items together was called the *Omnium*. For outsiders, it might seem strange that the sum of the face values of the three items was much higher than £100, but remember that the market prices of the Consols and Reduced Annuities were much below par.

When choosing the value of *B*, the bidders in 1807 had to perform some complex calculations, taking into account at least five different features (Grellier and Wade 1812, Appendix). First, of course, the current and the expected future market prices of the three constituent parts of the Omnium were highly relevant. Second, it was possible to pay promptly or in ten monthly instalments, the first instalment was due on 6 March 1807, the last one on 15 January 1808. Third, if full payment was made on or before 12 November 1807 the government gave a discount at the rate of five per cent per annum from the day of full payment to 15 January 1808. Fourth, even if several monthly instalments were still due, the Consols and the Navy Fives already produced interest from 5 January (hence two months extra), and the Reduced Annuities from 5 April. Fifth, the first half year's interest was tax free. Hence, submitting a clever bid for such a sophisticated financial product was not easy, but Ricardo was especially gifted and quick in performing all the necessary calculations.

On 3 March 1807 four different groups of candidates went to Downing Street 10 and delivered their sealed bids to the Prime Minister (Lord Grenville) and the Chancellor of the Exchequer, (Lord Henry Petty). The *Morning Chronicle* (4 March 1807, p. 3) wrote:

> The biddings, on breaking of the seals, appeared as follows;

Messrs. Barnes, Steers and Ricardo -- £.	10 12 0
Messrs. B. and A. Goldsmid -- --	11 3 0
Sir Francis Baring -- -- --	11 8 0
Messrs. Robarts and Curtis -- --	11 17 6

> The contract is therefore taken by Messrs. Barnes, Steers and Ricardo [...] Our readers will observe, that there was no combination in the biddings.

A similar report appeared in several other newspapers. The above report shows that Barnes-Steers-Ricardo delivered the cheapest bid to the government. The second in the bidding was the consortium of the brothers Benjamin and Abraham Goldsmid; already for many years the brothers were a prominent duo in the world of finance (Cope 1942). The third bidder was a partnership of the Barings group and some other financiers, including John Julius Angerstein and John Battye. The Angerstein Family Papers show that this consortium was dominated by the Barings and by Angerstein. In his history of the House of Barings, Philip Ziegler (1988) described the Barings as 'the sixth great power' in Europe (he meant: besides England, France, Prussia, Austria and Russia). Angerstein had been Chairman of Lloyd's, he was the wealthiest insurance broker of his day, and a major contractor for British loans in the period 1789–1815. After his death, his rich collection of paintings formed the nucleus of the newly opened National Gallery (Twist 2002). The worst bid for the 1807 loan was delivered by a consortium formed by Abraham Robarts, William Curtis, and some other prominent bankers. It is obvious that by signing the winning contract for the 1807 loan, Ricardo had entered the 'premier league' of Britain's financial community.

The above newspaper report of 1807 explicitly remarked that there was 'no combination in the biddings', because a year earlier, when the same four consortia competed for the 1806 loan, the situation was different. It was the first time that Barnes-Steers-Ricardo entered the competition and they failed to obtain the 1806 loan, because the three other candidates were experienced consortia that colluded to keep the newcomers out of the elite market for loan contracts.

3. Ricardo's Consortium and Its Unknown Fourth Member

In the beginning of the nineteenth century Ricardo and other jobbers and brokers of the Stock Exchange were often dissatisfied by the way the loan market was dominated by the consortia of a few big bankers and merchants, like the Barings, the Goldsmids, and Angerstein. This was the reason why in 1806 a few influential members of the Stock Exchange formed their own consortium.

In principle, such a consortium then compiled a list of subscribers, usually containing the names of a few hundreds of persons or companies that wanted to buy a small share of the loan. If a consortium failed to obtain the loan contract, its subscribers had to obtain their share of the loan elsewhere. Sometimes they were able to subscribe to two or more different lists, otherwise they had to purchase Omnium after the start of the loan on the Stock Exchange, where the opening price of Omnium was nearly always higher. In 1806 and earlier, the winning consortia of bankers and merchants often distributed the shares in the loan in an unfair way, for example, by keeping a large part of the loan for themselves if it was immediately denoted above par on the Stock Exchange (that happened often and was not illegal, but unfair).

When the Barnes-Steers-Ricardo consortium obtained its first loan in 1807, it behaved more ethically. The more than two hundred investors on its list were happily surprised by the unusually equitable way the loan was distributed among them. To show their satisfaction, the subscribers organised a special meeting and decided to offer a precious silver vase to each of the contractors in the consortium. The corresponding letter of thanks included a 'List of Subscribers to the Four Vases voted to The Contractors' (Cambridge University Library, Ricardo Papers, file ADD 7510/III/D.3). Sraffa, who enjoyed studying such detective problems, was unable to identify the fourth man and wrote: 'Of the four, only John Barnes and James Steers, besides Ricardo, are named in the contemporary newspapers' (Sraffa 1955, 125). The authoritative history of the Stock Exchange by Morgan and Thomas (1969, 49) describes the same open problem: 'Only three of the names, those of Barnes, Steers and Ricardo survive'.

Recently this mystery was solved (Parys 2020, 2021). It is possible to find the fourth name by combining the 1807 membership lists of the Stock Exchange, the diary notes of Joseph Farington (1978–1998) on his relations with the Steers family, the recently discovered correspondence by John Barnes on the 1806 loan, and the information provided by *The Genealogist* (1878, 186–87) on the Steers family. The combination of these sources leads to overwhelming evidence that the unknown fourth man was a certain Charles Steers. He was a brother of James Steers, but perhaps socially less visible because he suffered from a hearing problem, although Charles Steers, just like his brother James, and John Barnes and David Ricardo, belonged to several committees of the Stock Exchange. These four influential financiers remained loyally together in the same consortium for all future loans until the end of their lives (Charles Steers died in April 1810, John Barnes in January 1815, and James Steers in July 1817). The ironical conclusion of the search for the enigmatic fourth man is that the label 'Barnes-Steers-Ricardo' in the newspapers was less incomplete than Sraffa and other historians thought, because the consortium of four involved two Steers brothers.

Barnes had been elected as the first chairman of the new Stock Exchange in 1802 (Armstrong 1939, 373–78). Ricardo, James Steers and Charles Steers too appear regularly in the minutes of its committee meetings. In the following paragraphs, however, I will sometimes refer to the consortium of this influential quartet simply as 'Ricardo's consortium', because, from a financial point of view, Ricardo was a more powerful dealer than his three partners. The Stock Ledgers of the Bank of England reveal that Ricardo's turnover figures on the Stock Exchange were much higher. For example, with respect to the three per cent Consols registered in the period 1798–1804, it is possible to compute the following totals (Parys 2021, 563):

– John Barnes: £177,000
– Charles Steers: £230,000
– James Steers: £425,000
– David Ricardo: £6,965,000

Note that the first three turnover figures are not low, but normal. Ricardo's figures are exceptionally high.

4. Ricardo's Influence and Prestige on the Stock Exchange

In the beginning of the nineteenth century the Stock Exchange in London made several efforts to improve its reputation, for example by using a new building, and by limiting its membership, trying to exclude disreputable behaviour. On several occasions Ricardo helped to increase the quality of the Stock Exchange and to handle problems with frauds.

For example, on 5 May 1803, a notice at the Mansion House (the residence of the Lord Mayor in London) falsely suggested that peace negotiations between Britain and France were successful. The stock prices rose about 10 per cent, before the news was officially denied. The Stock Exchange was shut immediately, and it was agreed that all transactions of 5 May should 'be considered as null and void'. Ricardo was appointed as a member of the Select Committee that had to trace out the culprits of the forgery (*Morning Chronicle*, 7 May 1803, page 3).

In February 1814, a certain Charles Random de Berenger used sophisticated theatre tricks and complex logistics, suggesting that he just arrived at Dover from France, and carrying a report of Napoleon's death and the surrender of the French army. Berenger's clique, which had purchased a lot of stocks in the preceding period, earned big profits when the stock prices went up considerably after the 'good news' reached London. Then the frauds quickly took their profits. After the fraud became obvious, all were convicted in criminal court. To preserve its reputation, the Stock Exchange took special action. Its *Committee for the Protection of Property against Fraud* decided that the illegal profits would be transferred to different charities. One of the most respected and influential members of this Committee was David Ricardo (Duguid 1901, 108–16; Parys 2021, 564–66).

Sometimes Ricardo spent a considerable amount of time on seemingly minor problems, for example, with respect to the price lists that James Wetenhall regularly published in *The Course of the Exchange*. Wetenhall's lists recorded prices of transactions on the Stock Exchange, and many investors subscribed to these lists (Ricardo and Malthus sometimes used them in their correspondence). In the summer of 1811 Ricardo spent many efforts to insert a small correction in the lists, when he became aware that on 26 July 1811 Wetenhall had not recorded Ricardo's purchase of £14,000 Consols from Street & Andrews. Wetenhall considered the price paid by Ricardo as not representative, because Andrews had asked to be paid in cash. After long discussions, several meetings, letters, lobbying, extra information from several brokers, the *Committee for General Purposes* finally decided in September to accept Ricardo's request for inclusion of his transaction in Wetenhall's 'official price' lists, despite having refused it in earlier meetings in July and August (Parys 2021, 566).

Besides desiring high standards for the records of the Stock Exchange, Ricardo also tried to correct the often rude, noisy and chaotic behaviour of its members. When, after the short-lived Peace of Amiens, Britain and France started war again on 18 May 1803, many of Ricardo's colleagues of the Stock Exchange did not hesitate to 'astound the neighborhood with their yells' (*Sunday Times*, 14 September 1823, page 1). They enjoyed such news, because they hoped it would generate more war loans, and thus more business at the Stock Exchange. Ricardo rebuked his colleagues, because they welcomed news that would bring suffering to millions of ordinary people.

5. Silberling's Critique of Ricardo's Business Ethics

In May 1924 the *Quarterly Journal of Economics* published an influential paper by Norman Silberling (1924), who criticised Ricardo's ethics in the world of finance, especially in the competition with the Goldsmid consortium. After the suicide of Benjamin Goldsmid in 1808, his brother Abraham tried to continue business as usual. In 1810 Abraham and the Barings combined to make the winning bid for the 1810 loan. A few months later, Sir Francis Baring died of natural causes, Abraham was involved in a traffic accident in Lombard Street, and when the price of the loan went six per cent below par, Abraham shot himself. A special intervention by the government and the Bank of England was necessary to avoid a crash at the Stock Exchange.

Given this dramatic historical background, Silberling's accusations against Ricardo looked very serious. Silberling accused Ricardo of leading a 'bearish clique', i.e., a faction of the Stock Exchange that systematically tried to depress stock prices and by clever speculation derived large profits from it. Silberling even thought that Ricardo's monetary theories were heavily influenced by his private interests. He believed that Ricardo advised resumption of the convertibility of bank notes, because such an action would have decreased the gold reserves of the Bank of England, then decreased its possibilities to provide credit to investors, and ultimately depressed stock prices. For several decades, Silberling's ideas were repeated by other authors, for example, by Cope (1942) in his otherwise excellent article on the Goldsmids in *Economica*, and by Clapham (1944) in his standard work on the history of the Bank of England.

Sraffa's unpublished papers show that already in the early 1930s he had serious doubts about Silberling's article (Parys 2021, 568–70). Silberling was heavily influenced by an anonymous pamphlet on the Stock Exchange, which turned out to be written by a certain Joseph Lancaster (1821). Silberling treated Lancaster as a well-informed insider, but by a careful archival search Sraffa found out that Lancaster was a defaulter and had been punished by exclusion from the Stock Exchange. Lancaster's frustration then generated offending remarks about Ricardo's influential role in the politics of the Stock Exchange. Silberling seemingly did not know that Lancaster was unreliable. Moreover, Silberling surprisingly neglected that Ricardo often was involved in biddings for British loan, and therefore often was a not a bear, but a bull, i.e., not hoping for falling but for rising stock prices. Several decades after his discoveries, Sraffa (1955, 91–94) finally published his findings in *A Canard*, a short editorial section of his Ricardo edition. Sraffa's rehabilitation of Ricardo in this context is now widely accepted by most Ricardo specialists. For example, Jacob Viner once called Lancaster's pamphlet 'the product of a disordered mind' (quoted by de Vivo 2014, 308), and Samuel Hollander (1979, 499) referred to the 'ludicrousness' of Silberling's charge against Ricardo.

A recently discovered pamphlet by Barnes (1806) can be used to strengthen Sraffa's defence of Ricardo against Silberling (Parys 2021, 568–70). Barnes criticised the unusual and unfair methods that the Goldsmids used in 1806, when the newcomers Barnes-Steers-Ricardo tried to compile their own list of subscribers for the loan contract. According to Barnes (1806, 3–4, 7) Abraham Goldsmid then made the unusual announcement that any investor on the Barnes-Steers-Ricardo list would be excluded from his own list, and he regularly sent his son as a spy to Barnes's office to collect information about the names on the Barnes-Steers-Ricardo list. Ultimately Barnes sent a letter to the Chancellor of the Exchequer to complain about the problematic methods that were used by the powerful consortia that wanted to keep new competitors out of the elite market for loans. Maybe Silberling confused perpetrators and victims.

Loan contractors had a special status in the world of finance, and sometimes the Chancellor of the Exchequer asked their opinion about problems of public debt. For example, Ricardo and other would-be contractors were consulted in 1814 on the following two alternatives: either Britain could use its Sinking Fund and borrow only £12 million, or it could organise a Big Loan of £24 million. The latter was more profitable for the loan contractors. All of them advised a big loan, except Ricardo, who, contrary to his personal financial interest, recommended the small loan as being more advantageous to the country (Sraffa 1955, 81–82). In his theories with respect to public debt and several other policy problems, Ricardo was motivated by concern for the advantage of his country, rather than by any one particular interest (Churchman 2001, 91–110; Cremaschi 2022, 130–71).

6. Ricardo's Seven British Loans Contracts

The collusion and intimidation by the old consortia against Barnes-Steers-Ricardo had succeeded in 1806, but the next year Barnes-Steers-Ricardo submitted the best bid and took the whole British loan of 1807. Barnes-Steers-Ricardo did not obtain the contract in 1808, 1809 and 1810, but could take half of the loan of 1811, when it turned out that both Barnes-Steers-Ricardo and Robarts-Curtis had submitted exactly the same cheapest bid.

In 1812 the government wanted to raise a loan of £22.5 million, nearly twice as much as the year before, due to increasing war costs. Not a single consortium dared to take the whole loan on its own, but after difficult negotiations the government accepted that three consortia (Barnes-Steers-Ricardo, Baring-Angerstein and Robarts-Curtis) combined, and each took one third of the loan.

In 1813 Britain needed even more money and took the extraordinary step of launching not one, but two big loans: one in June and one in November. The ever-increasing risks explained why some prominent financiers no longer tried to form their own consortium. Only two consortia remained: Ricardo's consortium and the powerful Baring-Angerstein consortium. They combined to take the two loans of 1813 and the loan of 1814.

The biggest single loan (£36 million), later sometimes referred to as the Waterloo Loan, was launched on 14 June 1815, four days before the Battle of Waterloo (18 June). News travelled slowly in those days, and the official messenger of the Duke of Wellington arrived in London on Wednesday 22 June, just before midnight (Cathcart 2015). Many authors (for example, Sraffa 1955, 82; Heertje 2015, 266) suggest that in this turbulent month of June four different consortia had divided the loan contract, but this is wrong. The *Committee of Treasury Report Book, 1797–1832*, in the Bank of England Archives (file G8/7) mentions the same two (not four) consortia as in 1813 and 1814. The year 1815 was not different in this respect. Do also note that although the record loan of £36 million was launched in 1815, the record annual total was reached in 1813, when Britain had to organise two loans, generating a total of £49 million.

The five loans in the period 1812–1815 were all very profitable for the investors, especially the two 1813 loans (Parys 2020, 62). It is no surprise that at the end of 1813 Ricardo made plans to retire and to buy Gatcombe Park. The profits of the Waterloo Loan of 1815 were a big bonus for Ricardo, but without this extra he would not have altered his decision to diminish his involvement in transactions at the Stock Exchange and to spend most of his days on more scholarly questions of economic theory and economic policy debates.

7. Unregistered Transactions in Scrips and for Time

From the archives of the Bank of England it is possible to get some insight into the amount of Ricardo's sales and purchases (Sraffa 1955, 72; Parys 2020, 67). If yearly totals for Ricardo are computed, then his record figures appear in the year 1813.

Note that the Bank of England registered transfers of ownership, but not transactions involving so-called scrips. To explain the transactions in scrips, it is important to emphasise that most investors preferred to pay the loan in monthly instalments. After full payment, the name of an investor was registered in the Stock Ledgers of the Bank of England. Before full payment, however, investors received subscription receipts, usually abbreviated as 'scrips'. These scrips showed how many instalments had already been paid.

The scrips were marketable on the Stock Exchange, and speculators could generate large profits or losses by buying or selling them. Consider, for example, the scrips of the Omnium of a new loan, after the first monthly instalment of £10 had been paid, showing that £90 was still due in the next nine months, and suppose that on the Stock Exchange the Omnium was already quoted at £107 instead of £100 (hence at '7 per cent premium'). In this case the owners of scrips could sell them for £17 instead of £10, making a quick profit of 70 per cent. Such transactions in scrips were not registered. Hence, the data about such profits or losses are not extant. When Ricardo (for example) became the last holder of some scrips and paid the final instalment, he became the owner of the bonds in the basket of the Omnium, and then his ownership was registered by the Bank of England. When he had sold scrips before the final instalment, however, his transactions were unregistered.

A similar lack of registration can occur in case of 'transactions for time'. Suppose today A owns no Consols, although A agrees to sell Consols to B at a total price of £7,000, to be settled 20 days from now. Suppose at settling day the total market price has decreased to £6,600. Then A and B can settle their contract simply by a payment of £400 from B to A. Again, this is an unregistered transaction because neither A nor B is involved in a transfer of Consols or a change of ownership. Such time bargains were very common.

Ricardo referred to such time bargains when he was heard by a parliamentary committee in 1818:

> When preparations are making for a loan, large sales of stock are made, of which the seller may not be possessed, but which he may expect to replace by the share he may have in the loan to be contracted for. (V, 341)

In 1815, for example, the Omnium of the loan contained three different sorts of bonds: three per cent Consols, four per cent Consols and three per cent Reduced Annuities. Niles (1815, 67) computed that if a loan contractor had sold these three bonds a week before the new loan contract and then obtained the same bonds back via the loan basket, he gained about 10 per cent. In a letter to Malthus, dated 27 June 1815, Ricardo described such transactions in the context of the new loan of 1815:

> I have been a considerable gainer by the loan; in the first place by replacing the stock which I had sold before the contract with the minister at a much lower price, and secondly by a moderate gain on such part of the loan as I ventured to take over and above my stock. This portion I sold at a premium of from 3 to 5 pc.t and I have every reason to be well contented. (VI, 233)

The daily price statistics of the Omnium in June 1815 (Parys 2020, 64–65) reveal that Ricardo could have earned a higher premium of 13 per cent, if he had waited a bit longer, until London was informed about Napoleon's defeat in Waterloo, but taking maximum risks was not part of Ricardo's investment tactics.

8. Ricardo's Investment Strategies

Ricardo surely made many unregistered transactions in scrips and time bargains. Of course, information on such unregistered deals is scarce. Luckily, the numerous transactions that were registered by the Bank of England more than two centuries ago, can still be studied today in the Bank's archives, and show that Ricardo handled extraordinarily large quantities of Consols, Reduced Annuities, Navy Fives and other stocks. On the one hand the number of Ricardo's transactions was extremely high, but on the other hand he was not an extreme risk taker.

When the 1811 loan, co-contracted by Ricardo's consortium, went below par after one month, his friends James Mill and Jeremy Bentham were worried about Ricardo's finances, but he reassured his friends by the following remark on his tactics:

> there is one security which I always take on these occasions, and which I consider by far the most important. – I play for small stakes, and therefore if I am a loser, I have little to regret. (VI, 52)

Ricardo seemed to follow such cautious strategies not only on the special occasions when he had to handle a big new loan, but also in his routine day-to-day activities on the Stock Exchange. In this context, Sraffa (1955, 73) drew attention to the diary of Ricardo's friend John Lewis Mallet. After Ricardo's death in 1823, Mallet described Ricardo's business habits as follows:

> He is said to have possessed an extraordinary quickness in perceiving in the turns of the market any accidental difference which might arise between the relative price of different stocks, and to have availed himself of this advantage, so as to realise as much as £200 or £300 in one day, by selling out of one, and buying into another stock or *vice versa.* He is also said never to have carried his stock transactions to any speculative extent; but to have always, or generally sold out on the turn of the market, so as to realise a small percentage upon a large sum. (Mallet 1921 [1823], 205–6)

In a letter to John Sinclair, dated 31 October 1814, Ricardo suggested that he benefited from his superior knowledge of political economy:

> The Stock Exchange is chiefly attended by persons who are unremittingly attentive to their business, and are well acquainted with its details; but there are very few in number who have much knowledge of political economy, and consequently they pay little attention to finance, as a subject of science. They consider more, the immediate effect of passing events, rather than their distant consequences. (VI, 150–51)

When describing Ricardo's financial strategies, many authors referred to *The Great Metropolis* by James Grant (1837), a popular multi-volume work that offered entertaining information on London, and included a chapter on the London Stock Exchange, full of anecdotes about Goldsmid and Rothschild, and also one paragraph on Ricardo's business. Grant (1837, 81) suggested that Ricardo used the following three 'golden rules':

1. Never refuse an option when you can get it.
2. Cut short your losses.
3. Let your profits run on.

Sraffa (1955, 73) pointed out that the first rule is rather vague and useless, because it mentions nothing about the price of the option. This vagueness explains why many authors, for example, Duguid (1901, 118), Henderson and Davis (1997, 214), and Skousen (2016, 99) discussed only the second and the third rule. The second rule suggests that Ricardo quickly sold as soon as prices started to fall, instead of stubbornly waiting for better times. The third rule is controversial: did Ricardo really follow it systematically? How authoritative are Grant's stories about the Stock Exchange? Grant's authority becomes doubtful when we look at his statements about a so-called Mr. F—, who suddenly went from bankruptcy to riches after the Battle of Waterloo.

9. Grant's Legend about Mr. F— and Waterloo

Some amusing stories by James Grant about the effect of Waterloo on the Stock Exchange seem unreliable and imprecise, as they are not supported by the correct statistical data. A typical example is the story of the huge 'Waterloo profits' of a certain Mr. F—, which is described in colourful details by Grant (1837, 64–72). After dramatic losses on the Stock Exchange, the desperate Mr. F— headed for London Bridge, threw his last shilling into the Thames and wished that his own body too were at bottom of the river.

Before he could commit suicide, however, Mr. F— felt that someone seized him by the hand. His rescuer turned out to be an old French friend, who had just parted with the French ambassador and now gave Mr. F— exclusive news about the defeat of Napoleon in the Battle of Waterloo. Mr. F— immediately realised that stock prices in London would rise considerably as soon as the sensational news became known at the Stock Exchange, where traders behaved very nervously after Britain had just launched a record loan of £36 million. By returning hastily from London Bridge to the city and acting quickly, using his inside information on Napoleon's defeat, Mr. F— succeeded in making a big financial coup. Still according to Grant (1837, 71–72), the price fluctuations of the Omnium of the new loan were 'fully 100 per cent'. After collecting his enormous Waterloo profits, Mr. F— left business and purchased one of the most extensive estates in the county of Middlesex.

The above story is a typical example of a Waterloo legend that is not supported by historical evidence. Grant's reference to fluctuations of 100 per cent is contradicted by the empirical data published in various newspapers. Their daily statistics show that during the whole month of June 1815 the Omnium of the new loan was always 'at a premium', that is, it was sold at a higher price than its face value of £100. From the *Morning Chronicle* and other newspapers, the following data can be compiled (Parys 2020, 64):

- From 14 to 19 June: Omnium fluctuated between $102\frac{1}{4}$ and $103\frac{3}{4}$
- Tuesday 20 June: Omnium increased to $104\frac{5}{8}$
- Wednesday 21 June: Omnium fluctuated between $104\frac{1}{4}$ and $105\frac{3}{4}$, closing at $104\frac{3}{4}$
- The official report on Napoleon's defeat arrived in London just before midnight
- Thursday 22 June: Omnium started at 109, then fell to $107\frac{5}{8}$, and closed at 108
- Napoleon abdicated in Paris on 22 June; this news arrived in London on 26 June
- After this news reached London, Omnium peaked at 113 in the week of 26–30 June

Grant's strongly exaggerated reference to fluctuations of 100 per cent in this period, and other bizarre details, render his tale of the adventures of Mr. F— completely implausible. Moreover, this might also cast doubts on Grant's reference to Ricardo's three 'golden rules'. Ricardo (VI, 233) had informed Malthus that he sold a portion of his Omnium at 3 to 5 per cent premium, that is, at a price between £103 and £105. In the light of the price statistics given above, it means that Ricardo sold before and on

Wednesday 21 June, a few hours before the official news from Waterloo arrived in London. Investors who sold on Thursday morning 22 June or later obtained higher profit rates.

In this case, Ricardo surely did not 'let his profits run on' (the third 'golden rule'). His friend Hutches Trower 'let his profits run on' much longer and sold later at £110. Ricardo's correspondence (VI, 233, 237) with Malthus and Trower reveals the following remarkable situation: Trower was unhappy because he had missed the peak prices of £113, whereas Ricardo was 'well contented' with a smaller profit rate, but again I emphasise that a *small profit rate* on Ricardo's very large total investment generated *high total profits*.

10. Ricardo and Rothschild

Grant's story of the inside information and the spectacular Waterloo profits of Mr. F— is not unique. Similar legends exist about Nathan Mayer Rothschild, who is said to have earned one million on the Stock Exchange thanks to exclusive information about the Battle of Waterloo (Dairnvaell 1846, 11–12; Engels 1846; Reeves 1887, 173–175). Moreover, it is not difficult to find analogous Waterloo rumours about Ricardo. His obituary on the front page of *The Sunday Times* of 14 September 1823 had suggested that Ricardo 'netted upwards of a million sterling'. Such rumours are still mentioned in many modern writings, for example in remarks about inside information (Samuelson 2009, 25) or about 'the day Ricardo made 1£ million sterling' (Skousen 2016, 99). It is rather bizarre to find three similar stories about three different persons who are said to have made 'unique' Waterloo profits. All three stories are very readable, but none are reliable. Just like in case of the enigmatic Mr. F—, there is a serious lack of historical evidence for the parallel Waterloo legends about Rothschild and Ricardo (Parys 2020).

In contrast to the legends in the *Sunday Times* obituary about a sensational coup that should have brought Ricardo one million in a few days, the obituary in *The Morning Chronicle* (13 September 1823, page 3) was less sensational, but more plausible; it stressed Ricardo's talents and also his numerous days of hard work:

> Mr. Ricardo is supposed to have been worth upwards of half a million when he retired from business. He was remarkably successful, hardly ever sustaining any loss. Indeed the system on which he proceeded in some measure secured him against heavy losses, though it also prevented him from gaining much at any one time. His practice was to sell always at the turn of the market, and his gains, though small at any one time, by being often repeated became large in the end.

Although both Ricardo and Rothschild reached the top in the world of finance in the early nineteenth century, their characters were very different. For Rothschild the main enjoyment of his life was found in the processes by which he was making money (Bourne 1886, 464). For Ricardo, however, his business success was just a means of reaching a better quality of life, by being able to retire into the country and to spend more time on his favourite science, political economy (Sraffa 1955, 90). After he had bought Gatcombe Park, Ricardo wrote to Malthus:

> I believe that in this sweet place I shall not sigh after the Stock Exchange and its enjoyments. (VI, 115, letter of 25 July 1814)

In this sweet place Ricardo could finally concentrate his intellectual talents on more scholarly activities and produce the three editions of his magnum opus *On the Principles of Political Economy, and Taxation* in 1817, 1819 and 1821. Two years later he died unexpectedly at the early age of 51, because of an ear infection that probably could have been cured in a few days by twenty-first century medicines.

References

Armstrong, Frederick Ernest. 1939. *The Book of the Stock Exchange*. Third edition. London: Pitman.

Barnes, John. 1806. *Letter, Addressed to the Gentlemen who Subscribed to the List for the Late Loan, Formed by Messrs. Barnes, C. and J. Steers, and Ricardo*. London: B. McMillan.

Bourne, Henry Richard Fox. 1886. *English Merchants. Memoirs in Illustration of the Progress of British Commerce*. London: Chatto and Windus.

Cathcart, Brian. 2015. *The News from Waterloo. The Race to Tell Britain of Wellington's Victory*. London: Faber and Faber.

Churchman, Nancy. 2001. *David Ricardo on Public Debt*. Basingstoke: Palgrave.

Clapham, John. 1944. *The Bank of England. A History. Volume 1: 1694–1797. Volume 2: 1797–1914*. Cambridge: Cambridge University Press.

Cope, Sidney Raymond. 1942. 'The Goldsmids and the Development of the London Money Market during the Napoleonic Wars'. *Economica* 9, no. 34: 180–206.

Cremaschi, Sergio. 2022. *David Ricardo. An Intellectual Biography*. London: Routledge.

Dairnvaell, Georges. 1846. *Histoire édifiante et curieuse de Rothschild 1er, Roi des Juifs (The Edifying and Curious History of the First Rothschild, King of the Jews)*. Paris: Chez l'Editeur, Rue Colbert-Vivienne, 4.

De Vivo, Giancarlo. 2014. *Catalogue of the Library of Piero Sraffa*. Milan: Fondazione Raffaele Mattioli, and Turin: Fondazione Luigi Einaudi

Duguid, Charles. 1901. *The Story of the Stock Exchange. Its History and Position*. London: Grant Richards.

Engels, Friedrich. 1846. 'Government and Opposition in France'. *The Northern Star*, no. 460 (5 September): 27–29.

Farington, Joseph. 1978–1998. *The Diary of Joseph Farington*. Vols I–XVII, edited by Kenneth Garlick, Angus Macintyre, Kathryn Cave and Evelyn Newby. New Haven: Yale University Press.

Grant, James. 1837. *The Great Metropolis*. Vol. 2. Second Series. London: Saunders and Otley.

Grellier, John James, and Robert Watson Wade. 1812. *The Terms of All the Loans Which Have Been Raised for the Public Service*. Third Edition. London: Richardson.

Heertje, Arnold. 2015. 'Life and Activities'. In *The Elgar Companion to David Ricardo*, edited by Heinz Dieter Kurz and Neri Salvadori, 264–72. Cheltenham: Edward Elgar.

Henderson, John Patrick, and John Bryan Davis. 1997. *The Life and Economics of David Ricardo*. Boston: Kluwer.

Hollander, Samuel. 1979. *The Economics of David Ricardo*. Toronto: University of Toronto Press.

King, John Edward. 2013. *David Ricardo*. Houndmills: Palgrave Macmillan.

Lancaster, Joseph. 1821. *The Bank—The Stock Exchange—The Bankers—The Bankers' Clearing House—The Minister, and the Public. An Exposé, Touching Their Various Mysteries*. London: Effingham Wilson, and J. Ridgway.

Mallet, John Lewis. 1921 'Diary entries from 1823–1837'. In *Political Economy Club. Minutes of Proceedings, 1899–1920. Roll of Members and Questions Discussed, 1821–1920. With Documents Bearing on the History of the Club*, Vol. 6, 205–75. London: Macmillan.

Marshall, George W., ed. 1878. *The Genealogist*. Vol. 2. London: Golding and Lawrence.

Michie, Ranald. 2006. *The Global Securities Market. A History*. Oxford: Oxford University Press.

Morgan, Edward Victor and William Arthur Thomas. 1969. *The Stock Exchange. Its History and Functions*. Second edition. London: Elek Books.

Niles, Hezekiah. 1815. 'British Statistics. Expenditures, Loans, etc. for 1815'. *Niles' Weekly Register* 9, no. 5: 66–69.

Parys, Wilfried. 2020. *David Ricardo, the Stock Exchange, and the Battle of Waterloo. Samuelsonian Legends Lack Historical Evidence*. University of Antwerp, Research Paper 2020–009. https://repository.uantwerpen.be/docstore/d:irua:3740

Parys, Wilfried. 2021. 'Some Additions and Corrections for Sraffa on Ricardo in Business'. *Cambridge Journal of Economics* 45, no. 3: 559–75.

Reeves, John. 1887. *The Rothschilds. The Financial Rulers of Nations*. London: Sampson Low, Marston, Searle, and Rivington.

Ricardo, David. 1951–1973. *The Works and Correspondence of David Ricardo*, edited by Piero Sraffa with the collaboration of Maurice Herbert Dobb. Vols I–XI. Cambridge: Cambridge University Press.

Samuelson, Paul Anthony. 2009. 'An Enjoyable Life Puzzling Over Modern Finance Theory'. *Annual Review of Financial Economics* 1, no. 1: 19–35.

Silberling, Norman John. 1924. 'Financial and Monetary Policy of Great Britain during the Napoleonic Wars: Ricardo and the Bullion Report'. *Quarterly Journal of Economics* 38, no. 3: 397–439.

Skousen, Mark. 2016. *The Making of Modern Economics. The Lives and Ideas of the Great Thinkers*. Third Edition. New York: Routledge.

Sraffa, Piero. 1955. 'Ricardo in Business'. In Ricardo's *Works*, X, 65–106.

Twist, Anthony Frederick. 2002. *Widening Circles in Finance, Philanthropy and the Arts. A Study of the Life of John Julius Angerstein 1735–1823*. PhD thesis: University of Amsterdam.

Weatherall, David. 1976. *David Ricardo. A Biography*. The Hague: Martinus Nijhoff.

Ziegler, Philip. 1988. *The Sixth Great Power. A History of One of the Greatest of All Banking Families, the House of Barings, 1762–1929*. New York: Knopf.

Chapter 8

POLITICAL ECONOMY 'THROUGH A GLASS HIVE'? THE ENCOUNTER OF RICARDIAN IDEAS WITH NINETEENTH-CENTURY AUSTRALIA

William Coleman

'They have the strongest interest as capitalists in searching, deep into the foundations of economic science. They have the best kind of school the world can afford for such inquiries; a young community. [...] it was as if political economy were being acted out on a stage - for in a colony we may witness the growth of human society, as plainly as we can observe the operation of bees through a glass hive' (Lowe 1844).

In 1817 *On the Principles of Political Economy and Taxation* was first published. In the same year European settlement in Australia remained confined to a semicircular disk, centred on Sydney, with a radius of 50 km.[1] But, only shortly before, the labyrinthine ranges that had for 30 years hemmed in the Sydney settlement were sufficiently traversed to make out the open tablelands that lay beyond, and which would revolutionise world's wool trade, and make Australia 'rich and free'.

> And, as a meteor shoots athwart the night,
> The boundless champaign burst upon our sight Till nearer seen the beauteous landscape grew, Op'ning like Canaan on rapt Israel's view. (Wentworth 1823: 13).

In anticipation of exploitation of the new Canaan's 'boundless champaign', Australia's first bank was formed in 1817. In the same year Governor Macquarie, perhaps stirred by the quickening of prospects, successfully proposed that New Holland be henceforth known as 'Australia'. Thus, Ricardo's *Principles* appeared at a critical moment in Australia's economic history.

Ricardo's work offered food for thought for both the Colonial Office and colonists. Rent had nothing to do with land's productivity as such, and might be as free as air. And a 'new society', the *Principles* insinuates, would experience high average productivity of land and labour, scant rents and moderate wages, with the consequent high profits stimulating capital growth.[2] Finally, the *Principles* contained a pregnant proposition, which would especially engage an essentially agricultural community: 'A tax on rent would affect rent only; it would fall wholly on landlords, and could not be shifted to any class of consumers' (I: 358).

The Colonial Office, further, had a particular cause to give notice to thoughts of about land or revenue in 'new societies'; the cost of New South Wales (NSW) to the British government was in the post-Napoleonic period swelling alarmingly, from £583,000 in the 12 years before 1817, to £2,242,000 in the twelve beginning that year (Butlin et al. 1986: 37). The East India Company – where James Mill worked from 1819 and John Stuart Mill from 1823 – would have an interest, as the Company had a legal monopoly of NSW's trade with the rest of the world. The educated crust of NSW might be expected to have a sensitivity to Ricardian speculations. Certainly, Alexander Macleay, the learned Colonial Secretary of NSW from 1825 to 1837, and thus the second most important figure in the colony's executive in those transformational years, owned a copy of the second edition of the *Principles*. But to the local elite political economy overwhelmingly meant Smith; Adam Smith was the educator; he was political economist with a particular interest in colonies; the visionary of the great sweep of development from 'an early and rude state' to 'rich, industrious and commercial nations'. Accordingly, political economy titles offered for sale in Australia over the period 1805–1849 included 132 copies of *The Wealth of Nations*, but just four of Ricardo's *Principles* (Berg 2017: 9). To the local elite Ricardo was just one of 'the authorities', to occasionally quote amid some respite from the urgent strivings of a raw existence.[3] Not without reason did Edward Gibbon Wakefield contend, 'Literary men, men of science, philosophers, do not emigrate to new countries where their acquirements would be neither rewarded nor admired' (Wakefield 1829: 40).[4]

Not surprisingly the first engagement of political economy with Australia – *A Letter from Sydney* – came not from Sydney or anywhere in Australia. And it is not unaccountable that its place of composition was, in fact, Newgate prison, where its author Edward Gibbon Wakefield had much opportunity to reflect on punishment – including 'transportation' – owing to his earlier conviction for certain sensational frauds. His success in these frauds owed much to his 'spell binding', 'magnetic' personality, which, one acquaintance judged, could be resisted only by hating him.[5] Wakefield's insertion of his driven and visionary personality into the affairs of empire might bring to mind an East India Company adventurer of an earlier period, or a Cecil Rhodes of a later one; but he is better interpretable as an early case of the 'special advisor', and is reminiscent of L. F. McDougall (1884–1958), the ubiquitous, insinuating and persuasive apostle of empire food trade; never in office, but, thanks to his 'remarkable personal influence,' the constant consultant, counsellor and confidant of 'a great many significant figures' in the mid-twentieth century (Turnell 2006).[6]

Wakefield's persuasiveness was assisted by the informal education in political economy presumably supplied by his father, Edward, not only a land agent of David Ricardo, but an economic pundit of the day, who had 'formed close friendships with Francis Place, John Mill and Henry Brougham' (Moss 2004).[7] Current events were grist for Wakefield's mill. The fiasco of Thomas Peel's attempt to establish settlement at 'Swan River' (i.e. Western Australia) in 1829 was too late for the *Letter*, but was to Wakefield's mind a vindication of his theories, and was much exploited in his *England and America* of 1833.[8]

The *Letter from Sydney* directs itself to explaining why NSW seemed to struggle, in contrast to the implicit optimism about new societies of Smithian and Ricardian political economy. As the author relates, supposedly of himself: 'I have got 20,000 acres, and they did not cost me more than 2s. per acre. But I imagined that a domain of that extent would be very valuable. In this I was wholly mistaken. As my estate cost me next to nothing, so it is worth next to nothing' (Wakefield 1829: 177).

The first cause of this unfortunate situation was transportation costs; NSW being, as W.S. Jevons later observed, 'a large, wild, in many parts a very rugged tract of country, in which water-carriage non-existent, and even locomotion by ordinary methods very difficult' (Jevons 1857). The fictitious Sydney correspondent lamented that raw productions, timber and minerals, conferred no value on the 20,000 acres he supposedly owned. 'As for disposing of it […], that would be impossible, for want of roads […]. As regards the coal, though, I am mistaken; I might consume it by fire without much trouble. But what could I do with the iron ore, when, even though there should be means to convey it to Sydney, nobody would give me one Birmingham frying-pan for the whole of it?'. Ricardo, then, was mistaken in putting the value of land down its relative fertility.

> Mr. Ricardo's theory of rent is perfectly unquestionable as far as it goes. But it does not, as I imagine, go far enough to explain the nature of rent in new countries. In England, the most fertile land, be it where it may, will let for what is called a high rent: here the most fertile land will not, unless near a town, yield any rent

> at all. But, even in England, fertility is not the sole criterion of rent; as land near a town will let for more than equally fertile land situated far from any town [...]. All I mean by this is, that in speaking of rent according to Mr. Ricardo's theory, we are not to attribute to natural fertility *only*, what is in fact, *partly* due to situation and to the outlay of capital. In England, that part of the rent which is paid for superior natural fertility only is generally so large, in proportion to what is paid for situation and the use of fixed capital, that it may not be worthwhile to distinguish them with hair-splitting precision. But here, that is, in all new countries, the case is quite different. Wherever the most fertile land can be obtained for nothing, the superior fertility of land is worth nothing; and whatever is obtained under the name of rent, is paid *solely* either for vicinity to markets or as interest of fixed capital. (Wakefield 1829: 176)

The simplest analytical manoeuvre beckoned by the allowance for transport costs would be a spatial model where distant labour is less value-productive than near labour, with (to us) well-known implications for the ratio of labour to land.[9] Vindication of such a manoeuvre might be found in the fact that economic historians of Australia have seen a great explanatory power in distance (Blainey 1968). But there is not a hint of spatial model of economic activity in Wakefield's *Letter* or later writings.

Instead, Wakefield takes aim at the key Ricardian tenet of diminishing average and marginal product of labour; or, in Ricardo's language, 'the greater difficulty of obtaining the increased supplies, on account of the additional quantity of labour which the cultivation of inferior lands requires' (I: 8). Wakefield sweeps away such a premise.

> We may, indeed, presume that the produce of 500,000 inhabitants of Van Diemen's Land, would much exceed twenty times the produce of 25,000 inhabitants; because the different *proportion* of people to territory would cause a greater *division of labour*, which is the very soul of production [...]. In short, there is little division of labour. (Wakefield 1829: 195)

Wakefield was striking at Ricardo's neglect of 'division of labour', which is referred to in *Principles* only four times, once in quoting Smith and three other occasions very passingly.[10] But having raised the standard of 'the division of labour', Wakefield was a few years later to dismiss it as question begging, and obscuring of the more fundamental phenomenon: the *combination* of labour.

> Adam Smith has said that the greatest improvement in the productive powers of industry is division of labour; others have dwelt on the great effects of machinery [...]; but none of these improvements are primary causes, as some

> of them, and especially 'division of labour', have been considered by political economists; each of them on the contrary, though an immediate cause, is the effect of some antecedent cause.
>
> In the most simple operation of industry, – in that, for example, which savages perform when they hunt for subsistence, – two persons assisting each other would obtain more game in a given time than two persons hunting each by himself without concert; just as two greyhounds, running together, will kill more hares than four greyhounds running separately. The very first improvement, therefore, in the productive powers of industry, seems to be not division, but combination, of labour. Several individuals, by combining their labour, procure more food than they want. (Wakefield 1833: 16–17)

'The combination of labour', not the division of labour: here was the root of productivity. J. S. Mill, the Great Assimilator, acknowledged the significance of the phenomenon in the *Principles of Political Economy*. The 'productiveness of labour' is promoted by 'the combined action of numbers' such as 'the lifting of heavy weights, for example, in the felling of trees, in the sawing of timber, in the gathering much hay or corn during a short period of fine weather, in draining a large extent of land during the short season [...], in the rowing of large boats' (Mill 1885: 101). We might imagine two people rowing a boat might have more than twice the productivity of one.[11]

To Wakefield it is a lack of the 'combination of labour' that is enervating in Australia. 'The soil and climate of New South Wales appear admirably suited to the growth of tobacco, olive oil, silk and wine. [...] Why has it not grown any of these things? Because for the growth of any of these things constant and combined labour is required; an element of production wanting in New South Wales' (Wakefield 1833, 2: 115). But why is 'combination' so wanting? Because of the abundance of land in the presence of free labour. 'Under a system of free labour the landowner will be 'eager to collect labourers from all quarters, and to reward them with the most liberal wages. But those liberal wages, joined to the plenty and cheapness of land, soon make those labourers leave him, in order to become landlords themselves' (Wakefield 1829, 153). Thus: 'Cheapness of land is another expression for scarcity of labourers; and as land here is extraordinarily cheap, we may expect that [...] labourers for hire will be excessively scarce' (Wakefield 1829: 67). [12]

If cheap land and free labour is the root cause of a lack of combination, then a solution would be the elimination of free labour. Thus Wakefield commends slavery at length. Large plantation agriculture of the Americas, based on slavery, secures the precious 'proportion' between labour and capital.

The extra productivity more than compensates for the 'dearness'; so 'the labour of slaves, though dear compared with that of free labourers in most countries, is, being combined, much more productive, in proportion to the number of bands employed, than the divided labour of free- men wherever land is very cheap' (Wakefield 1833,1:248). The 'dearness' of slaves is taken to be a matter of benefit to the slave: 'American slaves, or convicts in New South Wales, are fat and happy compared with very many free-born Englishmen' (1833, 1: 59).[13] Published in the same year as *The Slavery Abolition Act*, Wakefield's *England and America* was political economy's ardent advocate of the economic benefits of slavery.

Another species of forced labour is convict labour, and to Wakefield's mind it has much the same benefit as slavery: 'The convict labourers, being forced to work in combination, raise more produce than they consume' (Wakefield 1833, 2: 67). 'Who built Sydney?' Wakefield asked in the *Letter*. 'Convicts [...] By whom is the land made to produce? By convicts' (Wakefield 1829, 75).

Regrettably, convictism was 'now coming to its end'. So what to do? After a throng of circling assertions in the main text, Wakefield gets straight to the point in the *Letter*'s appendix.

Article I: granting of land in Australia is to be abolished, and all land henceforth be sold

Article II: a tax on 'actual' rent be imposed, the revenue used

By these means small settlers are to be inhibited, and emigrants subsidised to work on large (plantation like?) agricultural enterprises.

Both these Wakefieldian policy propositions are based on the merits of 'proportion' and 'combination'. But does he mean by these terms? Wakefield's words afford three alternative interpretations.

'Economies of Synchronisation'

At points Wakefield appears to be referring to what might be called 'economies of synchronisation'; or what Torrens (a Wakefieldian) referred to as the benefit of 'many pairs of hands at the same time in the same place' (Torrens 1835: 21). Wakefield's hunting illustration quoted would appear to refer to this: he seems to be saying [that] two persons hunting for (say) one hour each – in the same time and same place – will catch more than a single person hunting for two hours. But 'economies of synchronisation' may be dismissed as a merely technological observation, comparable to some remark on the power of a lever (to use Mill's example of a merely technological observation): which is to say the phenomenon will be no part of economics, unless, synchronisation is somehow scarce.

'Economies of Intensity'

But perhaps synchronisation is scarce. Perhaps there is only one person available to row freight across the lonely banks of a 'wild' NSW river. The advent of a second person might more than double the mass of goods transported across the river.[14] Thus at low levels of labour input the average product of labour *rises* with the amount of labour per unit of other inputs ('land').[15] The contention can be conveyed by means of visualising a relationship between the average product of labour and labour per unit of land. At low ratios, the relationship is convex (bowed in), and the average product of labour *increases* with the ratio of labour to land. We might refer to this increase as the 'economies of intensity'. Only after the labour/land ratio has reached a certain critical level will the relationship assume an orthodoxly concave (bowed in) shape, and both marginal and average products begin to diminish, in the orthodox way (Coleman 2014).

But economies of intensity seem a feeble reed on which to suspend any imperative for the large (plantation-like) enterprises that Wakefield urged. Every enterprise, no matter how small, is able to reap the economies of intensity simply by not choosing a labour/land ratio lower than the critical ratio; by not operating, in other words, in the concave portion of the average product of labour function. If the supply of labour is insufficient to cultivate the entire supply of land at that critical ratio (or greater), then some land will be left uncultivated. And there is both every private and social incentive to leave land idle in such circumstances, since the marginal product of land worked with a labour/land ratio less than the critical one will be negative (see Coleman 2014). Wakefield's concrete illustrations of 'economies of intensity' may be faulted on such grounds.

> In Van Diemen's Land [= Tasmania], it is common to see one, two or three, thousand sheep all in one flock, the old and the young, the strong and the weak, all mixed together. While feeding, the strongest of a flock, so mixed, always take the van, the weakest always bringing up the rear. Thus a great number of the lambs or weaker sheep are starved to death; and, of course, the profits of the owner of the flock are by so much diminished. Why is this loss incurred? for want of more shepherds; of more labour. (1833, 2: 115)

The response might be 'not for want of labour, but for want of restraint in capitalisation; for the lands are evidently overstocked (i.e. over capitalised); to the point that the marginal product of capital (stock) is negative'. Thus 'losses'.

Economies of Scale

A third possibility is that Wakefield is referring to economies of scale; that is, 20,000 sheep and 20 shepherds yield a higher average productivity than 1,000 sheep and a single shepherd. But the possibility immediately begs the question: is Wakefield referring to scale of the industry, or scale of the firm? Mostly he is clearly referring to the firm.

> Twenty thousand convicts, divided amongst five hundred settlers, would give to each settler forty pair of hands, wherewith to obtain for his wife a superb landau and plenty of gunpowder; but divide the same number of convicts amongst ten times the number of settlers, and poverty, in respect to everything above mere subsistence, must be the lot of all. (Wakefield 1829: 78)

A 'returns to scale' interpretation is still plainer when Wakefield disposes of Ireland as a supposed counterexample to his contention that a lack of labour is stifling. 'In order to observe in the United Kingdom the bad effects of that division of capital and labour [...] one must travel to Ireland, where, in some districts, the separate fractions, of capital and labour are almost as numerous as the cultivators' (Wakefield 1833, 1: 28). The problem with Ireland is that each labourer is a smallholder.

But is hard to see how a desirable scale needs to be fostered by legislative inhibition of small agricultural enterprises. Why is not desirable scale secured by market forces? If such economies of scale are so lucrative, there would be an incentive to avoid the diversification of activities that would be fostered by constant or diminishing returns and instead devote all resources to a single exportable good; capture what scale economies one could, and export the whole, taking maximal advantage of the division of labour in the rest of the world. A 'plantation economy', in other words, where exports equal 100 per cent of GDP. That the ultimate salvation of NSW did, in fact, lie in its becoming a 'wool plantation' has been articulated by economic historians (McCarty 1964).

Whatever the defects in Wakefield's ideas, they nevertheless bore a fruit, wholesome or not, in the 'Ripon Regulations' issued by the Colonial Office in 1831 for Australia. Henceforth the grant of land (no matter how conditional on later improvement) would cease completely. Henceforth all Crown land ('waste land') would be auctioned, subject to a reserve price ('upset price') of 5s an acre; not nearly high enough for Wakefieldians, but better than 2s that the author of the *Letter* had supposedly paid. There has been some debate among historians about to what extent this apparent policy landmark was externally inspired, doctrinally based and rupturing in effect or was instead locally sourced, rooted in expedience, and evolutionary in impact (Phillip 1960). But the distinct tendency of commentators has been to judge the Ripon regulations a 'complete and sudden reversal of established policy', which 'could well have been written in parts by Wakefield himself' (Burroughs 1965: 455, 457). Here is, undoubtedly, and probably for the worse, 'the power of ideas'.

The response of local landowners was hostile. Thus 'Cultor's' own letter of 1831 to the *Sydney Gazette*:

> Returning from a tour into the interior, where I had been looking for a desirable tract of waste land, […] I, as usual, took up the Gazettes which had accumulated on my table. You will better imagine than I can describe the amazement, vexation, and disappointment which rushed through my mind upon reading the new Regulations for the disposal of land […] inquiring into the causes of this unexpected and direful measure, my recollection was awakened to a letter, […] purporting to be written by an inhabitant of Sydney, published in London 1829. In his letter and its appendix, Sir, we find the germ of these ruinous Land Regulations […] this dandy settler sets up for a Solon! and having failed in the management of his own 20,000 acres, sets himself down among the unintellectual people of Sydney to teach them political economy, and to direct their obtuse intellects

To Cultor the great error in Wakefield's scheme is its neglect to encourage capital:

> How is the wilderness to be made productive, unless capital be invested to provide these labourers with employment. On this important, I may say vital, point of the subject, our Sydney correspondent is silent; whilst, at the same time, the Government is recommended to withdraw a considerable portion of the capital from the settlers already established, the outlay of which would otherwise provide employment for those labourers who may arrive in the Colony. […] To see the effects of condensing population, even on a rich soil, without capital to direct, control, and cherish their labour, we need look no farther than Ireland. (Cultor 1831: 3)

Such protests were overridden, and the focus of contention shifted to the prospective settlement of South Australia, which involved Wakefield in some measure, and, more centrally, Robert Torrens. Despite their differences, Torrens was a convert to Wakefieldian vision, expounded its ideas publicity, implemented them in the scheme for settlement.[16]

The plan for the settlement of South Australia was occasion for another encounter of political economy and Australia. The scheme was heavily criticised by two articles in the *Westminster Review* (1834, 1835), partly on account of the natural disadvantages of South Australia, and partly on account of the scheme's Wakefieldian premises. The reviewer puts squarely his objection to discouraging the sale of land, so as to 'concentrate' labour and capital. 'There is nobody who does not see, that if beef and bread are scant, that is the reason why potatoes should be taken for support. In new colonies both capital and labour are scant, and there the facility of land to work on is what nature has given for a compensation' (*Westminster Review* 1834). Torrens declared in response 'The Reviewer has read Ricardo, without being able to understand him'. Torrens repeats this statement four times (1835: xi, 1, 11, 23, 25). 'Those who read Ricardo', announced Torrens, 'without understanding him, are opposed to the principles on which the new colony is formed' (Torrens 1835: 30). Ricardianism seemed to portend a conflict between wages and profits and not the 'win-win' that Wakefieldians intimated would be a consequence of their proposals. In dealing with this apparent inconsistency of Ricardo and Wakefield, 'the Author' says Torrens of himself 'was naturally, and, indeed, necessarily, led into some fundamental questions of political economy' (1835: ix), which were 'new' and 'not unimportant'. Torrens' 'new' result was that Ricardo, properly understood, taught that only money profits and money wages were in necessary antagonism, but real profits and real wages could both be increased by a concatenation of productivity shocks. The possibility of the last Ricardo would hardly have disagreed with the antagonism between profits and wages is a wages fund comparative-static. But Torrens seems not to have thought so and concludes, 'the doctrine of Mr Ricardo is not true, under the actual circumstances of the world' (Torrens 1835: 31). Thus Torrens defends Ricardian doctrine by declaring it is irrelevant to South Australia.

But with the 'new British province' of South Australia's ultimate bankruptcy in 1841, the focus of Wakefieldian controversies shifted again. New Zealand absorbed Wakefield's attention, and NSW returned to the front stage with the appointment of Sir George Gipps as Governor in 1838, and Henry Grey, 3rd Earl Grey, as Secretary of State for War and Colonies. The Governor's resolution to collect 'Quit rents' – or land tax – and Grey's policy of increasing reserve price to 15s were Wakefieldian in flavour. But local critics of such policies now had a heavy gun to turn in the shape of Robert Lowe, best remembered as Gladstone's Chancellor of the Exchequer, 1868–1873, and defender of deductive political economy against inductivist critics, but who on 8 October 1842 arrived in Sydney for what proved to be an eight-year stay. A former fellow of Magdalen at Oxford who 'knew his Ricardo' (Maloney 2005: 43), Lowe may be described as an intellectual in politics, like Mill, or even Ricardo, although his foray in politics went further than these, and his failure much deeper. Like Ricardo he had a clear resolution of what lay within his narrow field of vision; but unlike the dispassionate Ricardo, he was possessed by a vehemence, which spilled over into poetising, including one poem protesting Quit Rents.

Lowe was, he later recalled, not initially hostile to Wakefield's nostrums. 'Fresh from England, I was impregnated with Wakefieldian theory; but as I acquired colonial experience I saw its inapplicability to the colony' (Knight 1968: 22). Presently, however, Lowe dismissed Wakefield as a 'plausible theorist' and 'accomplished land jobber' (Lowe 1844). He used his position as leader writer of Sydney's *Atlas*, 'written for a well-educated audience with literary tastes' (Walker 1976: 38) to blast Wakefield. Thus one of the exercises in versifying in *The Atlas*:

Gibbon Wakefield

In London Lecture-room one day,
A magnetized patient lay
And wondrous things did do and say
All in mesmeric trance;
While Acland, Molesworth and Buller stood,[17]
And many more, in musing mood;
As this phenomenon they view'd
And Science's advance

When all at once, the spell was broke,
And very serious was the joke
It seemed that Death with subtle stroke,
The clair-voyance had ended;
For Wakefield stood behind the chair,
And, with the operator's air
His arm waved in passes there,
In mockery intended

To mock, to thwart to baffle still,
From what is good, to work out ill,
Has Gibbon Wakefield tried his skill,
Since before Newgate knew him,
Abduction there had lodged him fast,
But his deductions that surpassed,
And young Australia's hopes did pass,
When Russel listened to him[18]

> Thus bold assurance works its sway
> Life's cup to still - life's currents sway
> Or darken Science's dawning ray,
> a demon's art employing,
> To lead the gentle maid astray
> To mock young Science's dubious way
> Or with young colonies to play
> Deluding and destroying

A 'hard fierce man, with a great gift for enmity' (Maloney 2006: 403), Lowe's enmity extended to Governor Gipps, as he protested '… the inconceivable inequity of our Government, which has framed out of the specious fallacy of Mr Wakefield, a system which has abused even them to purposes of oppression from which the author shrank' (Lowe 1845a). Lowe put his finger on the means of oppression.

> The air we breathe is, thank God, at present of no exchangeable value at all [...] but place your head in a receiver, and place the hands of the air-pump of in the hands of Sir George Gipps, and that which was valueless will become the most costly of all luxuries. A few turns of the winch, and the patient will give all he had in the world for a single inspiration of that which a minute before he would ridiculed to purchase. So it is with land. (Lowe 1845b)

This is obviously reminiscent of Ricardo's remark very early in the *Principles*, 'nothing is given for the use of air and water, or for any other of the gifts of nature which exist in boundless quantity' (I: 53).

Lowe turned his own analytic winch on Gipps by asserting an equivalence between restriction of land sales and a tax on land sales. 'Lowe described an improbable imaginary conversation between David Ricardo and J.B. Say … to show that land restriction was similar to the imposition of a tax on pastoral operations; the British consumer, he maintained, paid for this folly by an increase in wool prices' (Goodwin 1966: 76). Adding an anti-imperial twist, Lowe declared the revenue from the regulated land sales – which wholly was paid to Whitehall – was simply 'tribute' (*Atlas* 22 March 1845).

Despite the failure of Lowe's own blasts, the influence of Wakefieldian nostrums receded with the decay of 'direct rule' from Westminster. With the attainment of self-government of all of Australia (save WA) in 1856, and the introduction of adult male franchise in NSW from 1859, the law would no longer be designed to foster large land holding. The land acts of 1861 of Premier Sir John Robertson (see Shann 1948; Coleman 2021) were a final and total refutation of Wakefieldian sentiments: their explicit intention was to create an agricultural yeomanry out of pastoral properties, by allowing anyone to 'select', occupy and ultimately own in freehold several hundred acres of any grazier's leasehold. It has been sharply observed that most 'selections' proved to be economic failures, and that the Robertson land acts actually facilitated the mass conversion of pastoral leaseholds into pastoral freehold, as graziers used various legal stratagems to 'select' their own leases (see Shann (1948) for a devastating appraisal). The upshot of this irony of history was that by the 1880s a small class of 'squatters' with secure title faced a numerous group of 'cockies'.[19]

There was evidently a problem shift between 1830s and the 1880s; from development to distribution. And this shift suited the renewed application of Ricardian economics; was not 'To determine the laws which regulate this distribution, … the principal problem in Political Economy'?

The most reverberant policy contention of Ricardo's principles of taxation had been articulated with eloquence by J. S. Mill, in Section 5, Chapter I, Book V of his own *Principles*:

> Suppose that there is a kind of income which constantly tends to increase, without any exertion or sacrifice on the part of the owners: those owners constituting a class in the community, whom the natural course of things progressively enriches, consistently with complete passiveness on their own part. In such a case it would be no violation of the principles on which private property is grounded, if the state should appropriate this increase of wealth, or part of it, as it arises. This would not properly be taking anything from anybody; it would merely be applying an accession of wealth, created by circumstances, to the benefit of society, instead of allowing it to become an unearned appendage to the riches of a particular class. Now, this is actually the case with rent. (Mill 1885: 629)

It remained for someone to take these words and radicalise them; to advocate the taxation not simply of the increase in rent, but all of rent; and not simply to tax rent, but to tax only rent: 'to abolish all taxation save upon land values' (George 2020 [1898]: 240) where the 'value of land' was to be distinguished from 'the value of improvement' (George 2020 [1898]: 252). Thus the doctrine of Henry George in *Progress and Poverty*.

The publication of *Progress and Poverty* was of huge interest in Australia. An electronic search of hundreds of Australian newspapers indicates that *Progress and Poverty* received 2206 mentions between 1880 and 1889. Some sort of benchmark for this number is provided by the number of mentions of a thinker who shared George's market liberalism and hostility to private ownership of land: Herbert Spencer. His *The Man versus the State*, appeared in 1884, but secured just 22 mentions over those ten years.

The author of *Progress and Poverty* also had a definite interest in Australia. Henry George's son records that Australia 'had been a country of peculiar interest to him' (George 1890). As the 'foremast boy' on the *Hindoo* Henry George had visited Melbourne for a month in 1855. George later recalled to his son that Australia 'was looked upon by most of the crew as the Land of Promise, where gold was to be had by all'. A few years later he married the Sydney-born Annie Corsina Fox. These details make it less surprising that in 1889, when a free trade member of the NSW parliament invited him to tour Australia, George readily agreed.

George's Australasian tour commenced in Auckland on 1 March 1890, and concluded in Perth on 15 June 1890. The elite gave him every welcome. In Auckland Sir George Grey, a past prime minister and governor of New Zealand, greeted him. In Sydney George Reid, a future prime minister, took him on a harbour cruise. In Queensland Samuel Griffith, a future Chief Justice of the High Court of Australia, was 'unable to discover any flaws in his arguments' (Griffith 1890). H. B. Higgins, later Justice of the High Court, and of profound influence in Australia's labour market institutions, made a patient, if not very interrogating, examination of *Progress and Poverty*. He was most engaged, and heartened, by George's contention that wage levels did not depend on capital.

George's message of The True Remedy was even more readily taken by the people. The 'Prophet of San Francisco' was warmly, sometimes rapturously, received. George's partisans, his wife claimed, were 'fairly delirious with delight', that his lectures were not stiff as some had anxiously apprehended. In these lectures he was not afraid of bringing out the basic Ricardian foundation of his ideas.

> Let the front rank represent land which produces 20 bushels of wheat, bags of potatoes, or anything else, that is the best from its quality and position. Rank No. 2 produces 19, and is therefore second best, and so on till the last, which is the worst. The labor on each class of land being the same, it is obvious that No. 1 is 5, 10, or 20 times better than inferior laud; or, in other words, a mail could give 5, 10, or 20 pence, shillings, or pounds more in proportion for it, as a stand upon which to employ his labor. Hence rent – economic rent – arises as a necessary condition of things, and is therefore called the law of rent. (George 1890: 2)

Stirred by his successful visit, the various Single Tax Leagues in Australia now made their presence felt in other political organisations. Especially the NSW Labor Party, where Georgites took, 'however briefly, control of the party executive' (Picard 1953: 63), and made a lasting impression on some of its leading personalities, including the future Prime Minister Billy Hughes. The free traders, too, were thick with single taxers. The ambitious B. R. Wise, later temporarily Premier of NSW, sought to harness this energy by launching a Free Trade and Land Reform party, which at one point claimed one fifth of the assembly (Australian Star 1894). But George Reid, the leader of the larger faction of free traders in NSW, stole Wise's clothes, and in 1895, as Premier, passed the *Land Tax Act*, which imposed a tax of one penny in the pound on unimproved value of land. It was not the first tax on unimproved values in Australasia, but it constituted a powerful example.[20] By fiscal year 1899 land tax raised almost 10 per cent of NSW tax revenues: hardly one hundred per cent, but a decent portion.[21]

At the level of the Commonwealth Government, in 1910 Andrew Fisher's Labor government passed the *Land Tax Act*, which imposed a graduated tax on the unimproved value of land, starting at a penny in the pound. Despite the rhetoric of legislators, this tax was soon put into the shade by the advent of income tax during the First World War. Georgist thought did have additional impact in the prohibition of freehold title throughout the new Australian Capital Territory, but this metamorphosed into a legal fiction long ago. A more enduring imprint of the 'Single-Tax moment' in Australia was the NSW *Local Government Act, 1906*, passed by the Liberal Reform government of Premier Joseph Carruthers, who told the press he was 'a warm admirer of Henry George' (George 1890). The act comprehensively established local government throughout NSW, and provided that the revenue of the various municipalities and shires be obtained by their taxation of the 'unimproved value' of land. In NSW the 'rating on the unimproved capital value on land has been the basic means of financing local government in NSW since the Georgist victory of 1906' (Clark 1980: 145).

Conclusion

There was, evidently, transaction between political economy and Australia in the nineteenth century: a two-way transaction. The difficulties of settlement left a mark on the doctrines of some of the inheritors of Ricardo, and the doctrines of some of the inheritors of Ricardo certainly left a mark on the new settlement – for bad and good.[22]

What is striking about the response of doctrine to the encounter with nineteenth-century Australia is how weak it was analytically: Wakefield's attempt to argue that an abundance of land and labour made for a market failure, which demanded legislation to discourage small land holdings, surely had no theoretical legs. But equally noticeable is how inconsequential were the rebuttals of Wakefield; consisting of *ad hominem* attacks, dogmatic assertion or irrelevant digression. There is a sense of lost opportunity to expand the intellectual horizons of classical economics. In analysing the New World, the inheritors of Ricardo were fascinated by Land, and yet found no interest in Space. It is unsurprising that Ricardo treated distance perfunctorily in the *Principles*: the most remote point from the sea in England is, we are told, the village of Coton, just 72 km from the nearest tidal water. The distances between the New England, New Holland, New Zealand and New South Wales were of a different magnitude. The town of Bourke, founded during the heyday of Wakefield's influence, and quickly growing to a great wool centre, is, in ordinary seasons, 1,000 km from the nearest tidal water. But after flourishing transport costs at the beginning of his *Letter*, Wakefield made no attempt to pursue their consequences. George too had little interest in transport costs, and he mentions railways to chastise them for fostering speculative cycles.[23] The huge impact of immigration and population density on the huge reduction in transport costs – with all their distributional consequences – was not something that caught their eye. It is suggestive of the difficulty of the theorist analysing a novel situation to capture the significant feature.

Notes

1 See Roberts (1964: 2).

2 'In new settlements, where the arts and knowledge of countries far advanced in refinement are introduced, it is probable that capital has a tendency to increase faster than mankind: and if the deficiency of labourers were not supplied by more populous countries, this tendency would very much raise the price of labour' (I: 98).

3 See, for example, the quotation from Ricardo among the copious enumeration of 23 'authorities against protective duties' in the *Sydney Morning Herald* (30 May 1843: 2), which also included Adam Smith, Jeremy Bentham, Colonel Torrens, James Mills (sic).

4 There was also a physical propagation beyond the intellectual one: Wakefield, four of his brothers and a son all emigrated to New Zealand. There was less physical propagation of the Ricardo family. Sidney Ricardo (1819–1896), the son of David Ricardo's younger brother, Benjamin, did emigrate in the 1850s to Victoria, where he became a magistrate, a pioneer irrigator, a member of parliament (briefly), and a life governor of the colony's Benevolent Institution. In its issue of 10 April 1891, *The Argus* recorded that 'amongst the applicants of admission [to the Benevolent Institution] was Sidney Ricardo, formerly a wealthy landowner'.

5 A telling survey of the changing history of judgements of Wakefield's psychology and achievement is supplied by Martin (1997: 3–8).

6 'Explaining precisely why McDougall was so successful in the propagation (if not the implementation) of his ideas is a none too easy task. One answer, by no means likely to be the least accurate but by all means most difficult to establish, would

give priority to personal factors - to wit, McDougall's proselytising skills. [...] it would also be less than historically accurate not to note the array of accounts attesting to the remarkable, personal influence McDougall had upon a great many significant figures of the inter-war years' (Turnell 2006: 66). These included Eleanor and Franklin Roosevelt.

7 One (highly hostile) profile of Wakefield describes him as 'friends' with J.S. Mill (Hasluck 1965: 122).

8 Thus in Wakefield's analysis of the Swan River 'The labourers, obtaining land very readily, and running about to fix upon locations for themselves, and to establish themselves independently, very soon separated themselves into isolated families, ... cottiers, ...and very soon fell into very great distress' (Wakefield quoted in Hasluck 1965: 125). It needs not be said that the difficulties at Swan River arose from many circumstances – especially Thomas Peel's selection of woefully unsuitable land for his settlement – and provide no simple verification of Wakefield's principle of concentration.

9 Transport costs also destroy any notion of 'the' wages fund. Even granting the Ricardian premise that the payment of wages constitutes an act of saving; the existence of transport costs will entail that there is no conceptually significant quantity of total saving (i.e. 'the' fund), as saving in different points of space must be distinguished from each other. So logically enough, 'the' wages fund is absent from Wakefield; though the logic of transport costs in destroying 'the' wages fund is not clear.

10 See Ch V 'On Wages'; Ch XVIII 'On Value and Riches, Their Distinctive Properties'; Chapter XIX 'Effects of accumulation on profits and interest'; and Ch XXIX 'Mr Malthus's opinions on rent'. The only substantive contention Ricardo makes regarding the division of labour is to suggest that increased division of labour will increase fertility of all grades the same, leaving rent unchanged.

11 Wakefield declares the '"division of labour" is an improper term as commonly used; and, what is of far greater consequence, that the use of this improper term has kept out of sight the first great improvement in the productive powers of labour, namely, combination of power (Wakefield 1833, 1: 20).

12 Wakefield: 'During forty years we have combined the fire and water of political economy—cheap land and cheap labour. The result is, no doubt, astonishing: but, as that strange union of contradictions is almost at an end' (Wakefield 1829: 78). But not 'fire and water' in Ricardian political economy: there is no simple antagonism between wages and rents in Ricardo; an increase in the wages fund will press down on profits, not rents.

13 'The peasant of the South of England suffers nearly all the evils, but enjoys none of the advantages of slavery' (Wakefield 1833: 1:48).

14 Why not have two people row for half a day, and devote the remaining half day to some other activity? To rebut this might require a reference to travel time between valuable activities.

15 Mill's 'productiveness' and 'efficiency' refer, surely, to the average productivity of labour. George is explicit in 'combination' increasing the average product: 'Soon there comes another immigrant ... And another, and another, until around our first comer there are a score of neighbours. Labour has an effectiveness which in the solitary state it could not approach. If heavy work is to be done, the settlers have a log-rolling, and together accomplish in a day what singly would requires years' (George [2020] 1898: 137).

16 'Torrens disputed a number of Wakefield's theories during the life of the National Colonisation Society… In fact, the Society virtually disbanded in mid-1830 when Torrens and Horton resigned due to disagreements on the Wakefieldian 'concentration' principle. But a year later Torrens rejoined, having been convinced that his own idea on the division of labour was the same as Wakefield's point' (Moore 1980: 75).

17 Sir Thomas Acland: Conservative MP and a figure in the Society for the Promotion of Colonization. Sir William Molesworth: Philosophic Radical MP and enthusiast of Wakefield's ideas. Charles Buller: Philosophic Radical MP and enthusiast of Wakefield's ideas.

18 Lord John Russell, Whig Secretary of State for War and the Colonies.

19 Shann (1948: 208): 'By 1881 ninety-six land-holders [in NSW] had freehold estates covering eight million acres, averaging 84,000 acres each. Such was the agricultural revolution effected by unlocking the land …'. Note: 'Cocky' = 'a farmer, especially one who farms in a small way'.

20 NSW's tax had been preceded in 1883 by South Australia's *Taxation Act* which, amid much airing of *Progress and Poverty* in the local press, imposed a tax of half a penny in the pound on the unimproved value of land. New Zealand's *Land Income Assessment Act* of 1891 amounted to imposing a tax of the same rate on the unimproved value of land and the value of the excess of any improvement over £3000. In 1897 an amendment abolished the taxation of all improvements, large or small in value, in accordance with Georgeite prescription (Le Rossignal and Stewart 1908). Victoria's *Land Tax Act 1890* was a conventional 'wealth tax', which did not exempt from taxation the value of any improvement.

21 Gross revenue from the NSW land tax in the fiscal year ending 30 June 1899 was £271, 000 (Wagga Wagga Express 1900). In SA the revenue from the land tax in the fiscal year ending 23 June 1900 was £71 000 (Narracoorte Herald 1900).

22 A *uniform* minimum price across Australian seems idiotic. In the judgement of one fierce critic, the Wakefieldian minimum price in WA from 1831 'hit Western Australia very hard. Variations in the quality of land there, both by reason of unequal fertility and lack of water necessitated large holdings to make farming and 'sheep walks' pay – … the colonists of Western Australia knew that no one was going to pay vast sums for vast acres … Emigrants came in less and less numbers, and the labour force dwindled … It took Western Australia some fifty years to recover from Wakefield crying his theories' (Hasluck 1965: 128). This critic is following the earlier observation of Shann: 'A price sufficient to put an end to settlement at Australind and in Western Australia generally was so low in South Australia as to invite the speculative purchase … even of good wheat land on the Plains …' (Shann 1948: 233).

23 'It is thus that the rapid extension of railroads is related to the succeeding depression' (George 2020: 277).

References

Australian Star. 1894. 'The Free-Trade and Land Reform Party'. *Australian Star*, 8 August, 6.

Berg, C. 2017. 'Adam Smith and Jeremy Bentham in the Australian Colonies'. *History of Economics Review* 68, no. 1: 2–16.

Blainey, G. 1968. *The Tyranny of Distance: How Distance Shaped Australia's History*. London: History Book Club.

Burroughs, P. 1965. 'Wakefield and the Ripon Land Regulations of 1831'. *Historical Studies: Australia New Zealand* 11, no. 44: 452–66.

Butlin, N. G., J. Ginswick and P. Statham. 1986. 'Colonial Statistics Before 1850'. *Source Papers in Economic History*, Vol. 12, Canberra: Australian National University.

Clark, D. L. 1980. '"Roasting the Landowner Before a Slow Fire": The Origins of Rating on Unimproved Land Values'. In *Twentieth Century Sydney: Studies in Urban and Social History*, edited by Jill Roe Sydney, 134–47. The Sydney: Hale & Iremonger.

Coleman, W. 2014. 'Theorising Optimal Population Between the Wars: The Contribution of Australian Economists'. *History of Economics Review* 59, no.1: 44–61.

Coleman, W. 2021. *Their Fiery Cross of Union: A Retelling of the Creation of the Australian Federation, 1889–1914*. Redland Bay: Connor Court.

Cultor. 1831. 'The New Land Regulations', *Sydney Gazette and New South Wales Advertiser.* 13 September, 3.

George, H. 1890. 'Henry George in New England'. *Glen Innes Examiner and General Advertiser*, 3 June, 2.

George, H. [2020] 1898. *Progress and Poverty*, 4th edition. Delhi: Lector House.

George, H. 2008. *The Life of Henry George*. New York: Doubleday, Doran and Company.

Goodwin, C. D. 1966. *Economic Enquiry in Australia*. Durham: Duke University Press.

Griffith, S. 1890. 'Sir Samuel Griffith on West Australian Land' [Sydney]. *Daily Telegraph*, 3 February, 4.

Henry George, H. 1890. 'Single Taxers and the Revenue Tariffists' [Sydney]. *Daily Telegraph*, 2 January, 7.

Hasluck, A. 1965. *Thomas Peel of Swan River*. Melbourne: Oxford University Press.

Jevons, W. S. 1857. 'Comparison of the Land and Railway Policy of New South Wales'. *Empire*, 8 April, 6.

Knight, R. 1966. *Illiberal Liberal, Robert Lowe in New South Wales, 1842-1850*. Melbourne: Melbourne University Press.

Le Rossignal, J. E. and W. D. Stewart 1908. 'Rating on Unimproved Value in New Zealand', *Journal of Political Economy* 16, no. 1: 13–22.

Lowe, Robert 1844. *The Atlas*, 7 December: 1.

Lowe, Robert 1845a. *The Atlas*, 1 March.

Lowe, Robert 1845b. *The Atlas*, 15 April.

McCarty, J. W. 1964. 'The Staple Approach in Australian Economic History', *Business Archives and History* 4, no 1: 1–22.

Maloney, J. 2005. 'Robert Lowe, The Times, and Political Economy'. *Journal of the History of Economic Thought* 27, no. 1: 41–58.

Maloney, J. 2006. 'Gladstone's Gladstone? The Chancellorship of Robert Lowe, 1868-73', *Historical Research* 79, no. 205: 404–28.

Martin, G. 1997. *Edward Gibbon Wakefield. Abductor and Mystagogue*. Edinburgh: Ann Barry.

Mill, J. S. 1885. *Principles of Political Economy*. New York: D. Appleton and Co.

Moss, D. J. 2004. 'Wakefield, Edward Gibbon, (1796–1862)'. In *Oxford Dictionary of National Biography*, edited by H. C. G. Matthew and Brian Harrison. Oxford: Oxford University Press.

Moore, P. L. 1980. 'Colonel Robert Torrens: Some Bicentennial Observations'. *Journal of the Historical Society of South Australia*, no. 8: 68–83.

Narracootre H. 1900. 'The Revenue', *Narracootre Herald*, 3 July, 4.

Phillip, J. 1960. 'Wakefieldian Influence and New South Wales, 1830-32', *Historical Studies, Australia and New Zealand* 9, no. 34: 173–80.

Picard, F. 1953. 'Henry George and the Labour Split of 1891'. *Historical Studies* 6, no. 21: 452–66.

Pullen, J. 2014. *Nature's Gifts: The Australian Lectures of Henry George on the Ownership of Land & Other Natural Resources*. Annandale: Federation Press.

Roberts, S. H. 1964. *The Squatting Age in Australia, 1835–1847*. Melbourne: Melbourne University Press.

Shann, E. O. G. 1948. *An Economic History of Australia*. Cambridge: Cambridge University Press

Torrens, R. 1835. *Colonization of South Australia*. London: Longman.

Turnell, S. 2000. 'F.L. McDougall, Eminence Grise of Australian Economic Diplomacy'. *Australian Economic History Review* 40, no. 1: 51–70.

Wagga Wagga Express 1900. 'General News', *Wagga Wagga Express*, 14 July, 1.

Wakefield, E. G. 1829, *A Letter from Sydney: The Principal Town of Australasia*. London: Dent.

Wakefield, E. G. 1833. *England and America. A Comparison of the Social and Political State of Both Nations*. London: Richard Bentley.

Walker, R. B. 1976. *The Newspaper Press in New South Wales, 1803-1920*. Sydney: Sydney University Press.

Wentworth, W. C. 1823. *Australasia : A Poem Written for the Chancellor's Medal at the Cambridge Commencement, July 1823*. London: G. and W. B. Whittaker.

Westminster Review. 1834. Review of 'The New British Province of Australia; or a Description of the Country' 21, no. 42: 441-476.

Westminster Review. 1835. Review of 'Colonization of South Australia', *Westminster Review* 23, no. 45: 213–39.

Chapter 9

RICARDO AND CLASSICAL POLITICAL ECONOMY

Alex M. Thomas

1. Introduction

The aims of this essay are twofold: (i) to understand Ricardo's economics in relation to other classical political economists, especially Smith, Sismondi and Malthus and (ii) to provide an alternative conceptual architecture for better understanding contemporary societies. Thus, it serves as a companion in the above two ways. While the locus of discussion is Ricardo's explanation of relative prices and income distribution (value theory), this shall be complemented by a discussion of his approach to economics and his theory of economic growth.

In Ricardo's index to the *Principles*, there are five entries on Malthus,[1] one entry on Sismondi,[2] and over 20 entries on Smith. Ricardo writes approvingly of Malthus for presenting 'to the world … the true doctrine of rent' and of Smith and Sismondi for having improved the 'science' of 'Political Economy' but notes that they have not grasped the principles of rent and therefore that of income distribution (*Works*, I, 5–6).[3]

The essay is organized as follows. Section 2 highlights the role of value theory in Ricardo's political economy and for economics in general. Section 3 provides an overview of Ricardo's method. Section 4 outlines Ricardo's critical engagement with use value and exchange value. Section 5 discusses Ricardo's theory of value and distribution. Section 6 engages with Ricardo's growth theory and the role of demand therein. Section 7 offers a conclusion.

2. The Raison d'etre of Value Theory

Before stating the raison d'etre of value theory, it is necessary to present the aims or 'objects' of political economy as laid out by Smith.

> Political oeconomy, considered as a branch of the science of a statesman or legislator, proposes two distinct objects: first, to provide a plentiful revenue or subsistence for the people, or more properly to enable them to provide such a revenue or subsistence for themselves; and secondly, to supply the state or commonwealth with a revenue sufficient for the public services. It proposes to enrich both the people and the sovereign. (Smith 1776, IV.1).

In short, it may be stated that Smith envisioned political economy as a science which has at its core the enrichment of the people. Therefore, the determinants and growth of wages and profits constitute a central part of political economy. Additionally, this understanding is useful for the purposes of taxation – which enriches the sovereign or government. According to Ricardo, as noted earlier, Smith and Sismondi did not offer a satisfactory theory of distribution, and consequently income distribution 'is the [remaining] principal problem in Political Economy' (*Works*, I, 5).[4] As Aspromourgos (2015, 476–77) rightly argues, Ricardo's statement is best viewed 'as a descriptive statement concerning what, in Ricardo's view, remains, in 1817, the key unsatisfactorily treated part of the science, and hence the principal remaining problem' and not 'as a prescriptive statement concerning what should be the primary purpose of the science'.

Despite devoting most of the chapters in *Principles* to the study of income distribution, we also find a discussion of economic growth which inter alia deals with exhaustible resources, technological progress and social consumption. To study economic growth, Ricardo and other political economists required engaging with the production, distribution and consumption of the social surplus – that portion of the aggregate output which remains once replacement requirements are met. The terms 'gross revenue' and 'net revenue' were used by Ricardo to refer to aggregate output and social surplus, respectively. As Ricardo writes, '[i]f five millions of men could produce as much food and clothing as was necessary for ten millions, food and clothing for five millions would be the net revenue' (*Works*, I, 348). Ricardo's practical questions related to taxation rested on a proper theoretical understanding of the social surplus or 'net revenue' because 'the power of paying taxes, is in proportion to the net, and not in proportion to the gross, revenue' (*Works*, I, 349).

The discussion of the social surplus is found in all the classical political economists, including William Petty and Richard Cantillon. The 'gross revenue' is comprised of wages, profits and rents whereas the 'net revenue' comprises profits and rents (*Works*, I, 347–48). In the *Wealth of Nations*, Smith had included in 'neat revenue' the 'subsistence' of the inhabitants (Smith 1776, II.ii.5) thereby rendering it a non-strictly surplus conception since by definition subsistence implies necessary or essential and surplus implies non-necessary or non-essential (see also Aspromourgos 2009, 163). However, it must be noted that the conception of subsistence in classical political economy is more cultural than biological. Ricardo makes this qualification in the third edition of the *Principles*: 'more is generally allotted to the labourer under the name of wages, than the absolutely necessary expenses of production' (*Works*, I, 348n); this suggests that a part of wages may be treated as 'net revenue'. In any case, Ricardo's definition of 'net revenue' is more conceptually coherent than Smith's (for a succinct discussion on this matter, see Aspromourgos 2015, 473).

Since both the aggregate output and the social surplus are made up of heterogenous commodities, a coherent economic accounting requires the knowledge of their prices. If an economy produces commodities y_1, y_2 and y_3, the aggregate output $Y = p_1 y_1 + p_2 y_2 + p_3 y_3$, where p_1, p_2 and p_3 represent the prices of the three commodities, respectively.[5] Consequently, the determination of prices/values is central for all the classical political economists (and for economists in other schools of thought').[6] In short, the practical question of taxation warrants a clear theoretical understanding of the social surplus, which in turn necessitates a coherent value/price theory (see also King 2013, 80). More generally, it may be stated that 'the analysis of value and distribution' provides 'the foundation for the analysis of accumulation' (Bharadwaj 1989, 2).

3. Ricardo's Method

Ricardo's method of doing political economy can be clearly grasped from the following chapters: 'On Natural and Market Price' (Chapter VII), 'Value and Riches, their Distinctive Properties' (Chapter XX) and 'On Gross and Net Revenue' (Chapter XXVI). Of these, we have already briefly engaged with the third method – the surplus approach – in the previous section.

The 'natural price' captured the persistent factors determining the 'exchangeable value of commodities' whereas the 'market price' also included 'accidental causes' (*Works*, I, 92). In this manner, Ricardo and the other classical political economists did not 'deny the accidental and temporary deviations of the actual or market price of commodities from … their primary and natural price' (*Works*, I, 88). A clear statement of this method of separating persistent and accidental factors goes all the way back to the work of Petty; as Smith also writes, '[t]he actual price at which any commodity is commonly sold is called market price. It may either be above, or below, or exactly the same with its natural price' (Smith 1776, I.vii.7). A similar method is visible in Sismondi's distinction between 'intrinsic' and 'relative' value: 'In political economy one must distinguish at all times, and this observation applies to the entire work of Mr. Ricardo, two types of value, one intrinsic, the other relative; one comes into being by production, the other by competition' (Sismondi 1819, 229). In contrast, Malthus conflates the distinction between permanent and transitory factors when he writes that 'the relation of the supply to the demand, either actual or contingent, is the dominant principle in the determination of prices whether market or natural' (Malthus 1820, 76); in other words, for Malthus, it is the transitory forces of supply and demand which determine *both* market and natural prices.

The methodological distinction Ricardo makes between value and riches allows the determination of prices and quantities to be *studied* separately as opposed to the simultaneous determination visible in marginalist economics;[7] that this is important for Ricardo is also perhaps seen from the fact that this is the second entry under 'Value' in the index, out of a total of more than ten entries, not arranged in any alphabetical order (*Works*, I, 441). One way to interpret this is to view Ricardo's theory of value (and distribution) as being separately determined from his theory of growth (and activity levels).[8] This interpretation does not preclude the possibility of a common factor influencing both value and riches. In fact, Ricardo discusses this precise issue when he writes that activity levels are 'increased by employing a greater portion of revenue in the maintenance of productive labour – which will not only add to the quantity, but to the value of the mass of commodities' (*Works*, I, 278); in this event, both value and riches increase.

'Riches', in Ricardo, have a physical manifestation in 'necessaries, conveniences, and amusements' (*Works*, I, 273). Consequently, an increase in 'riches' increases the use value. However, an increase in 'value' increases the exchange value (more will be said in Section 4). Ricardo argues that '[m]any of the errors in political economy have arisen from errors on this subject, from considering an increase of riches, and an increase of value, as meaning the same thing [...]' (*Works*, I, 274). More precisely, '[i]t is through confounding the ideas of value and wealth, or riches that it has been asserted, that by diminishing the quantity of commodities, that s to say, of the necessaries, conveniences, and enjoyments of human life, riches be increased' (*Works*, I, 276). In particular, Ricardo criticizes Say for 'considering value, riches, and utility to be synonymous' (*Works*, I, 281).[9] It is owing to this analytical separation that the classical/Sraffian theory of value and distribution and Keynes's principle of effective demand have been coherently synthesized (see Garegnani 1978, 340n). As Bharadwaj, writing about the surplus approach of the classical political economists, aptly puts it, 'a "given" level of social output does not connote fixity or stationarity. It underlies the fact that there are more complex historical forces affecting output levels and their composition which are not confined to the scheme of price-formation and hence for the purposes of price-determination, social outputs are taken as provisionally given' (Bharadwaj 1989, 288).

The interpretation of classical economics as a champion of methodological individualism owes to J. S. Mill (for his Ricardian traits, see Bharadwaj 1989, 65–69).

This is of course not to say that Mill is at fault; subsequent commentators perhaps adopted the linear view of intellectual progress and therefore saw the entire corpus of classical political economy through the lens of Mill. Ricardo adopted methodological holism – a fundamentally social standpoint. This is clearly visible in his discussion of income distribution and its central role in Ricardo's entire economics. The first sentence of Ricardo's *Principles* is a testament: 'The produce of the earth [...] is divided among three classes of the community' (*Works*, I, 5).[10] Such a method is visible in Smith too: 'all the commodities which compose the whole annual produce of the labour of every country, taken complexly, must [...] be parcelled out among different inhabitants of the country, either as wages of their labour, the profits of their stock, or the rent of their land' (Smith 1776, I.vi.17).

The identification of social surplus presupposes the categorization of activities into those which produce a surplus and those which do not; this is captured by the classical political economists' division of sectors and labour into 'productive' and 'unproductive'. The prefix 'social' is employed so as to underscore the structural interdependence production and consumption, that is, the 'productive' sectors *require* the 'unproductive' sectors and of course vice versa. As Smith writes, productive labour 'adds to the value of the subject upon which it is bestowed. It tends therefore to increase the exchangeable value of the annual produce of the land and labour of the country' (Smith 1776, II.iii.17). Unproductive labour 'produces nothing which could afterwards purchase or procure an equal quantity of labour' (Smith 1776, II.iii.2). They comprise some of the 'most important' professions: officers of justice, lawyers, physicians, academics (Smith 1776, II.iii.2; for a detailed discussion on the social significance of unproductive labour, see Aspromourgos 2009, 167–68). Ricardo possesses a very similar analytical conception as Smith.

> It must be understood that all the productions of a country are consumed; but it makes the greatest difference imaginable whether they are consumed by those who reproduce, or by those who do not reproduce another value. When we say that revenue is saved, and added to capital, what we mean is, that the portion of revenue, so said to be added to capital, is consumed by productive instead of unproductive labourers. (*Works*, I, 151n)

'The ordinary expenses of the State', writes Ricardo, 'are chiefly devoted to the support of unproductive labourers' (*Works*, I, 244). A similar conception is visible in Sismondi: 'labour, whose fruits are naturally incapable of being stored up for future consumption, is unproductive [...]' (Sismondi 1819, 63). However, Sismondi incorrectly treats all services as being produced by unproductive labour and durable capital goods by productive labour; consequently, durable luxuries occupy an uneasy existence (Sismondi 1819, 63, 95, 123–24). Like the others, Malthus struggles and fails to arrive at a coherent and consistent analytical distinction between productive and unproductive labour (Malthus 1820, 29, 36–39, 41; for a summary account of the various criteria Malthus adopts, see Pullen 2022, 207–9).

Another method of interest found in classical political economy is the socio-historical approach to the conceptualization of 'necessaries, conveniences, and enjoyments of human life' (*Works*, I, 276). For Ricardo, necessaries 'varies at different times in the same country, and very materially differs in different countries. It essentially depends on the habits and customs of people. [...] Many of the conveniences now enjoyed in an English cottage, would have been thought luxuries at an earlier period of our history' (*Works*, I, 96–97). This strongly echoes Smith's conception of necessaries: 'By necessaries I understand, not only the commodities which are indispensably necessary for the support of life, but whatever the custom of the country renders it indecent for creditable people, even of the lowest order, to be without' (Smith 1776, V.ii.k.3). Sismondi also possesses such a customary understanding of wages: 'These serious enjoyments of the spirit, as well as those of a more fleeting nature, such as reading poetry, music, theatre, are exchanged against the income of the poor classes as well as the rich [...]' (Sismondi 1819, 123). And as does Malthus, who allows for luxuries in wages: 'The real wages of labour consist of the necessaries, conveniences, and luxuries of life, which the money wages of the labourer enable him to purchase' (Malthus 1820, 217, '2nd edition'). In all, it may be stated that Ricardo's method of doing economics is erected on a strong social footing (see also Thomas 2021, 309–10, 320; for an overview of the criticism of being-too-abstract levelled at Ricardo by Alfred Marshall, Joseph Schumpeter, and Lionel Robbins, among others, see King 2013, 34–41). This position is in line with Stirati's, which underscores the 'central role of customary, historical and institutional factors in determining the natural wage' in Ricardo (Stirati 1994, 168) and in opposition to the marginalist interpretations advanced most notably by Hicks and Hollander (1977) and Samuelson (1978). Our sociological interpretation of wages in Ricardo also repudiates the wage fund theory very commonly but very mistakenly attributed to classical political economists (for a discussion, see Stirati 1994, 177–79, especially the role played by J. S. Mill (again!)). On one hand, the marginalist interpreters attempt to endogenize wages by positing labour supply and demand schedules (see also Hollander 1979). On the other, the wage fund interpreters render wages asocial. However, in the interpretation offered here, wages in Ricardo are exogenous as well as social.

4. Use Value and Exchange Value

It has already been seen that use value is determined by the volume of 'riches' or the 'necessaries, conveniences, and enjoyments of human life'. Ricardo begins his first chapter, 'On Value', with a proposition about exchange value: 'The value of a commodity, or the quantity of any other commodity for which it will exchange, depends on the relative quantity of labour which is necessary for its production [...]' (*Works*, I, 11). Is there a connection between exchange value and use value? According to Ricardo, utility 'is not the measure of exchangeable value, although it is absolutely essential to it' (*Works*, I, 11); he writes further:

> If a commodity were in no way useful – in other words, if it could in no way contribute to our gratification – it would be destitute of exchangeable value, however scarce it might be, or whatever quantity of labour might be necessary to procure it.

Ricardo's proposition, following Smith, that use values do not determine exchange values is notable because contemporary mainstream economics, built on marginalist foundations, views exchange values as being determined by use values.[11] Furthermore, it must be noted that Ricardo's value theory applies only to those commodities that 'can be increased in quantity by the exertion of human industry, and on the production of which competition operates without restraint'; it is thus not applicable to 'rare statues and pictures, scarce books and coins, wines of a peculiar quality [...]' (*Works*, I, 12).

After quoting Smith – '[i]t is natural that what is usually the produce of two days', or two hours' labour, should be worth double of what is usually the produce of one day's, or one hour's labour' – Ricardo approvingly writes that 'this is really the foundation of the exchangeable value of all things [...] a doctrine of the utmost importance in political economy' (*Works*, I, 13). However, the use of machinery and other fixed capital in production modifies this principle.

> [The] difference in the degree of fixed capital, and [the] [...] variety in the proportions in which the two sorts of capital may be combined, introduce another cause, besides the greater or less quantity of labour necessary to produce commodities, for the variations in their relative value [...]. (*Works*, I, 30)

Therefore, since 'some capital' is always necessary even in Smith's 'early and rude state of society', in general, it may be stated that the exchange value of commodities is determined by the quantity of labour directly *and* indirectly embodied in it (*Works*, I, 22–23; also 26). As a consequence, we cannot unequivocally claim that the exchange value of a commodity will increase if there is an increase in the quantity of labour employed in its production; such a claim can only be made if and only if the capital–labour ratios are uniform across sectors.

Ricardo criticises Smith for measuring exchange value of commodities 'by the quantity of labour for which they will *exchange*' and instead argues that they are determined 'by the *quantity* of labour necessary to their production' (*Works*, I, 15). It is this distinction that gets captured in the phrases 'labour commanded' and 'labour embodied'. Ricardo's point is that the labour commanded varies when the price of necessaries vary and therefore this 'measure of value' of Smith is also very much 'subject to fluctuations' like gold and silver (*Works*, I, 14). Ricardo then agrees with the following conception of Smith found in the *Wealth of Nations*: 'that the proportion between the quantities of labour necessary for acquiring different objects seems to be the only circumstance which can afford any rule for exchanging them for one another' (as cited in *Works*, I, 17). Malthus critically engages with Smith's and Ricardo's labour theory of value in Sections IV and VI of Chapter II titled 'On the nature and measures of value'; in particular, he argues that labour alone cannot be the sole determinant of value across all time and space. But, as Ricardo rightly notes, he has always qualified his claim. He clarifies further: Malthus 'proves then that quantity of labour is not a perfect measure of value; but what are its deviations from a perfect measure on account of the circumstances which he mentions? – if they are slight, as I contend they are, then we are still in possession of a measure tolerably accurate, and in my opinion more nearly approximating to truth, than any that has been yet proposed' (*Works*, II, 66). In the *New Principles*, Sismondi does not engage with value theory; according to Richard Hyse, his English translator, 'Sismondi gave a conventional Smithian exposition of the labor theory [...] [and] he is more interested to take up what he perceives as real economic problems [...] and considers any deeper analysis of value as of limited usefulness' (Sismondi 1819, xliii).

In order to measure value, Ricardo was in the search of a 'commodity which was invariable in its value'; as he had written in the first two editions of the *Principles*, it referred to a commodity 'requiring at all times, and under all circumstances, precisely the same quantity of labour to obtain it' (*Works*, I, 27, 27n; also see Sraffa's discussion at xlviii–xlvix). Moreover, such an invariable commodity measure of value would enable us to identify and separate the causes which 'had operated in producing the alteration of the relative value' of commodities (*Works*, I, 28). Ricardo devotes an entire section in the first chapter (*Works*, I, 43–47), absent in the first two editions of the *Principles*, to a discussion on the 'invariable measure of value'. Although Ricardo was not successful in his search mission, his account of the nature of the problem is relevant for contemporary attempts to fix a numeraire in both theoretical and empirical economics.

Ricardo uses the terms 'exchange value', 'cost of production' and 'natural prices' interchangeably. As Ricardo writes in his chapter 'On the Influence of Demand and Supply on Prices',

> It is the cost of production which must ultimately regulate the price of commodities, and not, as has been often said, the proportion between the supply and demand: the proportion between supply and demand may, indeed, for a time, affect the market value of a commodity, until it is supplied in greater or less abundance, according as the demand may have increased or diminished; but this effect will be only of temporary duration. (*Works*, I, 382)

From our earlier discussion on Ricardo's method, it seems like this criticism is aimed chiefly at Malthus. Owing to the assumption of free mobility of labour and capital, the market prices tend to gravitate towards their natural prices; as Ricardo writes, '[i]it is then the desire, which every capitalist has, of diverting his funds from a less to a more profitable employment, that prevents the market price of commodities from continuing for any length of time either much above, or much below their natural price' (*Works*, I, 91). A similar formulation is already visible in Smith: 'The natural price [...] is, as it were, the central price, to which the prices of all commodities are continually gravitating' (Smith 1776, I.vii.15; also see I.x.a.151). Although Sismondi recognizes the long-run tendency towards the uniformity of profit rates – 'If the profits rise above the mean rate, the producer will extend his enterprises; he will employ new hands and fresh capital, and striving to benefit by his extraordinary profit, he will soon reduce it to the common level' (Sismondi 1819, 255) – he criticises Ricardo for not focusing on the more general case of non-uniform profit rates (Sismondi 1819, 228; see also Arena 1998). Ironically, it is the conceptual clarity provided by Ricardo's uniform profit rates that makes Sismondi's analysis of labour and capital immobilities meaningful by providing it with an analytical benchmark.[12]

Smith's concept of 'effectual demand' – 'the demand of those who are willing to pay the natural price of the commodity' (Smith 1776, I.vii.8) – is also found in Ricardo.

> By natural price I do not mean the usual price, but such a price as is necessary to supply constantly a given demand. The natural price of corn is the price at which it can be supplied affording the usual profits. (*Works*, II, 227)

> No producer can have any interest in supplying his commodity in a greater abundance that it is demanded at its natural price. (*Works*, II, 110)

When the quantity supplied is equal to the 'effectual demand', the market price equals the natural price – the appropriate object of theoretical inquiry. In this Smith–Ricardo conception, an asymmetry between supply and demand, with supply adapting to demand, is visible (Thomas 2021, 306–7). In Sismondi, there is no explicit discussion of 'effectual demand'; such a conception appears to be absent implicitly too. Malthus, surprisingly, breaks away from the other classical economists in his value theory; for him, 'the relation of the supply to the demand, either actual or contingent, is the dominant principle in the determination of prices whether market or natural, and that the cost of production can do nothing but in subordination to it, that is, merely as this cost affects actually or contingently the relation which the supply bears to the demand' (Malthus 1820, 76). It must be the asymmetry between supply and demand in Ricardo (and Smith) is an important characteristic of their theory and must not be viewed as an inferior version of the symmetrical supply and demand schedules in marginalism.

5. Value and Distribution

That is, the questions of distribution and value are interlocked. For instance, rent refers to 'that compensation, which is paid to the owner of the land for the use of its original and indestructible powers' (*Works*, I, 69); and since 'the difficulty of production, raises the exchangeable vale of raw produce, and raises also the proportion of raw produce paid to the landlord for rent, it is obvious that the landlord is doubly benefited by difficulty of production. First he obtains a greater share, and secondly the commodity in which he is paid is of greater value' (*Works*, I, 83). Sraffa informs us that this view of rents is inspired by and borrowed from Malthus and first expounded in Ricardo's *Essay on Profits* (*Works*, IV, 4–6; for a very short history of rent theory prior to Ricardo's, see King 2013, 60–61).

Smith had argued that the natural price of a commodity is constituted independently by wages, rents and profits (Smith 1776, I.vi), or, as Sraffa puts it, 'the price of commodities is arrived at by a process of *adding up* the wages, profit and rent' (*Works*, I, xxxv). But Ricardo disagrees with Smith and advances a different argument: rents do not enter the natural price of corn (the most important wage good) and rents and wages are inversely related.

> the price of corn is regulated by the quantity of labour necessary to produce it, with that portion of capital which pays no rent (*Works*, I, 110)

> in all countries, and all times, profits depend on the quantity of labour requisite to provide necessaries for the labourers, on that land or with that capital which yields no rent. (*Works*, I, 126)

It is by eliminating rents that Ricardo is able to correctly establish the inverse relationship between rate of profit household and real wages (for a clear account, see Aspromourgos 2015, 471–72). Given the methods of production, only a change in the wage rate can affect the rate of profit. Moreover, Ricardo expected the inverse relationship between the rate of profit and to hold in changing technological environments (Kurz 2010). The insightful discovery of the inverse relationship also refuted Smith's claim that the competition of capitals will reduce the rate of profit; as Ricardo writes, 'Adam Smith, however, uniformly ascribes the fall of profits to accumulation of capital, and to the competition which will result from it, without ever adverting to the increasing difficulty of providing food for the additional number of labourers which the additional capital will employ' (*Works*, I, 289). However, Sismondi criticizes Ricardo for finding 'it impossible to explain how the profits of capital and the wage rates often fall at the same time' (Sismondi 1819, 278). And Malthus endorses Smith's idea of the 'competition of capitals': 'The competition of increasing capital in manufactures and commerce would reduce the rate of profits [...]' (Malthus 1820, 304). A coherent analytical foundation for the inverse relationship between the rate of profit and the real wage had to wait till Piero Sraffa's *Production of Commodities by Means of Commodities* (1960).

What determines wages in Ricardo? The 'natural price of labour' in Ricardo, as in Smith, is determined by customary subsistence. Thus, real wages are determined by 'the quantity of food, necessaries, and conveniences [which] become essential to him [the labourer] from habit [...]' (*Works*, I, 93).

> It is not to be understood that the natural price of labour, estimated even in food and necessaries, is absolutely fixed and constant. It varies at different times in the same country, and very materially differs in different countries. It essentially depends on the habits and customs of the people. (*Works*, I, 96–97)

Here too, we sense a strong sociological and historical awareness in Ricardo alongside his oft-discussed formidable logical prowess. Such an exogenous conception of wages is antithetical to that found in marginalist economics where wages are determined endogenously by the marginal product of labour. The exogeneity or historicity is rendered even more explicit in the following excerpt from the *Notes on Malthus*: 'it is not difficult to conceive that with better education and improved habits, a day's labour may become much more valuable estimated even in what are now called the necessaries of the labourer'

(*Works*, II, 115; for an extended discussion of customary subsistence *and* effectual demand in Ricardo, see Thomas 2021, 309–10).[13] The customary, that is, social and historical, foundation of wages is explicit in both Sismondi and Malthus (for an account of classical wage theory, see Stirati 1994, 172–75).

In Ricardo, profits are a residual claim on the social surplus. Moreover, since wages and profits are interlocked together in an inverse relationship, 'every diminution in the wages of labour raises profits, but produces no effect on the price of commodities' (*Works*, I, 133). Therefore, according to Ricardo, '[t]he rate of profits is never increased by a better distribution of labour, by the invention of machinery, by the establishment of roads and canals, or by any means of abridging labour either in the manufacture or in the conveyance of goods' (*Works*, I, 133).

6. Growth and Demand

A holistic understanding of Ricardo's economics warrants an engagement with his theory of economic growth. His account of growth may be rendered conspicuous through our discussion of productive and unproductive labour, Say's law, social consumption, extent of the market, exhaustible resources and technological progress. Of these, Say's law has unarguably received the most scholarly attention.

Following Smith, Ricardo defines productive and unproductive labour as follows (see also *Works*, I, 151n cited above).

> [...] by employing a greater portion of revenue in the maintenance of productive labour – which will not only add to the quantity, but to the value of the mass of commodities [...] a country would not only become rich, but the value of its riches would increase. It would become rich by parsimony; by diminishing its expenditure on objects of luxury and enjoyment; and employing those savings in reproduction. (*Works*, I, 278)

Thus, for both Smith and Ricardo, by devoting more of the social surplus to productive labour, aggregate activity levels can be increased. It was likewise for Sismondi: '[...] the distinction between the two classes is real: one always exchanges its labour against the capital of a nation, the other always exchanges it against a share of the national income' (Sismondi 1819, 124). The former creates capacity, the latter does not. Similarly, Malthus writes that unproductive labour 'replace[s] little or no capital' (Malthus 1820, 39). From the discussions on productive and unproductive labour found in classical political economy, it seems that they were moving towards the latter-day conceptual distinction between capacity-creating and non-capacity-creating expenditure.[14]

Ricardo's endorsement of Say's law is visible here: 'M. Say has [...] most satisfactorily shewn that there is no amount of capital which may not be employed in a country, because demand is only limited by production' (*Works*, I, 290). However, this view needs to be juxtaposed with his assumptions regarding the nature of social demand in the economy.

> The demands for the produce of agriculture are uniform, they are not under the influence of fashion, prejudice, or caprice. To sustain life, food is necessary, and the demand for food must continue in all ages, and in all countries. It is different with manufactures; the demand for any particular manufactured commodity, is subject not only to the wants, but to the tastes and caprice of the purchasers. (*Works*, I, 263)[15]

And when this excerpt is read alongside Ricardo's argument that 'Mr. Malthus's peculiar theory is that supplies many be so abundant, that they might not find a market. [...] *We all like to buy and consume*, the difficulty is in the production' (*Works*, II, 240; emphasis added), it is as if Ricardo is always assuming sufficient social taste for manufactures.[16] A piece of strong evidence for this interpretation is found in this admission by Ricardo: '*If* every man were to forego the use of luxuries, and be intent only on accumulation, a quantity of necessaries might be produced, for which there could not be any immediate consumption' (*Works*, I, 293; emphasis added).[17] Unlike Ricardo's highly muted admission, both Sismondi and Malthus strongly argue that there is no tendency for aggregate consumption to be in line with aggregate production (Sismondi 1819, 11, 306; Malthus 1820, 352–53, 468).

Much like Smith, in Ricardo too, we find a positive association between the 'extent of the market' (Smith's term) and aggregate activity levels, although it is not utilized systematically by Ricardo. According to Ricardo, 'the extension of the market [...] may be [...] efficacious in increasing the mass of commodities' (*Works*, I, 132) and 'by the discovery of new markets, where more advantageous exchanges may be made, a million of men may produce double, or treble the amount of riches, of 'necessaries, conveniences, and amusements,' in one state of society, that they could produce in another [...]' (*Works*, I, 273). These extracts are strongly suggestive of a view that places demand in the more autonomous position and therefore Ricardo cannot be viewed to possess a simplistic understanding of demand in relation to macroeconomic activity levels (for a detailed account, see Thomas 2021).[18]

When aggregate activity levels rise and the population increases, either existing lands are intensively cultivated or the lands under cultivation are extended to less fertile tracts. The rents arising from these two distinct routes are respectively termed intensive rent and extensive rent. But what causes or generates rents in general? According to Ricardo, 'when land is most abundant, when most productive, and most fertile, it yields no rent; and it is only when its powers decay, and less is yielded in return for labour, that a share of the original produce of the more fertile portions is set apart for rent' (*Works*, I, 75). The case of extensive rent is illustrated in the following excerpt.

> It is true, that on the best land, the same produce would still be obtained with the same labour as before, but its value would be enhanced in consequence of the diminished returns obtained by those who employed fresh labour and stock on the less fertile land. (*Works*, I, 74)

As an economy grows, over time, because of 'diminished returns' on land, while wages and rents rise, profits fall. This is because 'the laws which regulate the progress of rent, are widely different from those which regulate the progress of profits, and seldom operate in the same direction' (*Works*, I, 68). Besides highlighting the distributional conflict between landowners and capitalists, Ricardo's account is also telling on the link between exhaustible resources and economic growth (because the rate of profit declines as a consequence of increased rents until the capitalists have no motive left to accumulate). However, it must be noted that in the counteracting presence of technological progress (in the production of necessaries), the tendency of the rate of profit to fall will be delayed (Kurz 2010, 1194–96).

The 'application of machinery to any branch of production', Ricardo had maintained in the first and second editions of the *Principles*, 'was a general good' (*Works*, I, 386). In the third edition, he admitted to having been mistaken and added a new chapter 'On Machinery' where he argued that 'the substitution of machinery for human labour, is often very injurious to the interests of the class of labourers' (*Works*, I, 388). At the same time, 'the invention of machinery', 'improvements in skill' and 'a better division of labour' positively influence 'riches' or aggregate activity levels (*Works*, I, 273).[19] For Ricardo, as he writes in the index, '[a] *qualified* use of machinery [is] vindicated' (*Works*, I, 436).

7. Conclusion

Ricardo's economic ideas can be largely seen as a product of his agreements and disagreements with other classical political economists, most notably Smith and Malthus. However, this does not imply that Ricardo's political economy is *omnis facies* superior to that of Smith; such a naïve view of intellectual progress must be resisted. And partly because of this reason, the scholarship engendered by Sraffa's phenomenal editorship of Ricardo's works and correspondence cannot be reduced to a 'neo-Ricardian' label because of the various rich insights found in other classical political economists such as Smith, Sismondi and Malthus, which are absent in Ricardo. After all, Ricardo's primary aim was to provide a sound theory of income distribution.

In stark contrast to marginalist economics, Ricardo's integrated approach to value, distribution and growth offers an alternative conceptual architecture. It rejects the subjective utility theory of value, making schedules of supply and demand, and the functional relationship between wages and employment; instead, Ricardo espouses an objective labour theory of value, highlights social aspects of demand and treats wages an exogenous social variable. Ricardo's adoption, like other classical political economists, of methodological holism along with exogenous wages especially highlights the sociological footing of his economic theory, which has long been submerged.

Notes

1 In addition to this, Ricardo made extensive notes on Malthus's *Principles of Political Economy* which is published as the second volume of *Works*. Their friendship is well documented; for details of their visits to each other and their correspondence, see the various index entries under 'Malthus, friendship with Ricardo' in *Works*, XI, 54.

2 There is evidence of Ricardo meeting Sismondi twice: once in the House of Lords, introduced by Sir James Mackintosh, in April 1819 (*Works*, VIII, 22) and the second in Coppet, near Geneva, when Sismondi had gone to visit the Duke de Broglie (whom Ricardo was also visiting), in the latter half of 1822 (*Works*, IX, 242). The latter meeting is also mentioned by Hyse (Sismondi 1819, 297, n. 4).

3 While Say's work is also appreciated by Ricardo (*Works*, I, 6–7), I include him within classical political economy since he advances a subjective theory of value; this choice is also consistent with Karl Marx's list of classical political economists.

4 Book 1 of Smith's *Wealth of Nations* is titled 'Of the Causes of Improvement in the productive Powers of Labour, and of the Order according to which its Produce is naturally distributed among the different Ranks of the People'. The second phrase is about income distribution.

5 Bharadwaj clearly articulates this point in her discussion on Smith: '[...] Smith's concern was to explain how surplus originates and is accumulated in the 'commercial economy'. [...] Smith needed to develop an analytically satisfactory measure of surplus which constituted heterogeneous commodities. This brings Smith to the question of the determination of the exchange value of commodities, primarily as an upshot of the complex problem of measuring the real produce' (Bharadwaj 1989, 23). This larger point is absent in Sinha's exposition of Ricardo's value theory (Sinha 2018, 72–78); Sinha identifies only the immediate, as it were, point: 'the problem of value had to be studied before the question of distribution could be dealt with' (Sinha 2018, 107).

6 Subsequently, the rate of profit is equal to the net product minus wages as a proportion of the capital advanced. If the net product, wages and capital advanced are measured in corn, then, as Sraffa puts it, no 'question of valuation' is necessary (*Works*, I, xxxi). Although Ricardo never makes such an assumption explicit, Sraffa thinks that this is the 'rational foundation of the principle of the determining role of the profits of agriculture' (*Works*, I, xxxi) found in Ricardo's letters of 1814 and the *Essay on*

the Influence of a Low Price of Corn on the Profits of Stock of 1815. Or, the net product, wages and capital advanced could be reducible to homogeneous labour via the labour theory of value – as is the case in Ricardo's *Principles*; in this route however, the question of valuation is central (see Section 4).

7 Garegnani arrives at the '*separate* determination of real wage and social product' by focusing on the surplus approach visible in the classical political economists (Garegnani 1984, 296).

8 Such a distinction is also found in Ricardo's separation of the motive to produce from that of the motive to accumulate. While the latter is provided by the rate of profit, the former is given by social demand. However, if Ricardo had probed the interaction of social demand on the rate of profit, the analytical separation he made would have been more insightful (for a discussion, see Thomas 2018, 62–63).

9 While exchange values allow for comparison, use values do not: 'One set of necessaries and conveniences admits of no comparison with another set; value in use cannot be measured by any known standard; it is differently estimated by different persons' (*Works*, I, 429).

10 Surprisingly, and unconvincingly, Peach claims that Ricardo is not 'a *social* surplus theorist' and denies 'that the principal distribution analysis was conducted in terms of social aggregates' (Peach 1993, 290, 291).

11 Peach marshals ample textual evidence from Ricardo to refute the marginalist interpretations by Marshall and Hollander (Peach 1993, 241–49).

12 Peach rightly identifies the long-period standpoint when he writes that 'Ricardo's habitual inclination [was to] minimise the significance of 'frictions' [...]' (Peach 1993, 137).

13 Although Peach (1993, 104) recognizes the role of habits, he does not give it any analytical import in Ricardo's economics.

14 Pullen does not see such an analytical undercurrent in Malthus; according to Pullen, Malthus 'believed that the two sectors – material goods and personal services – could feed off one another, and become mutually supportive, and that policies could be designed whereby both sectors would flourish' (Pullen 2022, 221). This is a very literal interpretation of the distinction between productive and unproductive labour in Malthus. Aspromourgos, in his reading of Smith, comes close to the interpretation advanced here when he writes that productive labour 'is labour employed with capital goods (labour consumption goods and other inputs), to produce further capital goods' (Aspromourgos 2009, 170).

15 This characterizing is analytically speaking a close paraphrasing of Smith: 'The desire of food is limited in every man by the narrow capacity of the human stomach; but the desire of the conveniencies and ornaments of building, dress, equipage, and houshold furniture, seems to have no limit or certain boundary' (Smith 1776, I.xi.c.7).

16 For Ricardo, both the 'ability' and 'will' to consume are important (Thomas 2018, 64–65, 69). The assumption of sufficient social taste for manufactures ensures that the 'will' is always present. Indeed, as Pullen (2022, 29) points out in his book on Malthus, what ensures an 'adequate will to purchase'?

17 Underlying this admission is Ricardo's general assumption that the 'demands for the produce of agriculture are uniform [...] [and] not under the influence of fashion, prejudice, or caprice' whereas 'the demand for any particular manufactured commodity, is subject not only to the wants, but to the tastes and caprice of the purchasers' (*Works*, I, 263). Given the preceding discussion on demand, Pasinetti exaggerates

when he writes that Ricardo 'did not possess a demand theory' (Pasinetti 1960, 85). Although Peach (1993, 255–56) disagrees with this specific claim of Pasinetti (and Hollander's marginalist reading of demand into Ricardo), he does not pay attention to the sociological dimension of demand in Ricardo.

18 However, King does not identify any important analytical role for demand in Ricardo; as he writes, 'output is always supply-constrained, not demand-constrained' (King 2013, 117). Taking a different approach, Davis (2005) eschews theoretical explanations and advances empirical reasons (for instance, inadequate capital vis-à-vis population in Britain) for Ricardo's propositions on accumulation and growth (for a detailed critical discussion of Davis's interpretation, see King 2013, 114–19).

19 According to Sinha, this discussion 'cannot be taken as an argument for accommodating unemployment of labour in his theoretical system' (Sinha 2018, 88). However, the machinery argument does lend additional support to the view that capacity is not fully utilized in Ricardo (see also the brief discussion in Thomas 2018, 68). Moreover, insofar as additional machinery *continues* to be employed in a growing economy, it does suggest persistent labour unemployment in Ricardo's theoretical system.

References

Arena, R. 1998. Sismondi, Jean Charles Léonard Simonde de. *The Elgar Companion to Classical Economics, L–K*, edited by H. D. Kurz and N. Salvadori. Cheltenham: Edward Elgar.

Aspromourgos, T. 2009. *The Science of Wealth: Adam Smith and the Framing of Political Economy*. London: Routledge.

———. 2015. Ricardo on Adam Smith. *The Elgar Companion to David Ricardo*, edited by H. Kurz, D. and Salvadori, N. Cheltenham: Edward Elgar.

Bharadwaj, K. 1989. *Themes in Value and Distribution: Classical Theory Reappraised*. London: Routledge.

Davis, T. 2005. *Ricardo's Macroeconomics: Money, Trade Cycles, and Growth*. Cambridge: Cambridge University Press.

Garegnani, P. 1978. 'Notes on Consumption, Investment and Effective Demand: I'. *Cambridge Journal of Economics*, 2, pp. 335–53.

———. 1984. 'Value and Distribution in the Classical Economists and Marx'. *Oxford Economic Papers* 36, no. 2: 291–325.

Hicks, J. and Hollander, S. 1977. 'Mr. Ricardo and the Moderns'. *Quarterly Journal of Economics* 91: pp. 351–69.

Hollander, S. 1979. *The Economics of David Ricardo*. Toronto: University of Toronto Press.

King, J. E. 2013. *David Ricardo*. Hampshire: Palgrave Macmillan.

Kurz, H. D. 2010. 'Technical Progress, Capital Accumulation and Income Distribution in Classical Economics: Adam Smith, David Ricardo and Karl Marx'. *European Journal of the History of Economic Thought* 15, no. 5: 1183–222.

Malthus, T. R. 1820 [1989]. *Principles of Political Economy*, Variorum edition, 2 vols., J. Pullen (ed), Cambridge: Cambridge University Press.

Pasinetti, L. L. 1960. 'A Mathematical Formulation of the Ricardian System'. *The Review of Economic Studies* 27, 2: 78–98.

Peach, T. 1993. *Interpreting Ricardo*. Cambridge: Cambridge University Press.

Pullen, J. 2021. *The Macroeconomics of Malthus*. London: Routledge.

Samuelson, P. 1978. 'The Canonical Classical Model of Political Economy'. *Journal of Economic Literature* 16, no. 4: 1415–34.

Smith, A. 1776 [1976]. *An Inquiry into the Nature and Causes of the Wealth of Nations*, R. H. Campbell, A. S. Skinner & W. B. Todd (eds), *Glasgow Edition of the Works and Correspondence of Adam Smith*, 2 vols., Oxford: Clarendon.

Sinha, A. 2018. *Theories of Value from Adam Smith to Piero Sraffa*. Second edition (1st edition 2010). New Delhi: Routledge.

Sismondi, J.-C.-L Simonde de. 1819 [1991]. *New Principles of Political Economy: Of Wealth in Its Relation to Population*, transl. & annotated by R. Hyse, with a foreword by R. L. Heilbroner, London: Transaction Publishers.

Sraffa, P. 1960. *Production of Commodities by Means of Commodities*. Cambridge: Cambridge University Press.

Stirati, A. 1994. *The Theory of Wages in Classical Economics: A Study of Adam Smith, David Ricardo and their Contemporaries*, translated by Joan Hall. Aldershot: Edward Elgar.

Thomas, A. M. 2018. 'A Note on the Role of Aggregate Demand in Ricardo'. *History of Economics Review* 70, no. 1: 11–29.

———. 2021. 'On 'Effectual Demand' and the 'Extent of the Market' in Adam Smith and David Ricardo'. *European Journal of the History of Economic Thought* 28, no. 3: 305–23.

Chapter 10

RICARDO AND MARX

Michael C. Howard

1. The Place of Ricardo's Economics in Marx's Theory

Marx had great respect for Ricardo, both regarding his analytic abilities and his intellectual integrity, and Ricardo's influence on Marx's economics was greater than that of any other individual economist. Nonetheless, it is also the case that Marx was severely critical of Ricardo's propositions on value and on growth, as well as those pertaining to the coordination of economic activities under capitalist relations of production and exchange.[1] Moreover, the most impressive parts of Marx's economics lay in areas untouched by Ricardo, and all of Ricardo's economics were interpreted within Marx's own conceptual framework, which was very different from that of Ricardo's own classical liberalism.[2] This conceptual framework is explained in Section 2, and Marx's treatment of Ricardo's economics is elucidated in Section 3. Section 4 follows with an outline of those parts of Marx's economics which owed no debt to Ricardo and which were analytically much stronger than those which did. They are thus relevant for the overall assessment of both Marx and Ricardo as economists. Finally, in Section 5, the claims that it is possible to resurrect a so-called classical-Marxian approach to economic theorization based on the work of Piero Sraffa is assessed as it clearly relates to understanding the intellectual relationship of Ricardo and Marx (Sraffa 1960).

2. The Principal Influences in the Formation of Marxism

Marx's thought has often been described as combining German philosophy, French socialism and British political economy (see, e.g., Lenin 1913). The latter included the work of Ricardo, but the first two intellectual influences had the more profound effects, and these significantly affected Marx's evaluation of British political economy, including Ricardo's ideas. They determined how Marx interpreted Ricardo's economics and how he transformed some of Ricardo's propositions to suit his own purposes. Moreover, they help explain why Marx's most important contributions to economic theory occurred independently of the influence of Ricardo as they follow from Marx's historical perspective and his analysis of the mechanisms of change that are indebted to the first two influences on his thought. By contrast, Ricardo saw all of history as more or less imperfectly capitalist[3] and the other British economists that Marx studied were either similarly ahistorical or, like Adam Smith, anticipated strands of the historical materialism Marx developed from his understanding of German philosophy (see Meek 1977).

The German philosopher that had the greatest influence on Marx was Hegel, who presented world history as a sequence of stages in the understanding of human freedom and the actual attainment of that freedom. The former was deemed completed in Hegel's own philosophy and the institutional embodiment of freedom was claimed to reside in the post-Napoleonic Prussian state of the early nineteenth century. Furthermore, the historical process of understanding freedom and realising it were presented by Hegel as changing dialectically, and with the dual culmination regarded as the 'end of history'. This termination was interpreted to mean the elimination in consciousness as well as in reality of any rational basis for political conflicts, and not the cessation of happenings or the completion of all knowledge. For Hegel there were no longer any bases for contradictions in philosophy or of antagonisms in the sociopolitical order, as the full flowering of individual needs was understood and the capacity for their realization within the state had been achieved.

Hegel is typically and correctly classified as a philosophic idealist who concentrated upon the role of consciousness in human history. This does not imply that he denied the existence of any dimension of reality, including the reality of human relationships, independent of consciousness. Instead, as a post-Kantian, he stressed the active role of consciousness in shaping reality, albeit in a different way from Kant himself because Hegel sought to explain historical changes rather than the invariant ways that mind structured the understanding of reality. Thus, unlike Kant, he emphasised that the role of mind in shaping reality changed through time. Consciousness improved historically in a dialectical manner because of the contradictions it embodied. This in turn brought about changing structures of social reality. The process continued until all contradictions were finally eliminated in consciousness and all political conflict could wither away in reality. Thus, Hegel is an idealist only in the sense that he regarded consciousness as the primary active transformative force in historical change, not in the sense of denying a material reality independent of consciousness.

Marx was not alone in finding the historical panorama presented by Hegel as hugely impressive whilst also regarding his conclusions as deeply suspect. The so-called Young Hegelians all rejected the claim that the constitutional monarchy in Prussia and its supportive institutions, including the Church, were the end of history in the sense explained above.[4] However, Marx's critical position was especially radical in two respects.

First, it was uncompromisingly materialist and rejected Hegel's emphasis on the casual importance of consciousness in the process of historical change relative to actual events, structures of social relationships and the productive forces. Indeed, these were treated as the active elements in the historical process and consciousness was deemed to be derivative. Thus, there was a reversal of Hegel's causal directionality within the dialectical perspective he had employed. Marx himself once expressed this by saying that he found Hegel standing on his head and had to turn him right side up. His materialism was therefore a materialized Hegelianism. As such, Marx was also critical of the Young Hegelians either because they remained idealist or because the materialism which they adopted lacked historicity and reasoned in terms of a humanity abstracted from changing historical circumstances.

Second, under the influence of French socialists,[5] Marx adopted an uncompromising hostility to the economic, social and political conditions prevailing throughout Europe. The 'end of history', in the sense of attaining genuine freedom and the elimination of political conflicts, Marx argued, would occur only after proletarian revolution and the attainment of communism. Nonetheless, he criticized the most prominent French socialists in a similar manner to that of the Young Hegelians. He claimed that they too misunderstood the possibilities of change because they were insufficiently historical and, again, often thought in terms of an abstract humanity devoid of historical variation.

This perspective of Marx was fully formed by the mid-1840s, at the same time as his systematic study of British political economy began.[6] Thus, when Marx began a serious study of Ricardo's work, his interpretive principles were already established. These principles later became known as historical materialism, and the most succinct summary of the central propositions were provided by Marx himself some years later as follows:

> The general conclusion at which I arrived and [...] became the guiding principle of my studies can be summarized as follows. In the social production of their existence men inevitably enter into definite relations, which are independent of their will, namely relations of production appropriate to a given stage in the development of their material forces of production. The totality of these relations constitutes the economic structure of society, the real foundation,

> on which arises a legal and political superstructure and to which correspond definite forms of social consciousness. The mode of production of material life conditions the general process of social, political and intellectual life. It is not the consciousness of men that determines their existence, but their social existence that determines their consciousness. At a certain stage of development, the material productive forces of society come into conflict with the existing relations of production or – this merely expresses the same thing in legal terms – with the property relations within the framework of which they have operated hitherto. From forms of development of the productive forces these relations turn into their fetters. Then begins the era of social revolution. The changes in the economic foundation lead [...] to the transformation of the immense superstructure. In studying such transformations it is always necessary to distinguish between the material transformation of the economic conditions of production [...] and the legal, political, religious, artistic or philosophic – in short, ideological forms in which men become conscious of this conflict and fight it out. Just as one does not judge an individual by what he thinks about himself, so one cannot judge such a period of transformation by its consciousness, but, on the contrary, this consciousness must be explained from the contradictions of material life, from the conflict existing between the social forces of production and the relations of production. No social order is ever destroyed before all the productive forces for which it is sufficient have been developed, and new superior relations of production never replace older ones before the material conditions of their existence have matured within the framework of the old society. [...] In broad outline, the Asiatic, ancient, feudal, and modern bourgeois modes of production may be designated as epochs marking progress in the economic development of society. The bourgeois mode of production is the last antagonistic form of the social process of production – antagonistic not in the sense of individual antagonism but of an antagonism that emanates from the individuals' social conditions of existence [...]'. (Marx 1859: 20–22)

The influence of Hegelian philosophy and socialist theory is very evident here, and the sway of Ricardo's economics on Marx's thought occurs within the confines of this perspective. Dominant, then, were intellectual influences that played no part in Ricardo's own world view and of which he was likely wholly ignorant. As Ferdinand Lasalle once said of Marx's economics, one finds 'Ricardo become socialist; Hegel become an economist' (Sperber 2013: 388). Thus, Ricardo's labour theory of value is transformed into a theory of exploitation in which all property income is derived from the labour of the proletariat, and Ricardo's theory of the declining profit rate was reformulated as exhibiting a contradiction of capitalism. So, together, they provided an economic basis for proletarian radicalisation and evidence that capitalism was experiencing an impediment to its continual functioning, conclusions that most certainly would have horrified Ricardo and which he would likely have rejected.

However, Marx is employing the same procedure regarding Ricardo's work as he did with that of Hegel and the French socialists. He accepts the chief conclusions of all three but changes the mechanisms through which the conclusions are the result. This is a recognition by Marx of the respect he had for Ricardo, along with Hegel and the early socialists. From his perspective, they all exhibited an intellectuality of the highest quality but, nonetheless, could not properly understand the causal nature and historic significance of what they accomplished because the dialectical process remained incomplete. It thus awaited a further elimination of contradictions, both intellectually and in reality. Marx saw his own work as completing the process intellectually, and through this facilitating the completion in reality.

3. Marx's Treatment of Ricardo's Economics

Marx accepted the logic of Ricardo's reasoning in his treatment of value and profit.[7] But he rejected entirely Ricardo's commitment to the population principle of Malthus as an explanation for subsistence wages. And this was coupled to questioning Ricardo's pessimism as to the capacity of technical change to overcome the limits nature placed upon economic growth through diminishing returns in agriculture. Both wages and profits were instead explained by Marx in terms of the regularities resulting from capitalist social relations, not those of nature. In other words, and as indicated above, Marx accepted Ricardo's conclusions as to subsistence wages and the declining profit rate but changed the causal mechanisms in accordance with his perspective of historical materialism. This allowed him to interpret them as contributing to the radicalisation of the proletariat and the incapacity of capitalist social relations to sustain economic growth.[8]

Marx thus followed Ricardo in locating the origin of value in labour but gave the matter far greater significance by turning it into an exploitation theory in which all property income – profit, rent and interest – derived from the labour of the working class.[9] He also sought to improve Ricardo's value theory by tackling the problem Ricardo recognised concerning different capital–labour ratios in the production of different commodities leading to his labour theory of value not being strictly correct as prices deviated somewhat from labour values.[10] Marx did so by arguing that the labour theory of value held exactly only at the economy wide level. In other words, the aggregate magnitude of produced commodities came to the same total whether measured in labour values or in prices. Analogously, Marx claimed that the same held for total profits; they were invariant to measurement in values or prices.[11]

This was a conceptually clever move on the part of Marx as it appears to preserve the labour theory of value and the exploitation theory fully intact at the macro level while seemingly recognising their limits in explaining individual prices. It also fits very well with Marx's treatment of class and revolution in the context of his theory of historical materialism. Both the remuneration of workers and of capitalists are clearly shown to depend on the operation of the whole economic system, not just their sectoral locations within it. However, as is now well known, both Ricardo's labour theory of value and Marx's modifications incorporate major deficiencies.

First, there are difficulties in converting various kinds of labour into a common value measure. Second, there are further problems in dealing with non-competitive markets and the use of non-reproducible inputs in production processes. Third, there are multiple problems in dealing with services. Furthermore, even abstracting from all these difficulties, in general it will not be true that aggregate output measured in values will be equal to aggregate output measured in prices. And, likewise, property income measured in values will deviate from the same property income measured in prices. Moreover, if there are alternative processes of production so that a commodity can be produced in more than one way, and commodities are jointly produced in the same production process, value magnitudes may be undefined, zero or negative, while prices and profits are positive. This indicates that there are extremely serious deficiencies in the work of Ricardo and in that of Marx when he followed in the tracks laid down by him.[12]

Regarding the theory of the subsistence wage and the falling rate of profit that Ricardo explained in terms of the Malthusian population principle and diminishing returns in agriculture respectively, Marx followed the same procedure as he did in value theory. He agreed with the results but changed the mechanisms of causation from those of nature to those of historical materialism. He claimed that wages would not rise above subsistence because technical progress created a "reserve army of unemployed".[13] The rate of profit would also fall simultaneously, Marx argued, because the increase in profits resulting from more productive technologies would not be sufficient to compensate for the greater capital required by them. However, these arguments are flawed. While it is possible for technical progress to create a reserve army of unemployed, including one that expands over time, the empirical evidence shows no such increase as a proportion of the labour force over the very long run.[14] As for Marx's argument concerning a declining rate of profit, it is not possible for the rate of profit to fall because of technical progress unless the cost of non-capital inputs, namely labour and land, rise.[15] Thus, on these matters, Ricardo had the better logical arguments.[16]

The one component of Ricardo's economics that Marx did accept unconditionally was the support provided for free trade internationally. Not only did he agree with Ricardo that this would promote efficiency and therefore the development of capitalism, but he also believed it would enhance international solidarity of working classes. It would thereby contribute to promoting proletarian revolution.[17]

4. Marx's Economics beyond Ricardo

Marx's economics proved to be far more robust where the influence of Ricardo was non-existent or at its weakest. And much of what he produced here constitutes explicit or implicit critiques of Ricardo's own economics. This is the case regarding the overall theoretical framework of historical materialism summarised in Section 2, and particularly with regard to elaborating on the role of collective action and violence in bringing about economic change. Marx's analyses of the coordination problems that could be experienced in capitalism, including those arising from effective demand failures, are also acute. Thus, while Marx followed Ricardo quite closely in his analysis of value and distribution, as we have seen above, he moved outside the domain inhabited by Ricardo in examining methods of coordinating economic activity and coordination failures that extended way beyond markets and values. In the same vein, Marx recognized the progressive elimination of market relations in capitalist development, a trend evident since the 1870s and not reversed until a century later. This was in accord with historical materialism as changing technologies were held by Marx to be the chief cause of variation in the extent of marketized relations.

Historical materialism, of course, has been in receipt of an avalanche of criticisms alleging conceptual muddles in the theory and failures to explain relevant empirical events that the theory claims to fall into its domain (see, e.g., Plamenatz 1963). However, the vast bulk of both types of criticism have been shown to be misplaced, confused, irrelevant or wrong. And these defences of the theory have been joined together in making a persuasive case in favour of the theory's empirical relevance.[18] These include explaining the factors involved in the formation of solidarities that underpin collective action groups. The atomistic agents of Ricardo's economics, as well as those of neoclassical economics, do not typically inhabit most areas of economic life or figure prominently in historical changes and Marx's analysis helps explain why.[19]

Marx also clarifies why social, economic and political changes may not occur in pacified ways even if rationality prevails comprehensively and the deadweight costs of using force is also generally recognised. Differences in the interests between groups may well lack a basis for tradeoffs and compromises, particularly in circumstances involving indivisibilities and uncertainties, and also where agreements are neither self-enforcing nor secured by an external agency. The use of force therefore has an opening and, of course, has been endemic in historical change (see Howard and King (2001) and Howard and Kumar (2007)). Marx himself illuminated this in his analysis of the 'primitive accumulation' whereby capitalist relations of production emerged in Europe, as well as the subsequent imperialist conquests by capitalist powers (see Marx (1867), part viii, and Marx (1847–1882)). This is generally passed over in silence in Ricardo's economics as well as that of neoclassicals.

In addition, Marx went way beyond Ricardo's analytic perspective in specifying the conditions that must hold for the different sectors of an economy to be integrated even under fully pacified conditions and without any systemic change occurring. The 'reproduction models' outlined in Volume II of *Capital* show the conditions of coordination that must be met if the output of each sector is to be exactly sufficient to provide the inputs into other sectors as well as precisely satisfy consumption needs (see Howard and King (1985: chapter 11)). This is accomplished in abstraction from market relations and the price mechanism and thus applies to all types of economic systems. Consequently, they illuminate those matters involved in central planning and, indeed, inspired the techniques used in the Soviet Union that underpinned its exceptionally rapid growth from the late 1920s to the 1980s (Ofer 1987). And, under the influence of these techniques, the more sophisticated input–output analysis of Leontief emerged (see Nove (1972) and Nove and Nuti (1972)).

Of course, Marx recognised that in capitalist systems it is market prices that provide the main coordination mechanism And, here again, his treatment was acute, and very different from Ricardo's general orientation to the operation of markets as being unproblematic. Most particularly, Marx focusses on failures of effective demand that make no appearance in Ricardo's work. And, indeed, Marx's analysis of these demand deficiencies is brilliantly insightful and superior to everything prior to Keynes *General Theory* (Keynes 1936). For example, he writes, 'In all crises the following circular movement relates to the workers: the employer cannot employ the workers because he cannot sell his product. He cannot sell his product because he has no buyers. He has no buyers because the workers have nothing to offer in exchange but their labour, and precisely for that reason they cannot exchange their labour' (Marx (1847), p. 424; Marx (1862–3, Part II: 507–7)). Compare this with the following statement by Joseph Stiglitz, written in 1994. 'One of the central themes in recent macroeconomic work has traced economic slumps to "coordination failures". To put the matter baldly, there are no jobs because there is no demand for the output of firms, and there is no demand for the output of firms because people do not have jobs' Stiglitz (1994: 22). Both Marx and Stiglitz are pointing to the key aspect of the microeconomics that lies behind Keynesian effective demand deficiencies; namely, the mutually reinforcing quantity constraints applying to the demands and supplies of workers and capitalists. Neoclassical demands and supplies, by contrast, do not involve quantities different from those economic agents are *willing* to supply at the prevailing set of prices. These demands and supplies are merely notional and not necessarily effective.

Furthermore, effective demand failures have been a force constraining and eliminating market relations in capitalism, so modifying its structure as well as its performance. However, Marx also argued that there was a tendency for this to occur for other reasons that have also proved to be correct (see Howard and King (2008)). He was followed by an array of eminent non-Marxian economists, but there appears to have had no precursor. Most particularly, Ricardo is silent on the matter. However, from the 1970s and the emergence of a new general-purpose technology founded on the computer, the market-eliminating trend went into reversal. The new technologies have promoted market-type relations within corporations, as well as market relations between them, and with consumers. There is a powerful force of technological determinism operating here on both the decline of markets and their expansion in the later twentieth century. Marx appears to be the first major social theorist to begin understanding it. Of course, this was no accident as it is concordant with his theory of historical materialism (see Section 2).

None of the insights and analysis considered in this section figure at all in Ricardo's economics. This is not to claim that he was a minor pre-Marxian, but it does show that the characterization of Marx by Paul Samuelson as a 'minor post Ricardian' is absurd. It is true that in those areas where Marx did follow Ricardo, his economics was weak. However, when he departed the Ricardian tracks, the quality of his analysis vastly improved.

5. Sraffa and the Revival of the Classical-Marxian Approach to Economic Analysis

The arguments in the preceding section do not derive from the specific conceptual framework of Ricardian and Marxian analysis dealt with in Section 3 and are therefore not subject to the deficiencies encountered there. The most serious of these limitations were revealed in the application of the framework of analysis of Piero Sraffa's *Production of Commodities by Means of Commodities.*[20] However, this has also been claimed to provide the theoretical basis for a revival of a Ricardian-Marxian approach to economic analysis that avoids the weaknesses exposed in Section 3.[21] This makes sense in that Sraffa's conceptual framework has a similarity with those of Ricardo and Marx in abstracting from agent maximisations and the resulting concepts of supply and demand as relevant for understanding the properties of equilibria and, instead, focusses on the equalisation of wage rates, profit rates and input and output prices of each produced commodity. There is, however, no commitment to any labour theory of value from which many of the limitations of both Ricardo and Marx derive. Furthermore, the claim of seeking to revive a Ricardian-Marxian approach to economic theorisation derives cogency from the fact that Sraffa's framework has been used to launch a devastating attack on the neoclassical tradition founded on concepts of supply and demand. Most certainly, various versions of neoclassical theory lie in ruins because of Sraffa's work, which revealed logical mistakes in their formulation or the need for highly restrictive assumptions to ensure their validity.

This includes the aggregate production function tradition stemming from J. B. Clark (see Harcourt (1972) and the Austrian approach emanating from Bohm-Bawerk (see Howard (1980). Furthermore, the accomplishment of Sraffa here is buttressed when his earlier critique of the partial equilibrium method of Alfred Marshall is recognised (Sraffa 1926). Creating such wreckage is a phenomenal achievement and one without equal in the history of economic thought. As such, it suggests an alternative standard by which the relationship of Ricardo and Marx can be assessed. Instead of focussing on particular results, if the work of Sraffa is conceived as a recharged version of the paradigm common to Ricardo and Marx, their differences as explained above can be marginalised. Then the conclusion as to the relative merits of each and the absence of a positive influence on Marx by Ricardo is devalued. Ricardo and Marx can appear instead as comrades in arms in a joint project to replace the development of a supply and demand tradition that can be traced back to at least Adam Smith,[22] and Ricardo is the economist that put Marx on the right path.

However, such a verdict cannot stand for several reasons. First, Sraffa's work does not yield a complete destruction of neoclassical theory. Neither the temporary general equilibrium analysis initially developed by J. R. Hicks (1946) nor the intertemporal general equilibrium theory of Arrow-Debreu (Debreu (1959) and Arrow and Hahn (1971)) is affected by Sraffa's results. Moreover, the attempt to use Sraffa's work as a basis for reconstituting a Ricardian-Marxian approach to economic theorising [23] has proved to be a dead end (see Howard 1987). One reason for this is quite simple. All of Sraffa's models, just like those of Ricardo and Marx, assume a stationary price vector in equilibria, so that the input price of any commodity is the same as the output price. While there is no logical problem with this, the assumption is not general; it is instead a special case applicable only to very particular conditions such as steady state growth paths.[24]

It is true that some theorists claiming that Sraffa's work lays the foundation for a rejuvenation of the Ricardo-Marxian approach to economic analysis continue to believe a stationary price vector must characterize all genuine equilibria, but the case they make is exceedingly weak and there can be no reconstitution that is at all general based on Sraffa's own work (see Howard (1983: 142–43,149–53) and Howard (1987)). In addition, the full spectrum of economic forces from which the equilibria of Sraffa are supposed to emerge have never been elaborated. In particular, the matters determining the outputs of the economic systems and those determining the product requirements for the outputs involved have never been specified. This does not imply introducing neoclassical formulations of demands and supplies. They could be formulated instead in Keynesian terms as well as pay respect to the full spectrum of Weberian differentiations of class, status and power, also including those of the deplorables and the devout. However, the absences do mean that Sraffa's economics as it presently stands can only be used for critical purposes, not as the foundation of an alternative modality of analysis that is at all general.

Consequently, Sraffa's *Production of Commodities by Means of Commodities* has no impact on the conclusion of this chapter. Marx's achievements in political economy were made very largely independent of Ricardo's work, and Ricardo's influence on Marx proved not to be a productive one. The most important contributions of Marx to economic theory occur where the influence of Ricardo was non-existent or marginal. Of course, it is possible that Marx himself along with his followers may have taken a different view, but that can only be because they failed to recognise the limitations of Ricardo's thought and thus unwittingly emulated them.

Notes

1 In particular, Marx was critical of Ricardo's acceptance of Say's Law, and this criticism was part and parcel of Marx's anticipation of the main proposition of Keynesian economics. See Section 4.
2 See King (2013) for an analysis of Ricardo's politics, including his liberalism.
3 See King (2013: 157–59, 162–63, 175).
4 The Young Hegelians were also known as Left Hegelians, as distinct from the orthodox Right Hegelians. See McClellan (1980) and Barer (2000).
5 The most important of these were Charles Fourier, Pierre Joseph Proudhon, and Henri de Saint-Simon.
6 See Oakley (1983: 8,17, 34–36), as well as Sperber (2013: 119.
7 Marx erred here, failing to recognize that if diminishing returns operated such that the rate of profit fell asymptotically to a level equal to or greater than the minimally necessary rate to sustain positive accumulation, the stationary state need never be encountered.

8 Of course, Ricardo did recognize forms of class conflict, but the focus was on the different interests of capitalists and landlords. Only in the addition of 'On Machinery' in the third edition of the *Principles* was a basis for conflict between workers and capitalists recognized, and Ricardo did not elaborate on its political significance.

9 Ricardo adopted the labour theory of value as a means of generalizing his theory, which he had initially constructed in terms of the one sector corn model. He appears to have had no philosophic, sociological, or political reason for choosing labour as the basis of value. Marx, of course, did.

10 Stating the matter in this way, where numeric magnitudes are compared rather than ratios, makes sense only if units of labour value and of prices are measured in the same numeraire. Also, Marx like Ricardo conducts analysis in what are now often called competitive equilibria, involving equal wages for the same type of labour, equal rates of profit for all capitalists, and where prices are the same for any individual commodity whether it be an input or an output. In Section 5, reasons are given as to why the equality of input and output prices of commodities is an inappropriate condition in defining equilibria.

11 This can be expressed as follows. $\sum l_i e = \sum k_i r$ and $\sum q_i v_i = \sum q_i p_i$, where l_i represents the input of labour in industry $_i$, e is the rate of exploitation, r is the rate of profit and k_i is the capital in industry $_i$ measured in prices. Likewise, q_i is the output of commodity $_i$ and v_i is the value of commodity i and p_i is its price.

12 See Howard (1983) and Howard and King (1985) and Howard and King (2018: 324–25). It is possible to salvage Marx's exploitation theory, which arguably is the most important part of his economics when judged from the perspective of historical materialism. However, the theory has to be formulated independently of the Ricardian value categories employed by Marx himself. See Screpani (2001: 258) and Wright (2015: 84–87).

13 This was most certainly influenced by the chapter 'On Machinery' added by Ricardo to the third edition of his *Principles.* It also had some empirical support for much of the nineteenth century in Britain; see Allen (2017).

14 However, recently developed technologies may well change matters and Marx's claim of an increasing reserve army of the unemployed could become a reality. See, for example, Baldwin (2016) and (2019).

15 See Howard and King (1985: 200–207).

16 This is true also for the explanation of rent. Given his assumptions, the analysis of Ricardo was sound. The same cannot be said for Marx as his analysis was dependent on the labour theory of value. See Howard and King (1985: 104–7) and Samuelson (1992).

17 However, Marx's analysis of international trade extended beyond Ricardo's theory of comparative advantage. See King (2013: 96–106).

18 The outstanding works here are those of Cohen (1988), (2000) and Torrance (1995). See also Aston and Philpin (1985).

19 See Howard and King (2001). An attempt to incorporate collective action groups into neoclassical theory can be found in Olson (1965) and (1982).

20 Sraffa (1960). See Howard (1981) and Steedman (1977).

21 See Dobb (1973), Howard (1987) Meek (1977) and Kurz (2016). Sometimes the approach is simply described as "Classical", or as the "Surplus tradition", or as "Neo-Ricardian".

22 See Dobb (1973) and Meek (1967) and (1977). Other economists typically placed in this tradition include Vladimir Dmitriev, Ladislaus von Bortkiewicz and John von Neumann. See Kurz (2016).

23 Evidence for the claim that Sraffa intended his work to be interpreted in this way comes from Sraffa (1960) itself, and is buttressed by the fact that Sraffa spent several decades editing the collected works of Ricardo and was a close friend of Antonio Gramsci, the most innovative of Italian Marxist theorists.

24 Sraffian equilibria reflect those of Ricardo and Marx in this respect and, as a consequence, the critique of Sraffa (1960) on this matter apply to them too.

References

Allen, R. C. (2017). *The Industrial Revolution.* Oxford: Oxford University Press.

Arrow, K. J. and Hahn, F. H. (1971). *General Competitive Analysis.* Edinburgh: Oliver and Boyd.

Aston, T. H. and Philpin, C. H. E. (eds). 1985. *The Brenner Debate: Agrarian Class Structure and Economic Development in Pre-Industrial Europe.* Cambridge: Cambridge University Press.

Baldwin, R. 2016. *The Great Convergence: Information Technology and the New Globalization.* Cambridge: Harvard University Press.

Baldwin, R. 2019. *The Globotics Upheaval: Globalization, Robotics, and the Future of Work.* London: Weidenfeld and Nicolson.

Barer, S. 2000. *The Doctors of Revolution.* London: Thames and Hudson.

Brox, J. A. and Koveos, P. 2007. *Globalization, Governance and Public Policy.* Waterloo: North Waterloo Academic Press.

Cohen, G. A. 1988. *History, Labour, and Freedom.* Oxford: Clarendon Press.

Cohen, G. A. 2000. *Karl Marx's Theory of History: A Defence.* Princeton: Princeton University Press.

Debreu, G. 1959. *Theory of Value.* New Haven, Yale University Press.

Dobb, M. H. 1973. *Theories of Value and Distribution since Adam Smith.* Cambridge: Cambridge University Press.

Harcourt, G. C. 1972. *Some Cambridge Controversies in the Theory of Capital.* Cambridge: Cambridge University Press.

Hicks, J. R. 1946. *Value and Capital.* Oxford: Oxford University Press.

Howard, M. C. 1980. 'Austrian Capital Theory: An Evaluation in terms of Piero Sraffa's *Production of Commodities by Means of Commodities.*' *Metroeconomica* 32, no. 1: 1–23.

Howard, M. C. 1981. 'Ricardo's Analysis of Profit: An Evaluation in Terms of Piero Sraffa's *Production of Commodities by Means of Commodities.*'. *Metroeconomica* 33, nos. 1–3: 105–28.

Howard, M. C. 1983. *Profits in Economic Theory.* London: MacMillan.

Howard, M. C. 1987. 'Economics on a Sraffian Foundation: A Critical Analysis of Neo-Ricardian Theory'. *Economy and Society* 16, no. 3: 317–40.

Howard, M. C and King, J. E. 1985. *The Political Economy of Marx.* Harlow: Longmans.

Howard, M. C. and King, J. E. 1992. 'Marx, Jones. Rodbertus and the Theory of Absolute Rent'. *Journal of the History of Economic Thought* 14 (Spring): 70–83.

Howard, M. C. and King, J. E. 2001. 'Where Marx Was Right: Towards a More Secure Foundation for Heterodox Economics'. *Cambridge Journal of Economics* 25, no. 6, pp 785–807.

Howard, M. C. and King, J. E. 2008. *The Rise of Neoliberalism in Advanced Capitalist Economies: A Materialist Analysis*. Basingstoke: Palgrave Macmillan.

Howard, M. C. and King, J. E. 2018. 'Marx@200', *Review of Political Economy*, 30, no. 3: 31–38.

Howard, M. C. and Kumar, R. 2007. 'The Rationality of Violent Conflict'. In *Brox and Koveos*, pp. 3–20.

Keynes, J. M. 1936. *The General Theory of Employment, Interest and Money*. London: Macmillan.

King, J. E. 2013. *David Ricardo*. Basingstoke: Palgrave Macmillan.

Kurz, H. D. 2016. *Economic Thought: A Brief History*. New York: Columbia University Press.

Lenin, V. I. 1913. 'The Three Sources and Three Component Parts of Marxism', in Lenin 1977, pp. 21–28.

Lenin, V. I. 1977. *Collected Works, Volume 19*. Moscow: Progress Publishers.

Marx, K. 1847. 'Wages'. In Marx and Engels, 1976. pp. 415–37.

Marx, K. 1847–1882. *Karl Marx on Colonialism & Modernization*. Edited by S Avineri. New York: Anchor Books, 1969.

Marx, K. 1859. *Critique of Political Economy*. London: Lawrence and Wishart, 1973.

Marx, K. 1862–1863. *Theories of Surplus Value: Parts I – III*. London: Lawrence and Wishart, 1971–2.

Marx, K. 1867. *Capital: Volume I*. London: Lawrence and Wishart, 1970.

Marx, K. and Engels, F. E. 1976 *Collected Works, Volume 6*. New York: International Publishers.

McLellan, D. 1980. *The Young Hegelians and Karl Marx*. London: Macmillan.

Meek, R. L. 1967. *Economics and Ideology and Other Essays*. London: Chapman and Hall.

Meek, R. L. 1977. *Smith, Marx and After*. London: Chapman and Hall.

Nove, A. 1972. *An Economic History of the USSR*. Harmondsworth: Penguin.

Nove, A. and Nuti, D. M. (eds). 1972. *Socialist Economics*. Harmondsworth: Penguin.

Oakley, A. 1983. *The Making of Marx's Critical Theory: A Bibliographical Analysis*. London: Routledge and Kegan Paul.

Ofer, G. 1987. 'Soviet Economic Growth, 1928–85.' *Journal of Economic Literature* 25, no. 4: 1767–1833.

Olsen, M. 1965. *The Logic of Collective Action*. Cambridge: Harvard University Press.

Olsen, M. 1982. *The Rise and Decline of Nations*. New Haven: Yale University Press.

Plamenatz, J. P. 1963. *Man & Society, Volume II*. Harlow: Longman.

Samuelson, P. A. 1992. "Marx on Rent: A Failure to Transform Properly." *Journal of the History of Economic Thought* 14, no. 2: 143–67.

Screpani, E. 2001. *The Fundamental Institutions of Capitalism*. London: Routledge.

Sperber, J. 2013. *Karl Marx: A Nineteenth Century Life*. New York: Liveright Publishing Corporation.

Sraffa, P. 1926. "The Laws of Returns under Competitive Conditions". *Economic Journal* 36, no. 144: 535–50.

Sraffa, P. 1960. *Production of Commodities by Means of Commodities: Prelude to a Critique of Economic Theory*. Cambridge: Cambridge University Press.

Steedman, I. 1977. *Marx after Sraffa*. London: New Left Books.

Stiglitz, J. 1994. *Whither Socialism*. Cambridge: Harvard University Press.

Torrance, J. 1995. *Karl Marx's Theory of Ideas*. Cambridge: Cambridge University Press.

Wright, E. O. 2015. *Understanding Class*. London: Verso.

Chapter 11

MALTHUS AND RICARDO ON THE DISMAL SCIENCE

Bryan S. Turner

1. Introduction: From Political Economy to Sociology

There is general agreement that Thomas Malthus (1766–1834) and David Ricardo (1772–1823) are founders of political economy (Roll 1973: 173). Their status depends to a large extent on two, but profoundly influential, publications: *An Essay on Population* in 1798 and *Principles of Political Economy and Taxation* in 1817. Nevertheless, they produced a voluminous collection of publications. Pietro Sraffa's edition of Ricardo ran to eleven volumes. Malthus is also recognised in his own right as a founding figure of political economy, but his development of social science has in the past often been overshadowed by moral criticism that is blind to his real scientific contributions. In this chapter, I promote the idea that Malthus and Ricardo were also founders of sociology without whom there would be, for example, no Marxist sociology of social class. When Ricardo introduced the growth of manufacturing into the third edition of *Principles*, then wages cannot rise and the conflict between capitalists and landlords over rent evaporated to be replaced by a conflict between capitalists and workers as machines replaced labour (Davis 1993). Thus, the foundation of Marx's class theory was already well developed in classical political economy. Sociology in the case of Max Weber's generation emerged out of economics conceived as a 'science of man' that examined the 'conditions of existence' of people. Thus, sociology was already embedded in the Historical School of German 'political economy' (Hennis 1988: 105–45). German economists rejected Adam Smith's 'cosmopolitanism' in which nations freely traded with each other to their mutual benefit. For Weber, economics was a political science based on national struggle for domination. Weber was only too aware of issues around population growth and immigration from a national perspective (Tribe 1989). Prussian Junkers were hiring Polish workers to lower their costs of production, thereby displacing the German population. In his 1895 Inaugural

Address to the University of Freiberg, he criticised the policies that resulted in the displacement of German by Polish workers in the East Elbian provinces of Prussia with disastrous effects on German character and culture. Weber concluded: 'As usual, a large number of children follows hard on the heels of a low standard of living, since this tends to obliterate any calculation of future welfare. Economic advance (*wirtschaftliche Kultur*), a relatively high standard of living and Germanism are in West Prussia identical' (Weber 1989: 190). Malthus had the relationship in reverse: a low standard of living follows hard on the heels of a large number of children.

The context in which the first edition of *Population* was published in 1798 and in which Ricardo was developing his analysis of policies towards the Corn Laws is important for understanding their political reception. There was pervasive unrest among the working class relating both to economic problems, but also in relation to revolutionary movements and domestic chaos in France. There was also a fear regarding a possible military invasion from continental Europe. The French Revolution opened with the Estates General in 1789 and concluded with the French Consulate in 1799.The American War from 1763 to 1774 ended with the ratification of the independence of thirteen North American States. The decade leading up to the publication of *Population* was one of the most tumultuous periods in European history. Edmund Burke published his *Reflections on the Revolution in France* in 1790. While Burke offered an articulate conservative critique of the French Revolution based on his objections to the abstract notions of 'the rights of man', it was Malthus's *Population* that was embraced by the Whig opposition to political radicalism. The English elite came to associate radicalism with any 'levelling' of property, wealth and entitlement (McNally 2000). In this context, Malthus departed from the 'Ricardo School' by rejecting Jean-Baptiste Say's Law – production creates its own demand by generating wealth, employment and demand. For Malthus, the key to economic and political stability was to be found in population control where production could not keep up with fertility.

My position in this chapter contradicts the view of Joseph Schumpeter, who argued that the weakness of the classical period of economics was that it failed to produce any sociological understanding. The main problem according to Schumpeter was that economists saw society as simply a collection of separate individuals competing for advantage (Schumpeter 1954: 97). While this is a common criticism, philosophers of social science may equally claim that there is no alternative to methodological individualism. This accusation against Malthus is in any case incorrect, given his attention to the impact of social institutions such as the Poor Laws on the behaviour of individuals. He was only too aware of the role of institutions – law, parliament and land ownership – in conditioning economic activity. In the *History of Economic Analysis* (1987),

Schumpeter was equally critical of Ricardo. Inventing the notion of a 'Ricardian Vice', he complained that Ricardo's ideas did not address the complexity of actual social and economic activity and that his policy prescriptions were also based on assumptions that were not grounded in actual reality. The existence of such a 'vice' has been disputed (Viner 1954). However, all forms of sociological analysis involve the creation of models in order to simplify empirical complexity. The analytical power of Ricardo's three-class model of the social structure is precisely its simplicity. Why does this debate about Ricardo and Malthus and the early origins of sociology matter? There are at least three reasons as to why it matters. Firstly, recent historical research on Malthus has resulted in a re-evaluation of the importance and relevance of Malthus to contemporary social science, especially sociology and political theory. Malthus's stature as both a political economist and sociologist has grown in scholarship since the 1990s. Secondly, sociology and demography have become separate and specialised disciplines much to the disadvantage of sociology. The same problem confronts anthropology which also it is claimed neglects demography. 'Demography is basically concerned with changes over time in the structure of the population. Most anthropological studies have tended to be static cross-sections of a particular society at the point at which it was visited by the field-worker. Perhaps because of this, investigators have shown only a slight interest in demography' (MacFarlane 2018). Despite the great developments in modern demography, their research results have had little impact on how sociologists understand the history of modern societies. A re-evaluation of Malthus can only underline the importance of demography for both sociology and anthropology. The final reason is that it underscores the argument that the distinctions between economic and sociology are artificial. The history of the theory of money shows how sociology and economics were and are inevitably interwoven (Ingham 2004).

Much of the criticism of Malthus, and to a lesser extent Ricardo, was ethical rather than political. Malthus was in his time heavily criticised insofar as he stood outside the optimistic notion of progress in the Enlightenment. Turning to Schumpeter (1954: 472–73) once more, he condemned both Malthus and Ricardo for their pessimism in the face of significant economic progress in their lifetimes. Ricardo's version of the 'iron law of wages' was that, with population growth, wages would be just high enough to keep the worker from starvation. In *Population*, first published anonymously in 1798, Malthus proposed a simple formula that, while population multiplies exponentially, food supplies increase only arithmetically. The disconnect between the two processes resulted in a population disaster which would be eventually corrected in terms of famine or disease, by warfare and infanticide. This argument is in an if/then form. Given limitations on arable land, if population growth is not contained, then there will be starvation and disease. While Malthus offered simple solutions to the dilemma including late marriage and contraception, his analysis of the population issue changed over time with each new edition of *Population.*

2. Political Economy versus Enlightenment Optimism

Malthus's theory of population ran counter to the Enlightenment views of his generation such as the Marquis de Condorcet. In his *Sketch for a Historical Picture of the Progress of the Human Spirit* (1795), Condorcet argued that there was clear evidence of human progress and material affluence on the basis of advances in natural and social sciences. Humanity had moved from savagery to civilization. Enlightenment optimists about progress also included Jean-Jacques Rousseau, who was in turn connected to the intellectual circle around Daniel Malthus, father of Thomas Malthus. The Enlightenment philosophers such as Rousseau and Voltaire saw the Lisbon Earthquake and tsunami of 1755 as the end of any theodicy justifying God's relationship to humankind. Human reason rather than faith would drive societies on a progressive trajectory. Malthus and Ricardo saw the economic limitations to the prospect of endless progress. For the Enlightenment, the most troubling aspect of Malthus's essay for his times was his interpretation of poverty. While a generation of utopians imagined a bright and better future, Malthus proposed a much bleaker picture. Some poverty, he argued, was inevitable. As population increased when times were good, so the poorest would perish when times were bad. Disease and famine served as natural checks to overpopulation. With these uncompromising views, Malthus became the man we love to hate.

Malthus took orders in the Church of England and, following a period at Jesus College, Cambridge, he became a curate who corresponded widely. He began to publish pamphlets on topical issues in the crisis-ridden last decade of the eighteenth century. Malthus, as an Anglican priest in the Church of England, found himself outside the growing agnosticism of his enlightened generation. With a different background, Ricardo was by origin a Dutch Sephardic Jew who married the daughter of a Quaker and became an advocate of religious liberty (Henderson 1981). There is a long dispute as to whether Thomas Carlyle had Ricardo and Malthus in mind when in 1849 he called economics a 'dismal science'. Given his views on sexuality, population growth, the limitations on arable land and the food supply, Malthus concluded 'I see no way by which man can escape from the weight of this law which pervades all animated nature. No fancied equality, no agrarian revolutions in their utmost extent, could remove the pressure of it even for century' (Malthus 1798: 4). A similar theme occupied Chapter 4 ('The Gloomy Presentiments of Parson Malthus and David Ricardo') of Robert Heilbroner's *The Worldly*

Philosophers (1953). Although frequently described as 'parson Malthus', he was in fact a professor of political economy at the East India Company College. This position put him directly in touch with Britain's expanding imperial world, and for several generations he educated young men for service as company clerks in India (Tribe 1995).

Malthus's views on the sexual behaviour of the poor and the idea of a 'Malthusian catastrophe' – overpopulation, declining food supply, epidemics, plagues, famine and civil unrest – were roundly condemned by Charles Dickens, Percy Shelly, Samuel Taylor Coleridge, Willian Godwin, William Hazlitt and not least by Karl Marx who, on the basis of the first edition of *Population*, called Malthus the 'reverend scribbler' and the 'true priest' of the ruling class. The relationship between Marxism and Malthusianism is in fact more complicated. The principal criticism of Malthus was that, while his population theory might be valid in the natural world, it ignored the historical process of capitalist development. Engels and Marx accepted the fact that overpopulation crises existed among plants and animals, but not in social reality (Wiltgen 1998). While Malthus's critics condemned what they saw as a heartless attitude towards the poor, he was also critical of the rich, who had large families, and the poor suffered disproportionately. The elite had a moral obligation to have fewer children.

Ricardo also had to take a view of population in relation to economic activity. He included a discussion of population in Chapter 5 'On Wages' in the *Principles*; here he takes note of the influence of the supply of labour relative to the supply of capital and natural resources. Over the long run, wages converge towards their 'natural price' which is determined by the food supply, and other necessities required by the working class. When wages rise above the subsistence level, the worker is happy and content, but population growth depresses the wage level back to its 'natural price'. The inevitable privation of the worker brings about population decline and over time the wage level climbs back to a subsistence level. The economic principle is thus relatively simple: when labour is scarce, it is expensive; when labour is abundant, it is cheap. Improvements in agriculture and the discovery of new markets through colonial expansion may temporarily counter the rise in the price of necessities. The natural price of commodities will tend to fall with improvements in machinery, advances in science and improvements in the division of labour. With this argument as the background, Ricardo's theory of population is, following Malthus, pessimistic. When the market price of labour falls below its natural price, then the condition of the working class 'is most wretched: then poverty deprives them of those comforts which custom renders absolute necessities' (Ricardo 1988: 341). It is only with a decline in population through deprivation, that the circumstances of the worker can improve.

Auguste Comte (1798–1837) is often seen to be the founding sociologist, in part because he invented the term 'sociology' and also because he had a theory of social change resulting in industrial society which he developed in the six volume *Course in Positive Philosophy*. Society would pass through three stages: theological, metaphysical and positivism. Although he was critical of the age of the Enlightenment as a destructive period, Comte was impressed by the idea of modern 'development'. He noted that the idea of 'progress' was not widespread in social science, but notions of 'social evolution' and 'development' were synonymous with 'progress'. While Comte is often regarded as inventing sociology, a stronger case can be made for Malthus and Ricardo as the founders. Marx's theory of class is basically the analysis of the three classes – profit, rent and wages – that was first developed by Ricardo, despite the absence of satisfactory information on rent, profit and wages. Ricardo argued that the whole produce of society is divided among three classes of society and determining the laws by which that division takes place is the aim of political economy. Marx offered a more dynamic theory of social classes, claiming that, through social and political struggles, the two major classes of capitalism were workers and capitalists by which other classes – peasants and petty-bourgeoise – were undermined.

By the beginning of the nineteenth century, industrial machinery was already threatening the livelihood of the working class. The outcome was a classic conflict between capitalists and workers. The introduction of machinery into traditional production processes undermined the economic role of the worker. In 1811, power-driven mechanical frames for the manufacture of stockings were introduced into capitalist enterprises in Hucknall Torkard Nottinghamshire. The workers responded by breaking into local factories and destroying the frames. After the imaginary character Ned Ludd, they called themselves 'Luddites'. Ricardo had initially opposed the destructive actions of the Luddites, but in the third edition of *Principles of Political Economy* (1817) he recognised that the 'substitution of machines for human labour' was clearly 'injurious' to the working class. Luddite violence was not therefore based simply on error but was consistent with political economy. In response, a Bill was introduced into Parliament to make such behaviour a capital offence. In the parliamentary debate in 1812, Lord Byron, whose ancestral home was in Hucknall, spoke in his maiden speech to the House of Lords against the Frame Breaking Act. Nevertheless, many Luddites were hanged or deported to Australia. What is now known as the 'Luddite fallacy' claims that new technology does not result in overall unemployment. Rather than simply destroying jobs it simply changes the composition of jobs. In fact there is no settled economic view of the accuracy of the fallacy as technological innovations now include the use of robots (Ford 2016).

Despite the widespread criticism of Malthusian population theory, his ideas quickly found a widespread audience across Europe and the United States. By the 1880s, Neo-Malthusianism was being discussed in Sweden where poverty was seen to be the main cause of rising emigration. Malthus was also widely debated in the United States in the early decades of the nineteenth century (Cady 1931). *Population*, written and rewritten between 1798 and 1830, coincided with the height of the abolitionist campaigns, first against the slave trade and then against slavery. Malthus opposed slavery and asked William Wilberforce to inform the House of Commons that he was against the slave trade, in large part because quite a few slave traders were using his Principle of Population in their own defence.

It was not obvious that Malthus's arguments about population could have much relevance to colonial America – an immense land mass with a small colonial population and an indigenous population existing from the Arctic to Mexico (Hodgson 2009). Thomas Jefferson was seriously interested in Malthus and recognised the obvious differences between Europe and the Americas. The vast extent of uncultivated and fertile land allows any settler willing to work to marry young and raise a family of any size. He assumed over time America would become a society of land-owning farmers. In the period leading up to the Civil War, however, Malthusianism was used by both pro-slavery and anti-slavery advocates. It was argued that in a slave system the slave owner had an interest in the well-being of his slaves as the basis of labour power and furthermore the owner could control population growth by manipulating the sex ratio of his work force – for example by a predominance of male slaves.

In the emerging conflict, it was claimed that the regulated economy of the South was superior to the unrestrained capitalism of the North. However, there was an alternative conclusion. As population size and density increased in northern states, wages would begin to approximate subsistence levels and the labour costs of free workers would fall below the costs of slave labour. As the extensive landmass filled up with an ever-increasing population and the West was eventually closed, then America would become a land of over-crowded cities and the aristocratic vision of an orderly South was doomed. The pro-slavery argument came to an end with the end of slavery and then there was no alternative to the northern free-market capitalist system. Pessimistic versions of Malthusianism however periodically re-emerge in the United States with respect to immigration policies and debates about the overpopulating of America for example in the 1870s and 1880s (Hoff 2012; Robertson 2012). Malthusianism is also implicit in Donald Trump's election promise to build a wall to prevent further unwanted migration into the United States. Malthus believed that every country had a 'carrying capacity' that is a maximum number of people it could support and beyond that capacity a country was 'full'. Trump at various locations in California in April 2019 declared that 'America is full'. Attempts to develop Malthus's notion of a carrying capacity have explored a range of questions about intergenerational justice, individual preferences, cultural values and normative aspects (Hanssons and Stuart 1990).

3. Malthus and Historical Demography

The revival of interest in Malthus and the re-evaluation of work have, however, been driven by historians especially by historical demography over a period of some seventy years. In 1986, Tony Wrigley and David Souden published the complete works of Malthus. In 1964, Laslett and Wrigley created the Cambridge Group for the History of Population and Social Structure. Lasslett (1965) published *The World We have Lost.* His research demonstrated that the dominant family form in England from the earlies known records was nuclear, and that the extended peasant household had never been common. Laslett's aim was to integrate sociology and demography, and to do that he depended on the legacy of Malthus. According to Laslett, another important figure in this creation of an historical sociology of populations was David Glass, professor of sociology at the LSE, who published *Introduction to Malthus* in 1953. Wrigley argues that Malthus was in fact less pessimistic than either Adam Smith or Ricardo. He brings our attention to Malthus's view that western European societies had the advantage of an economically responsive marriage system and the slow oscillation in the economic-demographic balance allowed some evasion of the 'Iron Law of Wages' (Wrigley 1989).

Outside the Cambridge Group, Jack Goldstone has demonstrated the importance of Malthus to political history and political theory in an early publication – *The Demographic Revolution in England: a Re-examination* (Goldstone 1986) and more substantively in *Revolution and Rebellion in the Early Modern World* (Goldstone 1991). Goldstone's main argument is that an increase in population causes state breakdown by means of three mechanisms: it is responsible for a rise in prices, which habitually undermines state income; competition for position is strengthened by a growth in numbers, and this tends to lead, especially given the impoverishment of the state, to elite factionalism; finally, demographic pressures cause food shortages, and these in turn lead to those popular revolts, which massively exacerbate state crises. The analysis of these factors demonstrated that a relaxation of demographic pressures went together with a restoration of political stability. Goldstone also examined the political system of Tokugawa Japan when he argued that Japan managed to survive population increase, because state revenues came in kind rather than in cash. The overall thesis was that historical changes in society were the actual conjunction between social institutions and population.

These institutional factors have also been explored by historians in comparing the different trajectories of Spain and England. With the 'Great Discoveries' of the Americas, the Spanish monarchy, with the initial advantage of colonial bullion, evolved into a centralised, bureaucratic and absolutist political system. The new wealth also promoted extractive industries in the new world that further intensified centralised power. The paradoxical result was that the luxury of abundant natural resources delayed economic growth and industrialization. The Spanish experience was another example of the 'Dutch Disease' (Cordoba 2007). The disastrous failure of the Spanish Armada involving 130 ships in 1588 contributed to the emergence of England as a naval power with easy access to the North Atlantic. Spain was further weakened in the seventeenth century by the Dutch revolt and by wars with Italy, France and the Ottoman Empire. The rise of Europe between 1500 and 1850 was primarily confined to Atlantic Europe. Without new-world bullion, England eventually imposed parliamentary limitations on the monarchy through political struggles ending in 1688 with various rights enshrined in law.

Returning to Schumpeter's argument that Malthus lacked a sociological appreciation of the role of institutions in the regulation of population, this view has been overturned in the recent re-evaluations of Malthus. The role of the Poor Laws in England was an important feature in Malthus's work, in which Malthus was criticised for his 'de-moralisation' of political economy. It is true that Malthus objected to collective institutions in general, but he criticised the Poor Laws on the grounds that they offered a right of subsistence, which they could not in fact deliver. The policy of income redistribution in the Poor Laws through parish rates would only raise prices. The income of the poor would then be insufficient to cover the cost of food and, while these income transfers stimulated population growth, they did nothing to increase the food supply. Without an increase in outputs, the Poor Laws would increase the misery of the poor (Winch 1996). Malthus was also opposed to a proposal by Samuel Whitbread, who brought a (failed) bill before Parliament to empower parishes to build cottages for the destitute and extend the liability to pay parish rates to all types of property and not simply on the land. Malthus replied, in his 1806 edition of *Population*, that such legislation would only encourage landlords to destroy cottages rather than build new ones. These observations by Malthus do not, according to Richard M. Smith (2001), demonstrate Malthus's indifference to moral concerns. On the contrary, Malthus argued that private decisions for example to marry early and to have numerous children had negative effects on the wellbeing of the social group. Smith (2001: 408) concludes that recent interest in 'institutional determinants' of fertility and the importance of 'externalities' are well catered for in Malthus's *Population*, especially in later editions.

A comprehensive understanding of Malthus and the role of population and colonial power can only be grasped by seeing Malthus's population theories in a global perspective. While the research of Laslett and Wrigely was primarily concerned to understand the demographic history of England, in *The New Worlds of Thomas Robert Malthus*, Alison Bashford and Joyce Chaplin (2016) place Malthus in a global context that radically recasts our understanding of Malthus's famous essay. Challenging the widely held view that Malthus's population theory was a product of the English context in which it was written, it was the new world, as much as the old, that shaped Malthus's ideas. They explore what the Atlantic and Pacific new worlds – from the Americas and the Caribbean to New Zealand and Tahiti – meant to Malthus, and how he treated them in *Population* reveals how Malthus, long vilified as the scourge of the English poor, concluded that the treatment of native populations by European settlers was unjust. They argue that *Population* was based on his understanding of India from his role in the East India Company, but it included the Atlantic and Pacific new worlds. Malthus had benefitted from the extensive library at Jesus College which contained studies of expanding British global trade and exploration. It included records of Jesuit missions and journals of Pacific voyagers from the eighteenth century. He also had records from early settlements in Australia. Bashford and Chaplin conclude that we need to re-interpret Malthus's work in the light of colonial and imperial history. Malthus was writing his population theory in the context of world history. They also show that Malthus was not indifferent to the suffering of humanity with the expansion of European trade and colonialism. By 1803, Malthus anticipated and was critical of the fate that was awaiting the aboriginal populations of the 'new world'.

4. Conclusion: Unintended Consequences

I have argued that Malthus and Ricardo were sociologists avant la lettre, but what type of sociology? The theoretical framework of sociology, at least through the twentieth century, was formed around Max Weber's posthumous *Wirtschaft und Gesellschaft: Grundriß der verstehenden Soziologie* that was translated as *Economy and Society: An Outline of Interpretive Sociology*, edited by Guenther Roth and Claus Wittich in 1978 from which sociology inherited a rich vocabulary to investigate power and authority, class status and power, and a theory of social action and interaction. This publication was the foundation of his *verstehenden soziologie* as a measured responsive to methodological disputes in Germany. Weber defined sociology as a 'science concerning itself with the interpretative understanding of social action and thereby with a causal explanation of its course and consequences' (Weber 1978: 4). I draw attention to the idea of intended versus unintended consequences. It is the fatefulness of our actions and their unpredictable outcomes that demand meaningful interpretation from us (Turner 1996). Weber's sociology of religion was addressed to the problem of making sense of the world we live in, which gave rise to theodicy. The fatefulness of our world – the Lisbon earthquake – called for explanation, but Rousseau pointed to the unintended consequences of city design. Adam Smith used the idea of 'The Invisible Hand' on three occasions but apparently either ironically or sardonically (Rothschild 1994). The sardonic idea was that greedy and selfish behaviour of the rich can create employment for the poor. The 'Invisible Hand' had potentially good outcomes. With the exception of Robert Merton (1936) and Ulrich Beck (1992), sociologists have not in general terms been attentive to the unintended consequences in social action theory. Unintended consequences and the idea of 'bad outcomes' have not surfaced as a recognised area of Weberian study. However, the classic example of unintended consequences was *The Protestant Ethic and the Spirit of Capitalism.* These two articles are not the most important publications in Weber's sociology, but certainly the most famous. In their quest for certainty of salvation, the Protestant sects developed an ethic of hard work, discipline, self-restraint and the economic virtues of saving and careful investments. The unintended consequence was the construction of a 'spirit of capitalism' as the driving force behind rational capitalist enterprise.

We might argue also that Malthus and Ricardo developed a generally unrecognised sociology of unintended consequences. In the case of Malthus, it is obvious. The unintended consequences of human sexual activity and procreation with limited available arable land were the 'Malthusian catastrophe' – starvation, disease and epidemics. The population crisis also created conditions for social unrest. For Ricardo, the debate is less settled. One complication was that land was limited not by economic constraints but by social institutions, namely the laws of inheritance. However, insofar as Ricardo is the origin of the theory of the tendency of the rate of profit to fall (King 2013: 58–69), he also developed an economic sociology of unintended consequences. The implication of this Weberian legacy is that in human history unintended consequences are typically negative rather than positive – hence the underlying principle of the dismal science.

References

Bonar, James. 1887. *The Letters of David Ricardo to Thomas Malthus 1810–1823*. Oxford: Clarendon Press.

Bashford, Alison and Chaplin, Joyce E. 2016. *The New Worlds of Thomas Robert Malthus*. Princeton: Princeton University Press.

Beck, Ulrich. 1992. *Risk Society: Towards a New Modernity*. London: Sage.

Cady, George Johnson. 1931. 'The Early American Reaction to the Theory of Malthus'. *Journal of Political Economy* 39, no. 5: 601–32.

Condorcet. 2004. 'Sketch for a Historical Picture of the Progress of the Human Spirit'. *Daedalus* 133, no. 3: 65–82.

Davis, John B. 2012. 'Ricardo's Theory of Profit and the Third Edition of the Principles'. *Journal of the History of Economic Thought* 15, no. 1: 90–106.

Glass, David (ed.). 1953. *Introduction to Malthus*. New York: John Wiley & Sons.

Goldstone, J. A. 1986. 'The Demographic Revolution in England: A Re-examination'. *Population Studies* 40, no. 1: 5–33.

Goldstone, J. A. 1991. *Revolution and Rebellion in the Early Modern World*. Berkeley: University of California Press.

Hanssons, Ingemas and Stuart, Charles. 1990. 'Malthusian Selection of Preferences'. *American Economic Review* 80, no. 3: 529–44.

Hennis, Wilhelm. 1988. *Max Weber: Essays in Reconstruction*. London: Allen & Unwin.

Hodgson, Dennis. 2009. 'Malthus's Essay on Population and the American Debate over Slavery'. *Comparative Studies in Society and History* 51, no. 4: 742–70.

Hoff, Derek S. 2012. *The State and the Stork: The Population Debate and Policy in US History*. Chicago: University of Chicago Press.

Ingham, Geoffrey. 2004. *The Nature of Money*. Cambridge: Polity.

King, John E. 2013. *David Ricardo*. London: Palgrave MacMillan.

Laslett, David. 1965. *The World We have Lost. England Before the Industrial Age*. London: Methuen.

Laslett, Peter. 1985. 'Gregory King, Robert Malthus and the Origins of English Social Realism'. *Population Studies* 39, no. 3: 351–62

Macfarlane, Alan. 2018. *Thomas Malthus and the Making of the Modern World*. Cambridge: Cam River Publishers

Malthus, Thomas. 1798. *An Essay on Population*. London: J. Johnson St Paul's Church Yard.

McNally, David. 2000. 'Political Economy to the Fore: Burke, Malthus and the Whig Response to Popular Radicalism in the Age of the French Revolution'. *History of Political Thought* 21, no. 3: 427–47.

Merton, Robert K. 1936. 'The Unintended Consequences of Purposive Action'. *American Sociological Review* 1, no. 6: 894–904.

Ricardo, David. 2001. (3rd edition) *Principles of Political Economy and Taxation*. Kitchener, Ontario: Batoche Books.

Ricardo, David. 1988. 'Ricardo on Population'. *Population and Development Review* 14, no. 2: 339–46.

Robertson, Thomas. 2012. *The Malthusian Moment: Global Population Growth Birth of American Environmentalism*. New Brunswick, NJ: Rutgers University Press.

Rothschild, Emma. 1994. 'Adam Smith and the Invisible Hand'. *American Economic Review* 84, no. 2: 319–22.

Schumpeter, Joseph A. 1954. *Economic Doctrine and Method: An Historical Sketch*. Oxford: Oxford University Press.

Schumpeter, Joseph A. 1987. *History of Economic Analysis*. London: Routledge.

Smith, Richard M. 2001. 'Welfare of the Individual and the Group: Malthus and Externalities', *Proceedings of the American Philosophical Society* 145, no. 4: 402–14.

Sraffa, Piero (ed.). 1973. *The Works and Correspondence of David Ricardo*. Cambridge: Cambridge University Press.

Tribe, Keith. 1983. 'Prussian Agriculture – German Politics: Max Weber 1892–7' *Economy and Society* 12: 181–226.

Tribe, Keith. 1995. 'Professors Malthus and Jones: Political Economy at the East India College 1806–1858'. *European Journal of the History of Economic Thought* 2, no. 2: 327–54.

Turner, Bryan S. 1996. *For Weber: Essays in the Sociology of Fate*. London: Routledge & Kegan Paul.

Viner, Jacob. 1954. 'Schumpeter's History of Economic Analysis'. *Economic Analysis* 44, no. 5: 894–910.

Weber Max. 1978. *Economy and Society: An Outline of Interpretive Sociology*. Berkeley: University of California Press.

Weber, Max .1989. 'The National State and Economic Policy', in Keith Tribe (ed) *Reading Weber*. London and New York: Routledge, pp. 188–209.

Wiltgen, Richard J. 1998. 'Marx and Engel's Conception of Malthus: The Heritage of a Critique', *Organisation and Environment* 11, no. 4: 451–60.

Winch, Donald. 1996. *Riches and Poverty: An Intellectual History of Political Economy in Britain, 1750–1834*. Cambridge: Cambridge University Press.

Wrigley, E. A. 1989. 'The Limits to Growth: Malthus and the Classical Economists', in M. S. Titelbaum and J. M. Winter (eds), *Population and Resources in Western Intellectual Traditions*. Cambridge: Cambridge University Press, pp. 30–48.

FURTHER READING

John E. King

The first ten volumes of Ricardo's *Works and Correspondence*, edited by Piero Sraffa, appeared between 1951 and 1955, with an eleventh volume (published in 1973) providing a comprehensive index. They were published by Cambridge University Press for the Royal Economic Society. Volume I is a variorum edition of the *Principles*. Ricardo's critical notes on Malthus are in volume II, with his pamphlets and unpublished manuscripts coming in volumes III and IV. The lengthy volume V contains Ricardo's Parliamentary speeches and evidence to Select Committees, while his correspondence with Malthus, James Mill and many others can be found in volumes VI–IX. Volume X contains a great deal of biographical and bibliographical detail, beginning (as we have seen) with his brother Moses's tribute. The Chicago economist George Stigler described the *Principles* volume as

> a work of rare scholarship. The meticulous care, the constant good sense, and the erudition, make this a permanent model for such work. [...] The editorial notes are superb. They seem unbelievably omniscient; they are never obtrusive or pedantic; and they maintain unfailing neutrality. Their presence not only clarifies much of Ricardo's work but also provides a vast fund of information on the economics of the period. (Stigler 1953: 586–87)

Sraffa was awarded the Söderstrom Medal of the Swedish Academy of Sciences (a forerunner of the Nobel Prize in Economics) for his editorial labours.

There have been a number of different editions of the *Principles*, each with a different editor and hence a different editorial introduction (see King 2013: Chapter 7). The first appeared in 1846, edited by the well-known classical economist James Ramsay McCulloch. Then, in 1891, a new edition edited by E. C. K. Gonner was published, which saw eleven reprints between 1895 and 1929. The little-known F. W. Kolthammer took charge of the Dent edition which appeared in 1911, with later versions edited for Dent by Michael Fogarty (in 1965) and by Donald Winch (in 1973). The eminent American economist William Fellner edited the Irwin edition of the *Principles* in 1963, and another U.S. version appeared half a century later, edited in 2005 for Barnes and Noble by Robert E. Wright. Five years later the first Indian edition appeared under the editorship of R. N. Ghosh. But my favourite edition (other than the canonical work of Piero Sraffa) is the Penguin paperback version, published in 1971 with Max Hartwell as editor. I had studied economic history with Hartwell as an Oxford undergraduate in 1966–67, and although we seemed to disagree about almost everything I learned a great deal from him. His introduction to this, the cheapest edition of the *Principles*, is extremely good. The book has also been widely translated, including into French (the first edition appearing in 1819), German (1821), Polish (1826), Russian (1875), Hungarian (1892), Chinese (1921), Bengali (1928–30) and Japanese (1930).

The secondary literature is enormous: the bibliography to my volume on Ricardo's political economy in the Palgrave Macmillan 'Great Thinkers in Economics' series ran to no less than thirty-one pages (King 2013: 217–47). Articles on Ricardo continue to appear in the leading journals and, of course, in all the specialist history of economic thought journals, with five in the *Journal of the History of Economic Thought* between 2017 and 2019, ten in the *European Journal of the History of Economic Thought* (2015–2020), six in the Australian *History of Economics Review* (2016–2020) but – rather surprisingly – only two since 2013 in the leading journal in the field, *History of Political Economy*.

Books on Ricardo also continue to be published, including *Ricardo on Money and Finance: a Bicentenary Reappraisal* (Sato and Takenaga 2013); *200 Years of Ricardian Trade Theory* (Jones and Weder 2017); *Ricardo on Money: A Reappraisal* (Deleplace 2017); *Ricardo and International Trade* (Senga, Fujimoto and Tabuchi 2017); *Ricardo's Theory of Growth and Accumulation* (Salvadori 2021); *Before Method and Models: The Political Economy of Malthus and Ricardo* (Walter 2021); and *David Ricardo: An Intellectual Biography* (Cremaschi 2021).

If you are new to Ricardo, the best place to start would probably be the large and very scholarly edited volume, *The Elgar Companion to David Ricardo*, which has eighty-six entries, including several by contributors to the present volume (Kurz and Salvadori 2015).

References

Cremaschi, S. 2021. *David Ricardo: An Intellectual Biography*. Abingdon: Routledge.
Deleplace, G. 2017. *Ricardo on Money: A Reappraisal.* Abingdon: Routledge.
Jones, R. W. and Weder, R. 2017. *200 Years of Ricardian Trade Theory*. Cham: Springer International.

King, J. E. 2013. *David Ricardo*. Basingstoke: Palgrave Macmillan.
Kurz, H. and Salvadori, N. (eds). 2015. *The Elgar Companion to David Ricardo*. Cheltenham, UK, and Northampton, MA, USA: Edward Elgar.
Salvadori, N. 2021. *Ricardo's Theory of Growth and Accumulation*. Abingdon: Routledge.
Sato, Y. and Takenaga, S. (eds). 2013. *Ricardo on Money and Finance: A Bicentenary Reappraisal*. Abingdon: Routledge.
Senga, S., Fujimoto, M. and Tabuchi, T. (eds). *Ricardo and International Trade*. Abingdon: Routledge.
Stigler, G. 1953. 'Sraffa's Ricardo'. *American Economic Review* 43, no. 4: 586–99.
Walter, R. 2021. *Before Method and Models: The Political Economy of Malthus and Ricardo*. Oxford: Oxford University Press.

INDEX

accumulation of capital 51, 83
adding-up theory of value 57
agriculture, mechanisation of 56, 94
agriculture, Edward Gibbon Wakefield on productivity of 144
America, economic and social development of 201
Angerstein, John Julius 126
anthropology 197
Aspromourgos, Tony 164, 165, 167, 173, 178n14
Austen, Jane 127
Australia 143

Bank of England 22–24, 26n18, 77, 78, 126–128, 131, 133, 135–137
Bank Charter Act of 1844 24
bank money 10
banks 9, 17
Baring, Sir Francis 129, 130, 133
Barnes, John 130
Battye, John 129
Benetti, Carlo 11, 25n8
Bentham, Jeremy 76, 137
Berenger, Charles Random de 85
Berkeley, George 76
Bharadwaj, Krishna 165, 166, 177n5
Blaug, Mark 17, 102
Böhm-Bawerk, Eugen von 190
Bosanquet, Mr. 38
Bortkiewicz, Ladislaus von 63, 64, 119
Bray, John Francis 85–88
British Loans 125, 126, 134
Brougham, Henry 145
bullion controversy 77
Bullion Essays of 1809–11 9, 16, 22, 23, 25n12
Burke, Edmond 196
Byron, Lord 200

Cannan, Edwin 63, 68, 70n10, 97, 102
Cantillon, Richard 164
Capital, by Karl Marx 86
capital accumulation, Ricardo on 55, 56, 60, 68, 79
capital levy 79
capitalism, spirit of 205
capitalists 52, 56, 58, 63, 64, 66–68
Carlyle, Thomas 198
Carruthers, Joseph 157
Cartelier, Jean 11, 25n8
Castaing, John 18
charity, Ricardo's opposition to 82
cheap land, Edward Gibbon Wakefield on 147
Church of England 198
Clark, John Bates 190
class conflict 56, 192n8, 200
classical political economy 9, 165, 195
Classical-Marxian political economy 181, 189
Cobbett, William 85
Coleridge, Samuel Taylor 199
Colonial Office 144, 150
colonial powers and international trade, Ricardo on 84
Combination Acts 83
Comte, Auguste 200
commodity theory of money 10,11, 15
see also gold
comparative advantage, theory of 29, 32, 33, 36, 37, 39, 40, 42, 46, 46n6, 110, 116, 121
Condorcet, Marquis de 198

Consols 126–129, 131, 132, 136, 137
convertibility of bank notes into gold 77
Corn Laws 56, 57, 196
corn model 54, 59, 63, 68, 69, 192n9
cosmopolitanism 195
counterfactual reasoning in Ricardo 96
Course in Positive Philosophy, by Auguste Comte 200
crises, economic 86, 188
currencies, convertible and non-convertible 113, 114
Curtis, William 129, 134

Davis, Timothy 94, 179
deflation 16
demand, Ricardo on 166, 168, 171, 172, 174, 175, 178n8
demand, role in economic growth 163, 164, 174, 176
demography 197, 202
depression, economic 16, 17, 25n11
destabilising shocks 43–45
Dickens, Charles 199
differential rent 54, 55, 62, 94
diminishing returns in agriculture 53, 56, 150
dishonesty, alleged against Ricardo by Norman Silberling 133
distribution of income 11–15, 74, 84, 86, 94–96
distribution of wealth 74, 113, 121
division of labour 146, 147, 150, 159n10, 160n16
Dmitriev, V.K. 119n8
domestic trade 23, 31, 37

East India Company 199, 204
economic growth, Ricardo on 74, 163, 164, 174
economies of scale, Wakefield on 150
Edgeworth, Maria 76
Edmonds, Thomas Rowe 88
effective demand failures 82, 86, 87, 187, 189
Elements of Political Economy, by James Mill 33
Engels, Friedrich 199
England and America, by Edward Gibbon Wakefield 145, 148
England in Ricardo's day 74
Enlightenment liberalism 76, 197, 198, 200
equilibrium, global 35, 42–44
Essay on the External Corn Trade, by David Ricardo 83
Essay on Population, by Robert Malthus 195
Essay on Profits, by Ricardo 54–57, 60, 62, 65, 67, 172
Essays on Some Unsettled Questions of Political Economy, by David Ricardo 34
exchange value, Ricardo on 163, 169, 170, 177n5, 178n9
exhaustible resources 104, 105, 120n16
exploitation, theory of 184–186, 192n12

Faccarello, Gilbert 33, 35, 36, 46n2, 47n11
falling rate of profit 186
Farington, Joseph 130
Ferguson, Charles F. 107
fetishism of commodities 87
financial investments, Ricardo's 125–41
Fisher, Andrew 157
foreign trade, Ricardo on 93, 98, 110–115, 117, 120n18
Fourier, Charles 191n5
Fox, Annie Corsina 156
free market liberalism 75, 81
free trade, Ricardo on 83, 84
free traders, Australian 157
Free Trade and Land Reform Party 157
French Revolution 196
fiscal illusion 79, 80
full employment 78
fundamental law of distribution, Ricardo's 99

Garegnani, Pierangelo 166, 178n7
Gatcombe Park 125, 135, 141
Gehrke, Christian 46n6
George, Henry 79, 155
German Historical School 195
German philosophy 181, 182, 196
general equilibrium theory 11
General Theory of Employment, Interest and Money, by J. M. Keynes 73, 188
Gipps, Sir George 152, 154
Glass, David 202
Glorious Revolution of 1688 75

Godwin, William 199
gold standard 38, 40
Goldsmid, Abraham 129, 130, 133, 134, 138
Goldsmid, Benjamin 133
Goldstone, Jack 202
Gramsci, Antonio 193
Grant, James 138, 139
Gray, John 85–88
Grey, Henry 147, 152, 156
growth, economic 74, 163

Halévy, Élie 76
Hall, Charles 85
Hazlitt, William 199
Hegel, Georg Wilhelm Friedrich 182–185
Heilbroner, Robert 198
Hicks, John R. 168, 190
Higgins, H.B. 156
High Price of Bullion, The by David Ricardo 37
Hilferding, Rudolf 78
historical materialism 192n12, 182, 183, 185–187, 189
Historical School 195
holism, methodological 167, 177
Hollander, Samuel 18, 25n11, 26n15, 168, 178n11
Hotelling, Harold 93, 104–106, 120n16
Hotelling's Rule 104, 106
House of Commons 201
Hyse, Richard 170
Hughes, Billy 157
Hume, David 76

idealism, philosophical 182, 183
income distribution 9, 52–54, 57, 65, 68, 69, 74, 75, 79, 85, 86
induced innovation, Ricardo on 106–108
inflation 16
Inquiry into Rent, by Robert Malthus 54
international monetary economics 22, 23, 27
international prices 41
international trade, theory of 29, 30, 34, 35, 40, 46n2
Introduction to Malthus, by David Glass 202
investment, as determinant of saving 75, 77
investment strategies, Ricardo's 137
Ireland 150, 151
iron law of wages 197, 202

Japan 202
Jefferson, Thomas 172, 174, 175, 178n8, 178n15, 179n19
Jevons, William Stanley 91, 99
Johnson, Harry G. 102

Kaldor, Nicholas 73
Kant, Immanuel 182
Keynes, John Maynard 73, 75, 80, 92–94, 120n18, 188, 189, 191
King, John E. 165, 179n18
Keynesian economics 16, 17

Labor Party, New South Wales 156
labour market regulation 51
labour theory of value 57, 66, 170, 177, 178n6, 184–186, 190, 192n16
Lancaster, Joseph 168
land taxation 59, 66, 154
landlords, income share of 56, 58, 66, 68
Laslett, David 202
Lasalle, Ferdinand 184
law of diminishing returns 53, 56, 67–69
Letter from Sydney, A by Edward Gibbon Wakefield 144, 145
liberalism, classical 7, 181
loan contracts 82
Locke, John 76, 84, 86
London Stock Exchange 126, 127, 138
long-period method 184
Lowe, Robert 152, 154
Luddites 95, 200

machinery, economic and social effects of 105–107, 112, 121n22, 169, 174, 176, 199, 200, 202
Macleay, Alexander 144
Mallett, John Lewis 137
Malthus, Daniel 202–205

Malthus, Thomas Robert 29, 31, 37, 40, 43, 44, 47n12, 52–54, 57, 58, 59, 61–63, 65, 66, 68, 69n4, 69n9, 74, 80, 81, 86, 87, 92–94, 96, 97, 100, 101, 117, 127, 132, 136, 139–141, 163, 165, 166, 168, 170–177, 177n1, 178n14, 178n16, 195–205
Malthusian population principle 61, 186, 201
Maneschi, Andrea 36, 46n6,
'market price of labour' 61
Marshall, Alfred 63, 73, 92, 102, 118n2, 190
Marcuzzo, Maria Cristina 19, 26n21
marginalism 54, 172
market price, contrasted with natural price 165, 171, 172
Marx, Karl 64, 65, 70n12, 70n15, 70n17, 71n21, 73, 86–88, 91, 102, 109, 119n10, 120n16, 120n18, 177n3, 181–191, 191n1–7, 192n8–21, 193n22–24, 195, 199, 200
Marxism and Malthusianism 199
McCulloch, John Ramsey 33, 68, 69n7, 95, 100, 106
McDougall, L.F. 145, 158n6, 159n6
Menger, Anton 85
Menger, Carl 85
method of analysis, Ricardo's 93, 165–168, 171, 173
Milgate, Murray 77
Mill, James 33, 34, 39, 46n6, 76, 137, 144, 158n3
Mill, John Stuart 34, 35, 70n13, 70n18, 87, 144, 145, 147, 155, 159n7, 166, 168
monetary policy, 22, 23, 73, 77–79
money, theory of 9–24, 24n1–7, 25n8–14, 26n15–23, 78
'money wages', Ricardo on 53, 60–63
Money Standard Equation 21, 26n21
Morgan, Mary 94, 95, 119n10

Napoleonic Wars 77, 79
national debt 126, 127
nationalism 195
natural prices 41, 42, 60, 61, 165, 166, 171–173
neoclassical economics 187
neutrality of money 14, 16, 25
New Classical macroeconomics 79
New Principles [...], by Sismondi 170
net product 54
New South Wales 144, 147, 148, 158
New Zealand 152, 156, 158, 158n4, 160n20
Notes on Malthus, by David Ricardo 52, 59, 65, 66, 68, 80, 173, 177n1
numerical examples, Ricardo's use of 93, 96–98, 101–103, 110, 111, 113, 115, 116

obituaries of Ricardo 140
O'Brien, Denis 102
Old Corruption 75–77, 79, 85
over-production, partial and general 80

paper money 10, 15, 23
partial equilibrium 190
Pasinetti, Luigi 98, 119n8, 178n17, 179n17
Peach, Terry 178n10–13, 179n17
Peel, Thomas 145, 159n8
Penelope effect 22, 23
People's Charter 85
Petty, Henry Lord 129
Petty, William 119, 164, 165
philosophical radicalism 76
philosophy, German 181, 182
Piketty, Thomas 120n21
Place, Frances 145
Plan for the Establishment of a National Bank, by David Ricardo 23
political economy, Ri ardo's definition of 51–53
political theory 197, 202
politics, Ricardo on 75–77
policy, economic 73–88
population growth, theory of 60, 61, 68, 74, 82, 88, 195, 197–199, 201, 203
population of England 74, 82, 86, 88
poor relief 81, 82, 203
Portugal 29–33, 35–40, 45, 46n3, 110, 111, 113–117
price level 10, 11, 25
prices, international prices of production 41–42

Principles of Economics, by Alfred Marshall 73
Principles of Political Economy, by Robert Malthus 177n1
Principles of Political Economy and Taxation, The by David Ricardo 9, 29, 73, 141, 143, 195
Principles of Political Economy, by John Stuart Mill 87, 147
Production of Commodities by Means of Commodities, by Piero Sraffa 173, 189, 191
productive and unproductive labour 168, 174, 178n14
profit, rate of 52, 54– 60, 62–66, 68, 69n7, 70n13, 70n18, 186, 191n7, 192n11
profit, Ricardo's theory of 53–54, 100
profit share 60
progress, Enlightenment thinkers on 197, 198
Progress and Poverty, by Henry George 155, 156
Proposals for an Economic and Secure Currency, by David Ricardo 9, 17, 19, 23
Protestant Ethic and the Spirit of Capitalism, The by Max Weber 205
Proudhon, Pierre Joseph 191
Pullen, John 168, 178n14, 178n16

Quantity Theory of Money 10, 11, 16–19, 24, 25n9, 47n8, 78

radicalism 76, 84,
rate of profit 31, 41, 52–60, 62–66, 68, 69n7, 70n13, 70n18, 75, 83, 173, 174, 176, 177n6, 177n8
Ravenstone, Piercy 85, 86
'real value of wages', Ricardo on 52, 57–59, 64, 68
realism, philosophical 182
Reduced Annuities 126–129, 136, 137
Reflections on the Revolution in France, by Edmund Burke 196
Reid, George 156, 157
religion, Ricardo and 76
rent, Ricardo's theory of 54–56, 96, 98, 100, 103, 104, 106, 145, 163, 172, 175
rent, share of 52, 53, 55, 56, 60, 65–69
rent, taxation of 79 148, 155
Reply to Bosanquet 37–8
reproduction models in Marx 188
'Ricardian equivalence' 79, 80
Ricardian Socialists 73, 84–88
Ricardian-Marxian approach to economics 189, 190
'Ricardian Vice' 10, 91, 97, 197
Ricardo, Abraham Isaac 73–88, 125–141
Ricardo, David 1–24, 29–47, 51–69, 73–88, 91–118, 125–141, 143–158, 163–177, 181–191, 195–205 *passim*
Ricardo's consortium 130–131, 135, 137
riches, Ricardo on 166, 169, 176
Ripon Regulations 150, 151
Robarts, Abraham 129
Robbins, Lionel 168
Robertson, Sir John 154, 155
Rosselli, Annalisa 19
Rothschild, Nathan Mayer 138, 140–141
Rousseau, Jean-Jacques 198, 205
Ruffin, Roy 36, 120n18

Saint-Simon, Henri de 191n5
Samuelson, Paul A. 32, 168
savings and social class 73
Say, Jean-Baptiste 80, 154, 180
Say's Law 16–17, 25n9, 80, 81, 174, 175, 196
Schumpeter, Joseph A. 10, 17, 91, 97, 99, 107, 118n1, 168, 196, 197, 203
Sephardic Jews 75, 198
Shelley, Percy 199
Silberling, Norman 133–134
Sinclair, Sir John 79, 125, 138
Sinha, Ajit 177n5, 179n19
Sismondi, J.C.L. Simonde de 163–165, 167, 168, 170–175, 177n2
Sketch for a Historical Picture of the Progress of the Human Spirit, by Marquis de Condorcet 198
slavery 147, 148, 159n13, 201
Smith, Adam 22, 26n17, 26n23, 31, 51, 53, 57, 73, 84, 95, 96, 98, 104, 105, 114, 120n22, 121n23, 144–146, 158n3, 163–165, 167–177n4, 177n5, 178n14, 178n15, 182, 190, 195, 202, 205

social policy 76–84
socialism 85, 181
sociology 195–198
South Australia 151, 152, 160n20, 160n22
Soviet Union 188
Spain 203
Spencer, Herbert 155
Sraffa, Piero 9, 12, 13, 15, 24n4, 24n6, 25n8, 35, 46n1, 47n10, 53, 54, 57, 65, 66, 70n14, 71n20, 76, 98, 99–102, 119n8-n10, 120n18, 120n19, 125, 126, 130, 131, 133–135, 138, 141, 170, 172, 173, 176, 177n6, 181, 189–191, 192n20, 193, 195
Standard Commodity, Sraffa on 101
Standard system, Sraffa's 101, 102
Steers, Charles 128–131, 134
Steers, James 130, 131
Stiglitz, Joseph 188, 189
Stirati, Antonella 168, 174
Stimson, Shannon 77
Stock Exchange 125–128
surplus labour 86, 87
surplus product 7, 13–15, 24n6, 54–57, 60, 66, 97, 99, 100

Tabuchi, Taichi 46
Tasmania 149
taxation, Ricardo on 73, 79, 164, 165
taxation of land 143, 155, 157, 160n20
technical progress, Ricardo on 93, 95, 96, 102–105, 109, 111, 112, 117, 120n16, 120n21, 121n25, 186
Thompson, Noel 85–88
Thompson, William 85–88
Thornton, Henry 39
Torrens, Robert 34, 46n6, 148, 151, 152, 160n16
trade, theory of 29–47, 73–75, 77, 81, 83, 86, 87
trade policy 73–75, 77, 81, 83, 86, 87
trade unions, Ricardo on 83
Trower, Hutches 82, 140

under-consumption theory 74, 87
unintended consequences 204, 205
Unitarians 76
use value, Ricardo on 166, 169–172

value, theory of 9, 11, 21, 24, 31, 32, 40, 41, 57, 66, 68, 73, 78, 84, 91, 93, 98–102, 163, 166, 170, 177, 177n3, 184–186, 190, 192n9, 192n16
Viner, Jacob 133, 197

wages
- in Australia 147, 152
- in Britain 74, 85
- Malthus on 168
- Marx on 186, 200
- Ricardo on 24, 51–3, 56–70, 82, 91, 96–101, 106–9, 111–13, 119, 165, 172–4, 176, 178, 197, 199
- Sismondi on 172–4
- Smith on 172–4
- Sraffa on 24, 119, 172–4, 190
- state control of 81
- Torrens on 152
- Wakefield on 147, 152, 159

wages fund 61
Wakefield, Edward Gibbon 144–154, 157, 158, 159n8, 159n9, 159n11, 160n16, 160n17
Waterloo, battle of 125, 135, 137–140
Walras, Léon 91, 99, 125
wealth, distribution of 51–53, 60, 73–75, 79, 84–86
wealth, 'real value' of 51–53
wealth tax 60, 73–75, 79, 84–86
Wealth of Nations, by Adam Smith 31, 53, 73, 121, 144, 164, 170, 177n4
Weber, Max 191, 195, 196, 204, 205
Western Australia 145, 160n22
Wetenhall, James 132
Whitbread, Samuel 203
Wicksell, Knut 91, 92, 102, 118n1
Wilberforce, William 201
Wilkinson, Josiah Henry 125, 128
Wilkinson, Priscilla Ann (Mrs. David Ricardo) 125, 128
Wise, B.R. 84, 92, 157
workers, Ricardo on 52, 53, 56–62, 64, 67, 69n5, 73–75, 85, 87
World We Have Lost, The, by David Laslett 202

Young Hegelians 183, 191n4
Yukizawa, Kenzo 36

www.ingramcontent.com/pod-product-compliance
Ingram Content Group UK Ltd.
Pitfield, Milton Keynes, MK11 3LW, UK
UKHW041831100926
8556IPUK00002B/112